The Genius of Grace

the message of Ephesians

Sam Gordon

AMBASSADOR

BELFAST, NORTHERN IRELAND
GREENVILLE, USA

THE GENIUS OF GRACE
© 2003 Sam Gordon and twr-uk

All Scripture quotations, unless indicated, are taken from the Holy Bible: New International Version. Copyright © 1973, 1978, 1984, International Bible Society. All rights reserved.

ISBN 1 84030 136 8

Ambassador Publications
a division of
Ambassador Productions Ltd.
Providence House
Ardenlee Street
BELFAST
BT6 8QJ
Northern Ireland
www.ambassador-productions.com

Emerald House
427 Wade Hampton Blvd.
GREENVILLE
SC 29609, USA
www.emeraldhouse.com

Trans World Radio
Southstoke Lane
BATH
BA2 5SH
United Kingdom

01225 831390

www.twr.org.uk

Trans World Radio
P O Box 8700
CARY
NC 27512, USA

1 800 456 7TWR

www.twr.org

DEDICATION

to

David and Germania Logacho
and all my friends at
La Biblia Dice, Quito, Ecuador

*'Siempre estoy dando gracias a Dios al
hacer memoria de ti en mis oraciones ... tu
amor me ha proporcionado gran alegría y
consuelo, porque tú, has dado verdadero
alivio a los corazones de los santos.'*

(Filemón 4, 7)

Truth for Today

~ Mission Statement ~

*'To teach the entire Bible in a warm expository
style so that people's lives are influenced to such
a degree that they impact their world for Christ.'*

First Word

Grace! Amazing grace! Ever wondered, what is *so* incredibly amazing about it? To me, the answer is found in the unrivalled God we come face to face with in the book of Ephesians.

Here is a saving God—one who bends over backwards in order to draw sinful men and women to himself. A reconciling God—one who thinks nothing of going the third mile in his sterling efforts to break down the barriers man has erected. A gregarious God—one who enjoys the fellowship and company of his children. Grace!

Here is an exceedingly patient God—one who takes us the way that we are and makes us into the kind of people he wants us to be. A God with a cosmic shaped heart—one whose kingdom extends to the ends of the earth, whose family is a global family. Grace!

Here is a wonderfully generous God—one who trusts us and believes in us. A loving God—one who, through the ups and downs of life, longs to see us find our potential fully realised as we become a people of grace. All because we stake our future on him, and because we place our faith in his Son. Grace!

See what I mean! Here is a gracious God—one who dispenses grace fully, freely, and fairly. Where would we be without him? What would we do without it? That, it has to be said, is the genius of grace!

Sam Gordon

Contents

1

Big on Blessings

A mini course in theology, focused on grace, centred on the church! This is what Paul's extraordinary letter to the Ephesians is all about. When we take twenty minutes and read the epistle through, from cover to cover, we end up saying to ourselves:

'Great book! Great theology! Great grace! Great God!'

Ephesians is upbeat. Exciting and enriching. Exciting, because in every chapter Paul puts the spotlight on the Lord Jesus. We are transported into a whole new world for we find that our Saviour is one who is unrivalled in all his attributes. He is the incomparable Christ!

Enriching, because it shows us how we can be the kind of people God wants us to be. It helps us bridge the gap between what we believe and how we live. Paul blends some of the loftiest theology in Scripture with some of the most practical teaching in a letter bathed in love.

Charles Swindoll reckons that 'Paul lifts our heads above the smoke and dust of our struggles, and gives us a view of what Christ has done for us and why. He gives us a higher perspective, a new vision of our purpose and calling as the body of Christ, and how we are to live it out.'

A charm of its own

What is the special appeal of Ephesians?   In the space of half a dozen chapters, Paul presents the basic doctrines of authentic biblical Christianity—comprehensively, clearly, practically, and winsomely. In other words, we are told:

* who we are,
* how we came to be as we are,
* what we shall be, and
* what we must do now in light of that destiny.

John Stott draws the various threads together when he writes: 'The whole letter is thus a magnificent combination of Christian doctrine and Christian duty, Christian faith and Christian life, what God has done through Christ and what we must be and do in consequence.' Ephesians will change our lives. It is not so much a question of what we will do with the book, but what it will do with us. If read receptively, it is a bombshell!

You see, there are far too many of God's people who are living like paupers when Christ has made them rich. The bottom line of this tremendous letter:

---

why settle for skimmed milk when we can enjoy the benefits of full cream?

From a prison cell

It appears that Paul wrote this letter from a prison cell in Rome where he described himself as *an ambassador in chains* (6:20). Here is a man of grace and grit! The book was penned around the years AD 60-62 and was brought to the church by a low profile gentleman called Tychicus (*pronounced, Tik-i-kis*). What an awesome privilege was his (*cf.* 6:21, 22).

Besides Ephesians, Paul was prolific with his pen for he wrote three other epistles during this period of incarceration: Philippians, Colossians, and Philemon.

Isn't it good to remind ourselves that no matter how restricted our movements may be, there is always something we can do for the Lord. Inevitably, there will be times in your life and mine when we may be set aside from frontline ministry but, thank God, he never sees us as men and women who have passed their sell by date!

Little did Tychicus—a soul brother of Paul—realise that, in his hands, he held what Ruth Paxson exquisitely called 'the Grand Canyon of Scripture.' I suppose, in that sense, Ephesians is seen as terrifically beautiful and apparently inexhaustible to the one who wants to take it in. William Barclay called it 'the queen of the epistles.' The English poet, Samuel T Coleridge, termed this book as 'the divinest composition of man.'

John Mackay was converted as a young man of 14 in the Highlands of Scotland through reading the book of Ephesians. In later years, Mackay went on to become the highly respected president of Princeton Theological Seminary. Throughout his life, he never lost his fascination for Ephesians, often describing it as 'pure music'. Similarly, it was John Calvin's favourite letter. Dr A T Pierson called it 'Paul's third heaven epistle.'

Going higher

I like to think of Ephesians as comparable to a mountain range. By faith, we scale the heights of superb biblical truth. It is one summit after another ... but, the view from the top is worth it all—it is panoramic and breathtaking.

Ephesians is the Everest of Pauline thinking and theology, the apex of biblical revelation.

On the receiving end

The people who were the original recipients of this letter lived in and around the ancient city of Ephesus. I have spent many profitable hours walking around the splendid ruins of this old city, located as it is in modern day Turkey. Truly a fascinating place to be! It is even more intriguing when we realise that, in this environment, there was once a young and vibrant church—a church pulsating with life, oozing with energy, and overflowing with enthusiasm.

Ephesus was one of the five major cities in the Roman Empire, along with Rome, Corinth, Antioch, and Alexandria. It was recognised as the capital city of the province of Asia. It was renowned throughout the region for its opulence and was often referred to as the 'Vanity Fair of Asia' or 'the metropolis of Asia'. It was a well established centre for trade, business, and commerce. Merchants flocked to it from all over the place. Greek and Roman, Jew and Gentile, mingled freely in its streets.

Ephesus became a melting pot of nations and ethnic groups.

It had its own ample harbour and could boast a population of around 350,000 inhabitants. To all intents and purposes, it was a pagan city with all sorts of weird, wacky, and wonderful things taking place in the name of religion. You name it, they had it!

By all reports, Ephesus was a pot pourri of cultic influence.

Diana

The city's claim to fame is considerably enhanced because it had one of the seven wonders of the world within the city boundary—the famous temple of Artemis which housed the imposing statue of Diana—which they believed fell directly from heaven to earth. (In Roman mythology, Artemis was known as Diana.)

It measured 425 feet, by 220 feet, by 60 feet, making it almost four times the size of the Parthenon in Athens. We read that Diana was 'worshipped throughout the province of Asia and the world' (Acts 19:27).

William Barclay informs us that 'one of the features of the temple was its pillars. It contained one hundred and twenty seven pillars, every one of them the gift of a king. All were made of marble, and some were studded with jewels and overlaid with gold.' This shrine actually served as:

* the bank of Asia,
* an art gallery, and
* a sanctuary for the criminal community.

At the same time, it was notorious for all that happened behind closed doors—it was a seedy place, a centre for every expression of free love and superstitious influence that one could possibly imagine.

Sports mad

The city of Ephesus was also an important centre for sports. For example, the Pan-Ionian games, which was the most prestigious sporting event for miles around, were held there once a year in the month of May. I was interested to discover on a recent trip to Ephesus that the city boasted the largest of all Greek open air theatres, seating twenty five thousand spectators. There was a stadium for chariot races and fights with animals.

It is fascinating to note that, even back in Paul's day, the area was probably an ecological disaster zone—enough to send the Green lobby into a tailspin. The deforestation of the surrounding hills meant that the rain carried the topsoil into the rivers with far reaching consequences. It resulted in the harbour slowly silting up.

The extent of this calamity can be seen in the fact that Ephesus was lost for hundreds of years and was rediscovered only in 1869 below a swamp. By the time we come to the nineteenth century, the sea was six miles away—that nugget of information may help to explain why Paul, in his tearful farewell address, met the elders of the Ephesian church at Miletus (*cf.* Acts 20:17).

Seen one, seen them all

So, in more ways than one, Ephesus was your typical big city—a microcosm of London, Paris, Bangkok, Johannesburg, and New York. It has been described as:

- a sailor's favourite port,
- a prodigal's paradise,
- a policeman's nightmare, and
- a preacher's graveyard!

That is what makes Paul's letter so relevant to us as we face the daunting challenges of the third millennium, it is right up to date. It is so contemporary that we see life in the twenty first century mirrored in the perceptive comments of the apostle.

A closed door

We know from the Acts of the Apostles that Paul made three outstanding missionary journeys in the course of his lifetime. Something quite remarkable happened on the second when we read that he and his colleagues were 'kept by the Holy Spirit from preaching the word in the province of Asia' (Acts 16:6).

What happened was this: the Holy Spirit would not give Paul the go ahead to preach in the province of Asia at this point in time, he more or less said to Paul: 'You can't go down there now.' We are not told the specific reason why he closed the door, no divine explanation is given. But we do know that God's timing is always perfect. In his sovereign providence, he would send him there, at a later date, when he felt the time was right.

The story progresses for we read Paul travelled west into Macedonia, to Philippi, down to Berea and Athens, over to Corinth, and then, on his way back, he came by Ephesus. What a window of opportunity he saw there—he could hardly believe his eyes when he thought about the phenomenal potential of such a strategic place. He was staggered at the possibilities (*cf.* Acts 18, 19).

An open window

Paul was so impressed with the opportunities for missionary work in that area that he promised to return as soon as he could. True to his word, when the big day came, he made a beeline for the synagogue where he proclaimed the gospel of Christ for three months. Then he moved into the school of Tyrannus where he stayed for a further couple of years. At this venue, we are told, Paul held discussions in the lecture hall on a daily basis.

Acts 19:10 records the huge impact Paul's ministry had on the locals by confirming that 'all the Jews and Greeks who lived in the province of Asia heard the word of the Lord.' Is it any wonder that Paul wrote later to the church in Corinth with the humble comment that 'a great door for effective work has opened to me in Ephesus' (1 Corinthians 16:9).

God's river in spate

Such was the tidal wave of God's blessing upon his ministry—he was experiencing times of refreshing from the Lord. The Spirit of God was with him, using him in a spectacularly unique way. These were days when God was moving by his Spirit in the hearts of ordinary men and women. Dr Luke summarised it superbly when he wrote that 'God did extraordinary miracles through Paul' (Acts 19:11).

All that happened in sin city paid eloquent tribute to the grace of God, it was a clear indication of the ability of God to change men's lives for the better!

And so it is to these dear people—individuals who have experienced a new creation on a personal level that Paul picks up his quill and parchment to write about the genius of grace in God's new society.

Bite size chunks

Ephesians is a marvellous letter which can be neatly divided into three major sections. First, in 1-3, we read about the Christian and his manifold blessings. Second, in 4:1-6:9, we meet the Christian and talk about his behaviour in a whole variety of challenging situations. Third, in 6:10-23, we are introduced to the Christian and his battles for we are called to be soldiers in the army of the Lord.

www.

An easy to remember format favoured by R. Kent Hughes is:

- Wealth (1-3),
- walk (4-6:9), and
- warfare (6:10-24).

He has another snappy outline which I will share with you:

- Sit (1-3),
- walk (4-6:9), and
- stand (6:10-24).

Being church, doing church

We can look at the epistle from another angle. When we bear in mind that the first half of the book is all about the church and its heavenly calling and the second half deals with the church and its earthly conduct, it is clear that the main beam is focused on the nature of the church. It is painted for us with multifarious splendour—a kaleidoscopic presentation:

- In chapter 1—the church is a body,
- in chapter 2—the church is a temple,
- in chapter 3—the church is a mystery,
- in chapter 4—the church is a new man,
- in chapter 5—the church is a bride, and

● in chapter 6—the church is a soldier.

The two R's

Another outline of the epistle springs to mind when we look at it from a different perspective again. Chapters 1-3 are primarily doctrinal in content emphasising our riches in Christ. Chapters 4-6 are more down to earth and practical underlining our responsibilities in Christ.

A link with the past

It is a great little book, isn't it? It reminds us, in a succinct manner, that our treasures in Christ are of much more value than acres of diamonds. It shows us how we can claim our inheritance in the Lord. In many ways, what the general drift of the book of Joshua is to the Old Testament scene, Ephesians is to the New Testament.

As the redeemed people of God, we move forward by faith, we cross our Jordan river and we enter into all that God has for us in the person of his Son. Our multiple resources are in him.

The Lord is more than able to cover all our past debts, take care of our present liabilities, look after all our future needs, and still not reduce or drain the pool of heavenly assets.

That is the thrilling marvel of God's gracious provision for each of his children. In a deft touch, Paul gets a handle on our wealth in Christ by focusing on *the riches of his grace* (1:7) and *the riches of his glory* (3:16).

God's bank

The Christian faith is not an attractive, well put together set of ideas or a nice tree lined avenue to follow. Rather, according to Klyne Snodgrass, it is 'so deep an engagement with Christ, so deep a union with our Lord, that Paul can only describe it as living *in* Christ.'

Because we are *in Christ* (a phrase that appears 15 times in the book), it means we have access to all that he is and all that he has. It is a matter of each of us tapping the potential of heaven—we need to cash in the blank cheque, as it were, and discover again that our God *is able to do immeasurably more than all we ask or imagine* (3:20).

1:1

Hitting the right note

What can we learn from the opening phrase in chapter one where we read: *Paul, an apostle of Christ Jesus by the will of God.* Before we go any further, let me say that verses 1 and 2 tend to go together. It is what we generally refer to as the salutation. It is a warm and cheery personal greeting from his cell to their church.

R. Kent Hughes in his commentary suggests that 'Paul buoyantly begins a song (modelled on the Hebrew *berekhah* or blessing song) celebrating God's work in bringing us salvation. In quick order, Paul celebrates *himself*, the *saints*, their *God*, and *their blessings.*'

The question is, how did it all begin? These are words which we are so familiar with that the danger is we could read over them and skip on by. If we do that, we miss out on a blessing and we lose out on some of what Paul is trying to convey to the Christian community.

Paul's introduction is pithy and straight to the point. It all begins with a single word of four letters—*Paul*—and that tells us the identity of the writer. It was the accepted custom in those days for correspondents to sign their name at the start of a letter rather than at the end the way we do today.

Paul who?

• He was the prince of preachers in the early church.
• He blazed a trail for God in pagan darkness.
• He was Christ's flagship missionary to the regions beyond.
• He took the gospel where man had never taken it before.

- He held city wide crusades.
- He planted scores of churches.
- He was an articulate apologist and Christian statesman.
- He was prolific with his pen.
- He was in great demand across Asia, Europe, and the Middle East as a keynote Bible teacher.

Everyone wanted his services. The people then had the mindset which said: you have tried the rest, in Paul, you have the best!

Big name, wee man

Paul did not act like a prima donna who had to be worshipped. He does not come across on the pages of Scripture as a fragile hero who has to be treated with kid gloves. He saw himself as a servant, a bondslave, unafraid to take a towel in one hand and a basin of water in the other.

Before he met Christ on the Damascus off-ramp, he was Saul, named after the tallest (and vainest) of the Benjamites, King Saul, from whom he was descended (*cf.* Philippians 3:4-6). But now, after coming to know Christ, he takes the name *Paul* (*Paulos*). His name in Latin actually means 'little' or 'small'. No doubt about it, he lived up to his name.

'Paul's smallness became the medium for God's bigness, his weakness a channel for God's power.' (R. Kent Hughes)

Paul was definitely not interested in doing the evangelical circuit as a celebrity speaker. He did not run around the country holding seminars on the 'how to' or 'how not to' of Christian ministry. Unlike some I know, he was not a full time worker doing a part time job. So far as Paul was concerned, it could never be said that his was a luxurious lifestyle with all the attendant paraphernalia. The trimmings and trappings of ministry did not appeal to him—he just wanted to get on with the job!

Paul's clear vision and heart throbbing passion for mission was as big as the world he knew.

Unlike many of us lesser mortals, with a grasshopper mentality, it could never be said of Paul that he was guilty of dreaming too small. He knew that he served a great God who could do great things through him if he placed his life at his disposal.

What you see is what you get

In spite of Paul's unbelievable achievements in his illustrious career to date, he makes no attempt to enhance his own image. There are no spin doctors or PR men beavering away on his behalf. The impression we have is that of a man who is comfortable with himself—he comes across as someone who is totally relaxed with just a passing reference to his name.

No matter what success God allowed him to enjoy and experience, and the annals of history vouch for it, Paul stayed the same. He was plain Mr Paul. What staggering humility! There is a magnificence in his sense of insignificance. He had been liberated from the crushing bondage of ego. The lesson is:

we can be too big for God to use, but we can never be too small!

Out of sight, *not* out of mind

Just to mention Paul's name to the Christians in and around Ephesus would guarantee instant attention. People would sit up and take notice. His was a household name and even four or five years down the road, many would remember him with fond affection. It was there that Paul saw God work in a truly spectacular way—there were vast numbers of people won to the Lord. Ephesus became the centre of a spiritual awakening that embraced the whole area. Revival broke out in the community for we read of a people saturated with God.

It was a day of miracles and wonderful conversions. A day when public displays of allegiance to God were the norm, never more so than the moment when the locals burnt their books of magic on a bonfire. Dr Luke says with remarkable insight that 'in this way the word of the Lord spread widely and grew in power' (Acts 19:20).

What happened in the city of Ephesus was out of this world. When I read a story like that, my heart misses a few beats and I long for the Lord to move in such power in our day and generation. The plain fact:

God still takes ordinary people and uses them in extraordinary ways!

Commissioned by Christ

Having met the penman, we move on to immediately discover there is a series of four couplets in verses 1 and 2. The first is where Paul refers to himself as *an apostle of Christ Jesus by the will of God.*

What is an apostle? The role of an apostle is special—it is the highest office the church has ever had. The name means someone who is sent, someone who has been commissioned. He was handpicked by God for a special purpose. He is a man enthused and fired up with a sense of mission. He is an individual who has no qualms or quibbles about the future for he knows where he is going.

Paul is said to be an *apostle of Christ* in that he represents Christ at the coal face through his ministry.

As an apostle (*apostolos*), Paul is an emissary of the risen Lord— he represents the living God on planet earth. Now, not everyone could fulfil this particular casting. It was quite unique. There were two basic qualifications: one, an apostle had to see the risen Lord and, two, he had to be sent by him as well. That explains the logic behind Paul's argument in 1 Corinthians 9:1. These men had a wide ranging ministry which included:

- preaching the gospel of grace (*cf.* 1 Corinthians 1:17),
- teaching and praying (*cf.* Acts 6:4),
- working miracles (*cf.* 2 Corinthians 12:12),
- building up other leaders in the early church (*cf.* Acts 14:23), and
- writing the word of God (*cf.* Ephesians 1:1).

When we fast forward to our present day, it needs to be borne in mind that the apostles, as we know them, have come and gone. There is no thought here of apostolic succession. Theirs was a ministry unique to a particular age in that they were the foundation on which the church of Christ was built (*cf.* 2:20; 4:11, 12).

Round peg, round hole

The other side of the coin is that Paul is what he is *by the will* (*thelēma*) *of God*. This was God's supreme purpose for Paul and he lived his life in hot pursuit of that goal. His was a life lived in the centre of the will of God. That means he was not a round peg in a square hole. He was God's man for his day and generation.

Paul was in the place of God's appointment—the place where God wanted him to be.

For this ministry, Paul did not volunteer his services and expertise after attending an upbeat seminar on the way forward for the first century church, nor did the churches meet together in session and appoint him after taking a straw poll or conducting some kind of secret ballot. Not quite like that at all! On the contrary, his apostleship derived from the will of God and from the choice and commission of Jesus Christ. To the end of the day, Paul was amazed that God could have chosen a man like him to do his work.

How thou canst think so well of us,
And be the God thou art,
Is darkness to my intellect,
But sunshine to my heart.

Ripples in the pond

I think the implications of that statement are enormous for it means we see the book of Ephesians in an entirely new light. It is a book which demands our attention and deserves our obedience. When we flick through the pages of Paul's letter and read it for ourselves, we are seriously challenged.

John Stott in *The Bible Speaks Today* commentary writes: 'When we approach this great book, we must regard its author neither as a private individual who is ventilating his personal opinions, nor as a gifted but fallible human teacher, nor even as the church's greatest missionary hero, but as *an apostle of Christ Jesus by the will of God* and, therefore, as a teacher whose authority is precisely the author-ity of Jesus Christ himself, in whose name and by whose inspiration he writes.'

Saints with a small 's'

Number two couplet deals with the status and standing of believers. Paul addresses his letter *to the saints in Ephesus* and *the faithful in Christ Jesus*. This phrase contains three definitions of believers or what D. Martyn Lloyd-Jones called 'the irreducible minimum of what constitutes a Christian.'

They were real people, living in the real world—not icons sitting on mahogany pews.

These were no alabaster gurus standing on a pedestal! They are not cast in marble nor set in decorative stained glass in a Gothic cathedral window, neither are they statues sitting in an ornate city museum. Far from it! They are plain, simple, ordinary folk who have passed through an extraordinary experience—flesh and blood sinners, made of the same material as the rest of us—who have been saved by the grace of God.

Saints! That had nothing to do with them. It was God who set them apart for himself. That is the gist of what is behind the word *hagios*; the primary intent of the word is to set something/someone aside for God's exclusive use.

A little girl who attended worship in a place with a lot of stained glass windows was asked what a saint was. 'A saint is a person the light shines through,' she replied.

The expression was first applied to Israel as a 'holy nation' and it is one which came to be extended to the whole international Christian community, which is the Israel of God (*cf.* Galatians 6:16). God is the one who, in grace, seized the initiative and titled them because he had a special purpose for them. They are his exclusive people and he is happy to identify them as such.

They have not been canonised, however, they have been cleansed. They are not super pious, elitist individuals who are paid up members of an evangelical country club. They are not honours graduates in Christian living. No! they are everyday people made of the same stuff as the rest of us. This is the trademark of the people of God—we are saints! It means we belong to a different kingdom and, because of that, we have:

- a new nature,
- a new set of loyalties, and
- a new agenda.

It is no exaggeration to say that every Christian is a saint and every saint is a Christian. At times we may not feel like it, but we are—we may not look like it, but we are—we may not act like it, but we are. We are a people who belong to God!

We are members of the Church of Jesus Christ of present day saints!

Trusting and trusted

In the next breath, Paul says they are *faithful* (*pistos*). You see, saints are what we are from God's side for he is the one who makes us holy—faithful is what we are from man's side. In other words, we should be trusting in the Lord and trustworthy in relation to one another. We need to be both! There is no point in being one and not the other.

If we are trusting, looking for all that God has for us today, we must also be willing to be trustworthy, the sort of people that God can trust with all that he wants to give.

- What we are—*saints!*
- What we should be—*faithful!*

Location, location

Did you happen to notice where we are? We are supposed to be saints *in Ephesus* and faithful *in Christ Jesus*.

The first phrase tells me where I am geographically on the map—the second, where I am spiritually in the Lord.

Instead of Ephesus, you can write the name of your town in there, it could be anywhere in the world. The picture Paul paints here is quite staggering. He says we are in two places at once. We are here and we are there, at the same time! Our heart is up in heaven—our feet are down on terra firma.

There is a lot more to the phrase *in Christ Jesus* than meets the eye. As a root goes down into the ground, as a fish swims in the water, as a bird flies in the air, so the Christian is said to be *in Christ*—reason: that is our natural environment. It is where we find total security. I cannot think of a safer place to be. Can you? At this point in time, I would not want to be anywhere else.

It is so incredibly hard to explain. So profound. In all honesty, most of us are out of our depth. But we should not let that rob us of the joy of living in the good of it. All the central truths in Paul's dynamic letter revolve around this particular fact so we will come across it many times in the course of our study.

It is a turn of phrase which pops up nine times in 1:3-23 alone and it occurs no fewer than 164 times in all of Paul's writings. It means so much more than just believing on Christ or being saved by his atoning death at Calvary. It carries with it the idea of being joined to Christ in one spiritual body so that what is true of him is also true for us.

Union with Christ

I appreciate this is not the easiest concept to get a handle on— having said that, the Bible uses numerous images to teach it to us. For example:

- the union of a man and woman in marriage (*cf.* Ephesians 5:22-33),
- the union of the vine and the branches (*cf.* John 15:1-17),
- the wholeness of a spiritual temple where Christ is the foundation and we are individual stones (*cf.* Ephesians 2:20-22), and
- the union of the head and other members of the body in one living organism (*cf.* 1 Corinthians 12:12-27).

In one sense, our union with Christ is the very essence of salvation. Alister MacLean tells of a lady in the West Highlands of Scotland who lived a hard life, yet one of perpetual serenity. When asked the secret of it, she answered: 'My secret is to sail the seas, and always to keep my heart in port!' Wonderful! It does not matter where we are, we are still *in* Christ.

1:2

The twin towers of the gospel

Paul prays that the Ephesian believers might know a measure of *grace and peace* in their lives. Give or take a few words, this was the customary greeting with which Paul began all his letters. Paul reckoned there was no point in reinventing the wheel so he gave a distinctly evangelical slant to the contemporary Hebrew and Greek greetings.

Yet we dare not underestimate what Paul is saying for nothing from his pen was ever purely conventional—he was not in the habit of wasting words. On the contrary, both these nouns are particularly appropriate at the outset of a book like this. They are a double barrelled blessing—the twin towers of the Christian gospel.

First things first

We have *grace and peace*—two benefits from the open hand of God. I think the order is of supreme importance. We can never know the peace of God in our hearts without first experiencing the grace of God in our lives. Peace is a wonderful spin off from the grace of God. To use a different analogy, grace is the fountain of which peace is a flowing stream. Paul could not possibly have wished anything better for them. This was the aspiration of his heart that they might know both blessings. It was Paul's dream for them!

Grace is something that comes to us that we do not deserve and which we can never repay. Grace stoops to where we are and lifts us to where we ought to be.

Grace (*charis*) is God's kindness in our lives. Grace is also a token reminder to each of us in the family of God that that is where we stand. On the other hand, *peace* (*eirēnē*) is something which happens within us. It is a freedom from inner distraction, an internal rest. Peace is a profound feeling of well being, a kind of spiritual wholeness. It is a tranquillity of soul that frees us from fear and takes the sharp edges off our anxiety.

Charles Swindoll reminds us that 'peace produces a joy that transcends circumstances and all boundaries between fellow believers—whether it be race, class, gender, intellect, or anything else.'

- Peace with God,
- peace with ourselves,

- peace with our partner,
- peace with our neighbour,
- peace with our past,
- peace with our present, and
- peace with our future.

We need to realise that grace and peace do not come from ourselves, no matter how positive our thoughts may be. They certainly do not come from others, no matter how assuring their counsel may be. They come direct from God. So Paul takes this common greeting among Christians in the early church and lifts it to a higher plane.

This *grace and peace* has enabled thousands to lift up God even when their personal world is crashing around their feet. Consider H P Stafford (1828-88) who composed one of the greatest hymns of all time as he sailed over the watery grave of his close family, drowned on the *Ville du Havre*:

When peace like a river attendeth my way,
When sorrows like sea billows roll;
Whatever my lot, thou hast taught me to say,
'It is well, it is well with my soul.'

Two are better than one

Paul does this as we consider number four in this quartet of couplets. The rich blessing that is ours to enjoy is *from God our Father and the Lord Jesus Christ*. We remember, with fond affection, the words of the doxology: *Praise God from whom all blessings flow*. There is the secret for he alone is the source.

The fact that Paul includes the Father and the Son in one sweeping statement underlines the deity of Jesus Christ—it speaks of his oneness with the Father. Both of them are on an equal footing and they operate on equal terms.

What a wonderful greeting! What a great God!

It seems to me that the God of grace and peace who came to a local assembly of believers in the first century to meet their needs is the same God who comes to us, two millennia later, saying: *'Put your trust in me!'*

1:3

Be thou my vision

It is apparent from Paul's opening comments that the Lord Jesus Christ dominates his mind and fills his vision. It seems, almost, as if he feels compelled to bring the Lord Jesus into every sentence he writes—at least, at the beginning of his epistle. Paul knows full well that it is *through* him and *in* him that God's new community has emerged. As Augustine put it: 'He values not Christ at all who does not value Christ above all.'

You see, Paul's letter speaks as powerfully at the start of the twenty first century as it did early in the first. God's grace overflowed in their hearts, his peace reigned in their lives. And, it has to be said, that is why their brand of Christianity was so infectious and exciting.

With the salutation safely out of the way, Paul now moves into the body of the letter. In fact, verses 3-14 is one extremely long sentence in the original. It forms the longest sentence ever found in ancient Greek. Paul does not stop to punctuate, let alone pause for breath. What Paul says here flows from him like a great waterfall of cascading truth.

It is a splendid hymn of praise—a magnificent creed declaring all the blessings we enjoy in Christ. It is akin to a benediction packed full with truth. It is a eulogy to God, a primer for worship. It is doctrine set to music for if we discover who God is and what he has done for us, we will praise him. It is the logical thing to do!

These verses are a casket of distilled Christianity.

Lost for words

When it comes to this section in Paul's epistle, most commentators are lost for words. It has been feted as a 'magnificent gateway' to the rest of the epistle. To another it was 'a golden chain of many links.' One writer waxed eloquent when he spoke of it as 'a kaleidoscope of dazzling lights and shifting colours.' William Hendricksen compared it to 'a snowball tumbling down a hill, picking up volume as it descends.'

You can take your pick when it comes to the many metaphors; what matters is this, these few verses span the ages from eternity to eternity for they show to us God's masterplan for our salvation.

For example, in 1:3-6a we are shown the past aspect in election where the focus is on the Father and his will; in 1:6b-12 we are shown the present aspect in redemption where the attention is on the Son and his work; and, in 1:13, 14 we are shown the future aspect in our inheritance where the spotlight is on the Holy Spirit and his witness.

From start to finish, it is his story—a story that comes to us with a trinitarian feel woven into the fabric of it.

Yellow pages

What a wonderful chapter—a sweeping panorama of the eternal purpose of God in salvation—a window that enables us to look into eternity and see the heart of God—an A to Z of redemption. What good old yellow pages are for business in the UK, Ephesians 1 is for the Christian.

The apostle starts the ball rolling by blessing God for blessing us with every blessing imaginable.

Paul takes us to the throne room of heaven to show us the greatness and the vastness of the blessings and treasures that belong to all those who are in Christ Jesus. It is the fly on the wall syndrome for we are able to catch a breathtaking glimpse of his redemptive purpose and plan in eternity past. He lets us eavesdrop as God planned to save us, not only long before we were born but long before the earth was born.

And so, with his own inimitable style, the apostle reminds the believers in Ephesus of three unassailable facts. He shows them:

- where they have come from,
- where they are, and
- where they are going.

Praise be

We notice something of unbelievable importance in verse 3 for Paul said: *Praise be to the God and Father of our Lord Jesus Christ.* We are to praise him, we are to bless him. We praise him for his goodness for the Lord is good. It seems to me that God enjoys blessing his people. What has he done? He has made us rich in Jesus Christ.

When we were born again into God's global family we were born rich. Through Christ, we share in the riches of his grace (*cf.* 2:7), the riches of his glory (*cf.* 3:16), and the riches of his mercy (*cf.* 2:4). An appreciation of this is contained in that all inclusive phrase where Paul refers to the *unsearchable riches of Christ* (3:8).

All of these point in one direction and they intimate that our heavenly Father is not poor. He is rich and, wonder of wonders, he has made us rich in him. He is the true source of our many blessings. This is something we should never forget. God has blessed us. Richly.

During an evening walk, a son asked his father: *'Dad, will we ever be rich?'* Affectionately, the father replied: *'Son, we are rich. Perhaps someday we will also have money!'*

We praise him with our lips because he first made us blessed. Our blessing is a declaration. His blessings are deeds. We pronounce him blessed. He makes us blessed. This is something we can sing about for it is happening in our lives in the here and now. It is not reserved for the there and then. Nothing is more appropriate for God's people than to rejoice in him for his unfailing goodness—even the melancholic Jeremiah reminds us in Lamentations 3:23 that his compassions are 'new every morning'.

Blessings galore

In a sense, Rev Johnson Oatman's (1856-1922) hymn says all that needs to be said:

> *Count your blessings, name them one by one,*
> *Count your blessings, see what God hath done;*
> *Count your blessings, name them one by one,*
> *And it will surprise you what the Lord hath done.*

When we say to a brother or a sister in the family of God, 'the Lord bless you', we could wish nothing better for them. Thank God, he will bless them, and he does bless them!

The bottom line: God *really* wants to bless us!

The big question which springs to mind: how has he blessed us? The answer is found at the end of verse 3 where Paul says: *with every spiritual (pneumatikos) blessing (eulogia).* A most beautiful phrase that can be translated to read: 'all the blessings of the Spirit'. A dynamic saying. Indeed!

Then and now

Remember what happened to the nation of Israel. When God promised to bless them, he guaranteed to do it with material blessings. Today, in the dispensation of grace, he will bless us with all the blessings of the Spirit—a brand new dimension. He will meet our individual needs and our corporate needs.

The Lord does not promise to shield us from the troubles, traumas, and trials of this life. Why should he, when all that we need for a satisfying and successful Christian life is found completely in him. He is all we need. As Graham Kendrick says: *For this, I have Jesus!* He is the one who channels our riches to us from the Father through the Son. In a supra-mundane world we need to draw from the infinite resources we have in him. Why? Because there is a superabundance of wealth in the Spirit.

Out of this world

Right at the heart of this tremendous verse is a gentle reminder of the sphere of our blessings—they are said to be *in the heavenly (epouranios) realms*. This is the first of five instances where Paul uses this remarkable expression in Ephesians. It is worth noting, however, that we do not find it in any of his other writings.

What does it mean? The word 'heaven' is used in the Bible in several different senses. Ancient authors used to differentiate between the 'heaven of nature' which is the sky, the 'heaven of grace' which is eternal life already received and enjoyed by God's people on earth, and the 'heaven of glory' which is the final state of the redeemed.

Having said that, when Paul speaks of the *heavenly realms* it is significantly different from all of these. It applies to the unseen world of spiritual reality. When Paul employs this expression in Ephesians, it indicates the sphere in which the principalities and powers continue to operate (*cf.* 3:10; 6:12), the sphere in which Christ reigns supreme and his people reign with him (*cf.* 1:20; 2:6), and the sphere in which God blesses us with every spiritual blessing (*cf.* 1:3).

The contrast is patently obvious when we look at the nonChristian. He is primarily interested in that which is earthly— that is where he lives. The Christian, on the other hand, has a totally different focus for his life is centred in heaven. We are aliens in this world, we are citizens of the kingdom of God.

Our real orbit is in the supernatural.

- Our Father is there,
- our Saviour is there,
- our family and loved ones are there,
- our names are there, and
- our eternal home is there.

Paul challenges us in Colossians 3:2 when he says that our affection should be there as well. There is the huge tension we face as the people of God—we are here and we are there, at one and the same time. If you like, we live our life on two different levels. It is a two tiered experience.

The heavenlies, where Christ is now, at the Father's right hand and, because of grace, we are there sitting beside him (*cf.* 2:6). The whole scenario is nothing less than a paradox for we are down here as well! You see, it is a matter of striking a balance between them, it is all about maintaining a spiritual equilibrium.

It is a fine line we are walking, I know that! On the one hand, Paul suggests we inherit our wealth by faith and, on the other hand, in the next breath he implies that we invest that wealth by works. Basically, they are two sides of the same coin. It simply means all that the Lord Jesus has, those who are in Christ also have. We share everything together. Let me show you what I mean:

- Christ's riches are our riches,
- his resources are our resources,
- his power is our power, and
- his righteousness is our righteousness.

Fantastic! It is not the end of the story though, there is more!

- His position is our position—where he is, we are;
- his privilege is our privilege—what he is, we are;
- his possession is our possession—what he has, we have;
- his practice is our practice—what he does, we do.

When we pull each of these strands together, we get a little idea of what is entailed when we say we are *in Christ*. The sheer wonder of it all blows the mind of the average believer because we are transported by faith into another world.

1:4, 5

The blessing is in the detail

So far in verse 3 Paul has set out the groundwork, he has established a general principle, now he moves on to the small print. He fills us in on the particulars. I cannot help but wonder, what are these stupendous blessings which have come our way? The incredible splendour of each of them is adequately highlighted for us in verses 4 and 5.

Paul is speaking about a doctrine that we will never be able to understand this side of heaven—a truth far beyond our comprehension. In moments like these, we have to face reality for the chances of us finding a simple solution to a problem which has baffled the best brains of Christendom for centuries is fairly slim.

I am extremely grateful to the Lord that the doctrine of election was not invented by Augustine of Hippo or Calvin of Geneva. Aren't you?

On the contrary, it is, without doubt, a sound scriptural doctrine. The fact is, no biblical Christian worth his salt can afford to ignore it. The doctrine of election can be viewed as the cornerstone of our faith for it ensures that God gets all the glory for his deep work of grace in our hearts. In a sentence, it lets God be God!

Paul took one brief look at the believers in Ephesus and, without exaggeration, he was hugely impressed. He saw the intrinsic quality of their abundant life in Christ, the fruit of the Spirit in their personality and interpersonal relationships and, immediately, he sensed in the depths of his own heart, they really are the people of God. Paul recognised three telltale traits:

- God called them,
- God chose them, and
- God claimed them.

In other words, they are numbered among the elect of God! Now, sit back and relax, for I realise the moment I mention election, some people are frightened and begin to panic, others are totally confused on the issue but, thank God, there are some who are thrilled with the sheer wonder of it all—they joyfully declare: 'It's a knockout!'

Coming to terms with God's choice

What do we do when we find ourselves sandwiched between a rock and a hard place? How do we handle it? I suppose, it is true to say, we are walking through a potential spiritual minefield. Do not worry, we will pick our steps carefully. Circumspection is the name of the game! One thing we cannot do is pass by on the other side and pretend it is not there. The fact is, it is in the chapter, it is in the word of God.

The notion of election is not a weird fantasy of men, it is a truth which God himself has revealed. Warren Wiersbe has wisely observed: 'Try to explain the doctrine of election and you may lose your mind, try to explain it away and you may lose your soul.' I do not think that should deter us from studying it. It certainly should not detract us from seeking to come to terms with it. I have to be upfront and tell you that even though I cannot explain it, I can still enjoy it.

If it does nothing else, it emphasises the wonderful grace of Jesus. There is the mystery of the grace of God—the marvel of the love of God—and the miracle of the salvation of God.

Think of it: we are chosen *in* him, chosen *by* him, and chosen *for* him.

A quick look at a Bible concordance reveals that the words 'elect' or 'chosen' together with their variants appear numerous times in the Old and New Testaments. Generally speaking, they could be translated: 'to pick out, to select, to choose'.

Election is a sovereign act of God whereby he freely *chose* (*eklegō*) certain human beings to be saved. Such an idea is applied initially to the fledgling nation of Israel, we have a record of God's sovereign dealings with her in Isaiah 65:9. Another link is added to the chain when we realise it is also used with explicit reference to the Lord Jesus Christ in Isaiah 42:1 and 1 Peter 2:6. Similarly, in Romans 8:33 and Colossians 3:12, the term is associated with the people of God. It is, in that sense, which Paul is using it here in verse 4.

God is presently calling out from among the nations of the world, a people for himself, a people for his praise, and a people for his name. In today's world, the Lord is choosing an international community to be his saints.

God does what he does because God is who he is

The six million dollar question on everyone's lips: 'It's all very well talking about election—what I want to know is, how does God do it?' It seems to me an excellent illustration of this truth is found in God's selection of Israel who, when it happened, were living under the regime of the old covenant.

We read: 'The Lord did not set his affection on you and choose you because you were more numerous than other peoples, for you were the fewest of all peoples. But it was because the Lord loved you … that he brought you out with a mighty hand and redeemed you from the land of slavery' (Deuteronomy 7:7, 8). How did God do it?

- He did it in love, and
- he did it in grace!

The principal reason why he chose them was in himself, it was not in them. That same truth is hammered home elsewhere in the word of God. When we fast forward to the New Testament epistles, what do we read? Of some it is said: we are chosen 'in the Lord' ... we are chosen 'to be saved' ... we are chosen *in him before the creation* (*katabolē*) *of the world* (*cf.* Romans 16:13; 2 Thessalonians 2:13; Ephesians 1:4).

Who is Paul specifically referring to in these verses? Surely he is speaking about the same people who are mentioned in the high priestly prayer of Jesus in John 17—they are those whom the Father has given to the Son. It is not that God's sovereign act of election prevents man from making up his mind and exercising his own choice in faith. Far from it!

Divine sovereignty and human responsibility are an integral and an inseparable part of the component of salvation. Exactly how they operate together, only the infinite mind of God knows. Any teaching which diminishes the sovereign, electing love of God by giving more credit to man also diminishes God's glory and, when it does that, it strikes a lethal blow at the real purpose of our salvation.

The eminent Baptist preacher, C H Spurgeon, was reportedly asked on one occasion how he reconciled God's sovereignty in election with man's personal responsibility to make an informed choice. Spurgeon apparently answered: 'I never have to reconcile friends!' For us, we should be satisfied, simply to quote the words of the hymn penned by James Grindlay Small (1817-88):

> *I've found a Friend, O such a Friend!*
> *He loved me ere I knew him;*
> *He drew me with the cords of love,*
> *And thus he bound me to him.*

I love the story told by the late Dr Harry Ironside of Moody Church, Chicago. A little boy was once asked: *'Have you found Jesus?'* The little fellow scratched his head, thought for a moment, and then he answered: *'Sir, I didn't know Jesus was lost. But, I can tell you what I do know, I was lost and he found me!'*

Before time, beyond time

I have another question lurking in the front of my mind: when did this business of election all transpire? Answer: it happened away back in the distant aeons of eternity. Yes, it is true to say, it was born in the heart of God before time began—it was a key thought on the mind of God before the world was made. I think we need to mark well the statement in the text of verse 4 where we read: *he chose us in him.*

The juxtaposition of the three pronouns is emphatic. God put us and Christ together in his mind. He determined to make us (who did not yet exist) his own children through the redeeming work of Christ (which had not yet taken place).

Prior to the fall of man in the idyllic environs of the garden of Eden, our eternal Father had fallen for us in love.

Because, in God's plan, Christ was crucified before the world was made, that means we were designated for salvation by that same plan, at that same time (*cf.* 1 Peter 1:20). It was then that our inheritance in the kingdom of God was determined. We belonged to God before time began and we will still be his after time has long since run its course.

It becomes intensely personal when we enter into the liberating reality of it in our own lives. It is that magic moment when we come face to face with majesty—when we say 'yes' to the Lord Jesus. Even though our salvation was planned in eternity past, it is realised in time.

When I stand before a congregation of people, I have not the faintest idea who the company of the elect are, that is why I preach my heart out when I tell them of Jesus my Saviour, that is why I proclaim with passion the gospel of redeeming love. And when people respond to the claims of Christ and embrace God's offer of salvation, then I can turn around and say to them: 'Hey, my brother (or sister), welcome to the global family of God, you didn't know it, and neither did I, but you're among the elect!'

The American evangelist D L Moody, a household name, put it like this: *'The whosoever wills are the elect and the whosoever wont's are the non-elect.'*

Maybe we can look at it from a different perspective:

* so far as God the Father is concerned, I was saved when he chose me in Christ before the world began (*cf.* 2 Timothy 1:9),
* so far as God the Son is concerned, I was saved when he died for me on the cross at Calvary (*cf.* Galatians 2:20),
* so far as God the Holy Spirit is concerned, I was saved on Sunday 11ᵗʰ February 1968 in Bangor, Co Down (*cf.* Titus 3:5).

Chosen not for good in me

Over the years in my capacity as a minister of a local church, it has been my delight and privilege to conduct quite a number of wedding services. Now and again I have had the misfortune of hearing a stage whispered comment from someone in the crowd: 'What did she ever see in him?' I sometimes cannot help but think to myself that when I stand in glory and see the King in his impeccable beauty, that I may be tempted to turn the question on its head and ask myself: 'What did he ever see in me?' And that says more about him than it does about me!

Every time I stop and reflect on it, I am bowled over with the unsurpassed wonder of it all. I often join hands with the apostle Paul and exclaim from a full heart: 'Oh, the depth of the riches of the wisdom and knowledge of God! How unsearchable his judgments, and his paths beyond tracing out!' (Romans 11:33). When your head spins with the mystery of election, let your heart also swell with the reality of grace.

C H Spurgeon said on one memorable occasion in the Metropolitan Tabernacle pulpit: *'If God hadn't chosen me before the creation of the world, he wouldn't choose me now!'*

John Chadwick expressed it well when he wrote:

I sought the Lord,
And afterwards I knew
He moved my soul to seek him,
Seeking me!
It was not that I found,
O Saviour true;
No, I was found by thee.

The reason why

Why did God do it in the first place? The answer is located in verse 4 for Paul boldly declares that he has chosen us so that we might be *holy and blameless in his sight.* In other words, he chose us for a clearly defined purpose—holiness. The doctrine of election is an incentive to holiness, it is not an excuse for sin!

For millions of people in our world the very word *holy* conjures up an image of pale faced, miserable individuals who are negative about most things and who are trying to be negative about the rest. Paul takes a totally different view! When we know Jesus and we are walking a path of holiness we are like a bunch of grapes on a vine (*cf.* John 15:5-8). If I know anything about grapes, they are most refreshing, very attractive, and can reinvigorate anybody's day.

His aspiration is that when his children stand before the Lord that they will be *blameless (amōmos)*—with no blemish on their lives; he longs that they will be *holy*—with no spots on their character.

Actually, when we turn back to the Bible, we discover that election is always *unto* something. It is consistently portrayed as a rare privilege that carries an enormous responsibility with it. That is the prime reason why God has saved us, that we should be like his Son, the Lord Jesus. I challenge you to find a more noble goal than that!

These great Bible doctrines are earthed to reality, they have to be lived out in the rough and tumble of everyday life. Where the rubber of your life hits the road, people should see something of the beauty of the Lord Jesus shining through. We are marching to the beat of a different drum. Let me share with you five great blessings of election:

- it eliminates boasting for we have nothing to write home about,
- it gives assurance of salvation for our focus is on the Lord,
- it leads to holiness of life,
- it promotes evangelism, and
- it encourages missionary endeavour to the ends of the earth.

Election is God's work—all of grace—from beginning to end!

1:5

Pre ... what?

In verse 5 we have another major hurdle to overcome. We come face to face with a truth that has caused huge problems among the people of God. Sad to say, it is a doctrine which has been bandied about all over the place by well-meaning people! Predestination.

Every time we come across that word in the Bible, we do ourselves no favours by shying away from it!

There is no point in walking away from it. Believe it or not, it does not spell trouble!

All we need to remember is this—it is talking principally about what God does for those people who are saved. I think we can draw a few helpful comparisons by looking at it from a fresh perspective:

- election refers to people—predestination refers to a purpose,
- election deals with the past—predestination deals with the future,
- election focuses on what we were chosen from—predestination focuses on what we were chosen for.

The word actually means 'to define, to mark out, to set apart, to horizon' like a blueprint. Let me explain: if we were to go outside and look around, we only see as far as the eye will let us, i.e. the horizon. In that position, from a technical perspective, we are said to be horizoned—we are fenced in within a given area. As the word implies, because God chose to elect us, he placed a special mark on us—he predestined us with the knowledge that he would one day adopt us.

Allied to that, when it refers to God, predestination (*proorisas*) has to do with God's loving eternal purpose with those whom he chooses. Paul echoed the same truth when he said that we are predestined to be conformed to the likeness of his Son' (Romans 8:29). In other words, God's goal for your life and mine—to be like Jesus.

Dr Reuben A Torrey used to say that *'this truth is a wonderfully soft pillow for a tired heart.'*

Raison d'être

Why has God acted in this manner towards us? What is the divine rationale? When we begin to unpack the teaching we discover the thinking behind it—it is because we are adopted. In a masterstroke of grace, God has removed all our sins and remade us as his sons. Here is our status symbol in the international community of God. It highlights our standing as a believer. We are sons!

How did it all come about? Well, none of us entered God's family by adoption, we got there by regeneration—the new birth, as outlined by Jesus himself to Nicodemus in John 3:7.

Adoption is the act by which God places us as adult sons in his expanding family.

Why does he do that? Well, a baby cannot enjoy an inheritance but an adult son can, and should. That means whether we are one month saved, one year saved, one decade saved, or even more years than we care to remember, we are all on precisely the same level. We do not have to wait until we reach a certain age before we claim our riches in Christ. John MacArthur writes: 'Christians not only have all of the Son's riches and blessings but all of the Son's nature.'

When we see ourselves as children in his global family, that brings into focus our membership of God's family. When we see ourselves as sons—a different issue altogether—the torch shines on our maturity in the family. That is what God has earmarked us for—if you like, we become mutual partners with him in his eternal purposes.

Here is the good news: he does not adopt people of proven worth, nor does he give his treasure to people who are outstanding. Adoption is not a reward for holy living.

- God adopts wrongdoers.
- He enriches failures.
- He makes rebels his heirs.

A young mother wrote: 'I stayed with my parents for several days after the birth of our first child. One afternoon, I remarked to my mother that it was surprising our baby had dark hair, since both my husband and I are fair.

'She said: "Well, your daddy has black hair." "But, Mama, that doesn't matter because I'm adopted."

'With an embarrassed smile, she said the most wonderful words I've ever heard: "I always forget!"'

Marvellous grace—grace that is greater than all our sin!

Like Father, like son

Paul will return to this vital theme later in his epistle for he writes: *Be imitators of God, therefore, as dearly loved children* (5:1). Because we are his sons, each of us has a solemn responsibility to fulfil this side of heaven. John Stott spells it out when he writes: 'It is inconceivable that we should enjoy a relationship with God as his children without accepting the obligation to imitate our Father and cultivate the family likeness.'

1:6

A sense of belonging

Look again and be thrilled with the significance of all our blessings—it is *to the praise of his glorious grace, which he has freely given us in the One he loves.* That means we are 'accepted in the Beloved' as one older translation has it. We are accepted!

God sees the believer in Christ and he accepts the believer just as he receives his own Son. Fantastic!

Jesus gave his life *for* us at Calvary, then he gave his life *to* us.

We cannot make ourselves acceptable to him, but he can do it for us. That is our eternal position and it will never change. We are taken the way that we are and we are made into what he wants us to be. We feel wanted, so much so, we can sing with Norman Clayton from overflowing hearts: *Now I belong to Jesus.*

Once a son, always a son

To fully understand what this means we need only think of the familiar parable of the prodigal son. Far from home, destitute, and feeding the pigs, the prodigal decided to return back home. He would not ask to be received back into the family, he would only ask his father to take him on as a hired servant. But this was not to be. Luke 15:20 says: 'But while he was still a long way off, his father saw him and was filled with compassion for him; he ran to his son, threw his arms around him and kissed him.'

Moments later the son's shame was covered by his father's best robe. A ring on his hand testified to all in the family circle that he had been fully reinstated as a son. Shoes on his feet witnessed that he was a free man and in no sense could he be regarded as a slave. His genuine repentance and return were greeted with scenes of exuberant joy and wild celebration. The father was so excited that he threw a party in his son's honour!

Why did the father treat his wayward boy the way he did? There is only one explanation—he was his son. And because he was his son, his acceptance could not be anything else but unconditional and complete. Thank God, this is how our heavenly Father treats us.

Welcome home!

We end each day with our lives stained by sin. Our thoughts have not been totally pure, our lips have spoken unwise and often unkind words. We have not done what we should have done. The chances are, we have done what we should not have done. And when we come to him in true repentance, he throws his arms around us and treats us as dear children. He never hesitates. We approach him with tears only to find that his home is a house of joy.

How can God give us such a warm reception as this? It is because his eternal Son, the Lord Jesus, has never disappointed him in any way, and he sees us as being in him. He accepts us for his sake.

It has nothing to do with us, it has everything to do with him!

We are back to where we started—it is all down to the grace of God and it is all done for the glory of God.

The genius of grace

That is why Paul breaks out into this psalm of praise. He cannot contain his feelings any longer. He is so excited and moved by such a mountaintop experience. All is achieved on the basis of his amazing grace and the ultimate end is the glory of God.

'The inception is grace, the conception is adoption, and the reception is for his glory.' (Anonymous)

And ... it was his great idea in the first place! That is why all the glory goes to him. It was his dream and for us it has become a wonderful reality. His plan it was to seek us, save us, sanctify us, and one day to see us in heaven. He alone gets all the credit.

In moments like these I often reflect on the words of the Rob Hayward song, how relevant they are:

I'm accepted, I'm forgiven,
I am fathered by the true and living God.
I'm accepted, no condemnation,
I am loved by the true and living God.
There's no guilt or fear as I draw near
To the Saviour and Creator of the world.
There is joy and peace as I release
My worship to you, O Lord.

Win some, lose some

Adoption as sons and daughters of our heavenly Father brings both a plus and a minus into the equation of our salvation—there is an immense gain and that is offset by a necessary loss. The positive side—we gain access to him as our Father through redemption. On the negative side—we lose our blemishes through his sanctifying work in our lives, and that unique ministry continues until we are finally made perfect in heaven.

All in all, it underscores God's phenomenal, long term commitment to us as his children for he has lavished his love upon us in so many wonderful ways.

1:7, 8a

Turn your eyes upon Jesus

What do I mean? Aren't they the opening two words in verse 7 where Paul says: *in him.* That is the key phrase, the focus is exclusive to him, the spotlight is shining on the Lord. He is the centre of attention, and rightly so! It begs the question: what has he done for us?

We have seen in verses 3 to 6 all that the Father has done—he planned the church—it was his brainchild from day one. What about the Son? Do we have any indication of the level of his commitment to the project? Well, he is the one who paid the price for the church when he purchased it with his own blood (*cf.* Acts 20:28).

- There is redemption (*cf.* 1:7),
- there is revelation (*cf.* 1:8, 9), and
- there is royalty (*cf.* 1:10).

Redemption

We read: *in him we have redemption.* That means the Lord Jesus is the person involved. Basically, we are speaking here about the atoning work of Christ on Calvary's cross. Jesus is our Redeemer.

Remember the lovely story unfolding in the life of Ruth? It was amidst alien corn that she was redeemed by Boaz, a kinsman redeemer. What was so special about his role? One, he had to be qualified in that he had to be regarded as a near kinsman. Two, he had to be able. And, three, he had to be willing. The Lord Jesus was a combination of all three! Melody Green writes:

There is a Redeemer,
Jesus, God's own Son,
Precious Lamb of God,
Messiah, holy One.

A poet has expressed the magnificent grandeur and reality of redemption in the words:

Near, so very near to God,
Nearer I could not be;
For in the person of his Son,
I'm just as near as he.

Dear, so very dear to God,
Dearer I could not be;
For in the person of his Son,
I'm just as dear as he.

Our praise is 'to him who loves us and has freed us from our sins by his blood' (Revelation 1:7). We join with those around the throne in heaven and sing unto him: 'You are worthy ... because you were slain, and with your blood you purchased men for God from every tribe and language and people and nation' (Revelation 5:9). We share in a joyful anthem with angel voices when we say: 'Worthy is the Lamb, who was slain' (Revelation 5:12). We stand beside that great multitude that no one could count and we cry in a loud voice: 'Salvation belongs to our God, who sits on the throne, and to the Lamb' (Revelation 7:9, 10).

Oh yes, Frances Jane van Alstyne (1820-1915) was right when she declared: *Praise him, praise him, Jesus our blessed Redeemer.*

Grace is free, not cheap

It is one thing talking about the person, the Lord Jesus Christ, but what was the price involved? It was *through his blood*. Peter could say we are 'redeemed ... with the precious blood of Christ' (1 Peter 1:18, 19). The word *lytroō* means 'ransomed'.

It refers to the payment made to free a slave, a hostage, or a prisoner of war. It can be used to describe the experience of a man set free from the death penalty. When we go back to the Old Testament there were two possible means of redemption. One was by power and the other was by purchase.

The book of Exodus illustrates the first for that was how God delivered his people from their bondage and slavery in the land of Egypt. He redeemed them by power in that he brought them out.

As I mentioned earlier, the story of Ruth illustrates the second. That was redemption by purchase. Boaz simply said: 'I have bought all' (*cf.* Ruth 4:9, 10). We have no idea how much he paid for Ruth— so it is with the Lord Jesus. It is beyond our grasp for redemption is a costly business. He bought them out. For Jesus, it meant a cross. Well may we sing the Frances Jane van Alstyne (1820-1915) classic:

Redeemed, how I love to proclaim it,
Redeemed by the blood of the Lamb,
Redeemed through his infinite mercy,
His child and forever I am.

In a city on the shore of a great lake lived a small boy who loved the water and sailing. So deep was his fascination that he, with the help of his father, spent months making a beautiful model boat, which he began to sail at the water's edge. One day a sudden gust of wind caught the tiny boat and carried it far out into the lake and out of sight. Distraught, the boy returned home inconsolable.

Day after day he would walk the shores in search of his treasure, but always in vain. Then one day as he was walking through town he saw his beautiful boat—in a shop window! He approached the proprietor and announced his ownership, only to be told that it was not his, for the owner had paid a local fisherman good money for the boat. If the boy wanted the boat, he would have to pay the price.

And so the lad set himself to work doing anything and everything until finally he returned to the shop with the money. At last, holding his precious boat in his arms, he said with great joy: *'You are twice mine now—because I made you, and because I bought you!'*

Forgiven

When we are pardoned for our sin we experience *the forgiveness of sins*. I came across a lovely bumper sticker recently: 'I'm not perfect, just forgiven!' What a great blessing to know we can be forgiven. That is the essence of the gospel of sovereign grace—he forgives all our sins in the sweeping grace of salvation.

* Forgiveness is free,
* it is full, and
* it is felt.

The word that Paul uses here for *sin* (*paraptōma*) means 'a falling by the wayside'—it is a stepping aside from the path that we should be taking. We are out of bounds!

When God forgives, he puts us back on the right track!

Forgiveness is a fascinating word. To understand it, we really need to go back to the Old Testament. It refers to the regular remission of debts that happened every seventh year and in the year of jubilee. On top of that, every slave in a Hebrew household would serve for six years and then be freed in the seventh year. As well as that, at the end of a seven year period, every creditor would have to release all his debtors. The money could no longer be exacted from them, the slate would be wiped clean—the same word Paul uses here for *forgiveness* (*aphesis*). It means 'remission'. This is what enabled Charles Wesley (1707-88) to write:

Long my imprisoned spirit lay
Fast bound in sin and nature's night;
Thine eye diffused a quick'ning ray –
I woke, the dungeon flamed with light;
My chains fell off, my heart was free.
I rose, went forth, and followed thee.

So, in that sense, a quickie summary informs us that the death of Christ has cancelled—released—liberated—and discharged us from any spiritual obligation resulting from our sin. Grace!

Augustine (354-430), Bishop of Hippo in North Africa, succinctly said: *'Christ bought the church foul that he might make it fair.'*

No half measures

How has it been given to us? Well, we find the answer at the end of verse 7 and the beginning of verse 8 where Paul says it is *in accordance with the riches of God's grace that he lavished on us.* Some of those words are well worth thinking about. For example:

- *riches (ploutos)* speak of wealth and abundance,
- *grace (charis)* tells us it is undeserved and unmerited,
- *lavished (perisseuō)* suggests we are generously showered with forgiveness in a totally unrestrained way.

With a few carefully chosen words, the apostle paints for us a powerful picture of forgiveness that we need to rediscover in our day.

On the Day of Atonement—the solemn feast of Yom Kippur—a goat was sacrificed to take away the sins of the people of Israel. These sins were then symbolically transferred to a second goat which was dispatched into the waste howling wilderness, never to be seen again. It was called, appropriately, the scapegoat (*cf.* Leviticus 16:7-10).

As the solitary animal disappeared into the distance, this was a graphic picture for the people that their sins were carried away and gone for ever. The same truth is reflected in the New Testament when John the Baptist pointed to Jesus and said: 'Look, the Lamb of God, who takes away the sin of the world' (John 1:29).

The enemy strikes back

It seems to me when the devil comes along and reminds us of our past, as he often does, we should take a moment and remind him of his future! We have been forgiven! In Shakespeare's *King Richard III*, the king laments:

My conscience hath a thousand several tongues,
And every tongue brings in a several tale,
And every tale condemns me for a villain.

That is not true of Christians! We are forgiven! And 'there is now no condemnation for those who are in Christ Jesus' (Romans 8:1). Our past is behind us! John MacArthur sums it up well when he writes: 'God's forgiveness is infinite; it takes away our sins to the farthest reaches of infinity.'

What an unthinkable horror it would be if God had revealed himself as a God of infinite power, infallible wisdom, and inflexible holiness, a God devoid of compassion and sympathy for lost sinners, like us.

We take enormous comfort from the fact that there are no second class Christians in God's grand scheme of things. There are no deprived citizens in God's kingdom. There is no underclass when it comes to being a child in his extended family.

Every sin of every believer is forgiven forever!

God knows how we were, how we now live, and how we will live the rest of our lives. We may fool each other but we cannot fool him. He sees everything about us in stark naked reality. Yet in grace he says to us: 'I am satisfied with you because I am satisfied with my Son, to whom you belong. When I look at you, I see him, and I am well pleased.' That is what it means to be *in Christ*—we have forgiveness.

Accepting ourselves

Because God accepts us as he accepts his own Son, we should accept ourselves in the same way. Sometimes it is not the easiest thing to do—however, that is the rationale behind the truth of forgiveness. We should accept ourselves as forgiven sinners and as righteous saints for that is what God himself declares us to be.

To think otherwise is not a sign of deep humility, but of shameful arrogance. You see, any other attitude undermines the redemption price paid for us by the Lord Jesus. When we question the reality of our forgiveness through him and in him, and when we have lingering doubts about our relationship with Jesus, we end up pouring litres of cold water on the work of Christ on our behalf at Calvary. If we matter to God—and we do—we certainly ought to matter to ourselves and to one another.

His gracious work in granting us redemption covers every era and every eventuality!

- It is hugely effective today,
- it is efficient for all time, and
- it is eternal.

Forgiven much

The sheer vastness of our forgiveness is seen in Paul's statement at the end of verse 7 that it is *in accordance with the riches of his grace.* God's grace, like his love, his holiness, his power, and all his other attributes, is boundless. His grace is an expression of his munificence.

If you were to go to a multimillionaire and ask him to contribute to a worthy cause and he gave you a cheque for £50, he would only be giving to you *out of* his riches. Many poor people give that much, some give even more. If, instead, he gave you a cheque for £50,000— he would be giving to you *in accordance with* his riches.

I know that is a terribly small picture of God's extravagant generosity but it shows the largeness of his heart. He has a big heart, an expansive heart, a cosmic heart, and it is beating for you and me.

I get quite excited when I realise that our sins will never outstrip God's gracious forgiveness (*cf.* Romans 6:1-14). We cannot sin beyond God's grace, because as wicked and extensive as our sins might be or become, they will never approach the greatness of his grace. The least we can do is fall down on our knees and celebrate his love, and praise him for *the riches of [his] grace!*

1:8b, 9

Insight for living

The second 'R' is the 'R' of revelation. We read all about it in verses 8 and 9 where Paul informs us: *[It has been] lavished on us with all wisdom and understanding. And he made known to us the mystery of his will according to his good pleasure which he purposed in Christ.* Here is another wonderful blessing flowing from our salvation—we are a people who have been enlightened.

Wisdom (*sophia*) emphasises an understanding of ultimate things—an appreciation of those things that really matter—wisdom concerning the things of God. It is an ability to see life from God's perspective. *Understanding* (*phronēsis*, or insight) refers to an ability to prudently handle the nitty gritty affairs of everyday life.

God not only forgives us, he goes on to give us the equipment that we need to understand him, and to walk with him day by day. He gives us the ability to understand his word and to know how to obey it. The bottom line:

---

right thinking will lead to right actions.

Another vital perspective is that of the divine purpose. This is the truth so powerfully expressed in verse 9. Remember the memoirs of Moses when he wrote about Israel: 'The Lord did not set his affection on you and choose you because you were more numerous than other peoples, for you were the fewest of all peoples. But it was because the Lord loved you' (Deuteronomy 7:7, 8).

He was simply saying—he loved you because he loved you! Whether we realise it or not, that is the divine logic, the mindset of heaven. We should not dissect the love of God, we should enjoy it. Why did he do it? Why did his heart reach out to sinful man? Why did his grace touch and transform my life? Why did his mercy come to me where I was? Tell me why! My only answer is found in this amazing verse: he is God.

At the risk of sounding simplistic, God does what he does because he is who he is. Yes, we know that he really loves us, but we cannot comprehend it, neither can we understand it. We can never unravel the mystery of his perfect will, we are out of our depth. What a revelation!

1:10

Countdown to zero hour

The third 'R' in this amazing trio of R's is linked to royalty and we find that alluded to in verse 10 where Paul writes: *to be put into effect (oikonomia) when the times (kairos) will have reached their fulfilment (plērōma)—to bring all things in heaven and on earth together under one head, even Christ.*

What on earth is Paul referring to? Yet again, for the umpteenth time, the apostle is reminding us that history is neither meaningless nor purposeless—it is advancing towards a glorious goal when time merges into eternity again. Our God has a masterplan that finds its focus in the Lord Jesus Christ.

In the fulness of time, God's two creations, his whole universe and his whole church, will be unified under the cosmic Christ who is the supreme head of both.

We can say with robust confidence that he has set the agenda and all is going according to his schedule. Better still, it is on track! And on time!

All hail King Jesus

On the cross at Calvary, they nailed a piece of paper—the first gospel tract—above his head declaring Jesus to be the King of the Jews (*cf.* John 19:19). Today, our risen exalted Lord sits on a throne of majesty in heaven where he is hailed as the King of the saints and the King of all the ages (*cf.* Revelation 15:3). When Jesus returns in scenes of power and great glory he will be seen as the King of kings and Lord of lords and Prince of princes—that is what Paul anticipates here in verse 10. This is the day:

- when history is wound up,
- when God calls time to an end, and
- when he pulls the plug on man.

Follow the leader

There is no doubt about it, God controls events on planet earth. Paul speaks here about a moment when he will bring *all things in heaven and on earth together under one head, even Christ*—the picture here is of Christ being up front, at the head. In that day, Jesus Christ will be seen to be ruling and reigning.

This is the day when Satan will be cast down into a bottomless pit. It is the hour when the Lord's enemies will be crushed so that they become his footstool. This is the dawning of a brand new era for the millennial kingdom will be ushered in, and to the ends of the earth, and from the ends of the earth, Jesus Christ will be acknowledged as King over all the earth!

Jesus Christ is the goal of history!

No matter what direction the prevailing wind may blow, at the end of time it finds its resolution in him. The paradise lost in Adam is fully restored in Christ.

It is very easy for our hearts to sink when we watch the breaking news stories on television or hear them rehearsed on the radio. So much is happening around the world that causes us enormous concern. But no matter how tragic and heart rending these events are, we need to learn to look by faith behind secular history to see the spiritual account of things.

History is *his* story

Macbeth pessimistically declared that history is 'a tale told by an idiot, full of sound and fury, signifying nothing.' Nothing could be further from the truth!

History belongs to God, not to the puny plans of man or the perverse power of Satan. History is written and directed by its Creator and he will see it through to the very end—it will climax as the final fulfilment of his own ultimate purpose.

God is resolute. He is actively at work. Even though we live in a world damaged and bruised by sin, God is gathering his people into his eternal kingdom. No matter what takes place in today's world, we rest on the unassailable fact that God is behind the scenes directing the scenes he is behind. We gladly affirm that he has the whole world in his hands! And wait for it, he has you and me there as well. Exciting!

Seeing the big picture

That is just a little of what the Lord has graciously done for us—and the end is not yet. The best is yet to be! I think this is probably a good point in our study to pause for a moment and consider how much all of us need to develop Paul's broad perspective. It did not matter where he was or what he was doing, Paul always kept his eye on the big picture!

As my American friends tell me: *'When you are up to your ears in alligators it is hard to remember that the original intention was to drain the swamp!'*

Here was Paul—a prisoner in Rome, handcuffed to a big burly Roman soldier—times were incredibly tough! Even though his wrist was chained and his body cramped and confined, his heart and his mind inhabited eternity. He peered back *before the creation of the world* (1:4) and on to the fulness of time (*cf.* 1:10)—he grasped hold of what *we have* (1:7) and, consequently, what we ought to *be* (1:4) in the light of those two eternities.

Spiritual myopia

How blinkered is our vision in comparison with his! How small is our mind! How narrow are our horizons! It is so easy for us to slip into a preoccupation with our own petty little affairs where we see no further than our nose. The problem is, we are so often wrapped up in our personal tiny world. But we need to see time in the light of eternity. We need to see our present privileges and obligations in the light of our past election and future perfection.

Then, if we shared Paul's perspective, we would also share his praise.

Doctrine leads to doxology—doxology leads to duty!

When that happens, our lives becomes an altar of worship and we bless God 24/7 for having blessed us so richly in Christ!

Sensational stuff

This really is a chapter that blows the cobwebs from our lives—it is a fast moving account of all that the grace of God is doing in the lives of ordinary people. To me this is the greatest news story of all time, it is headline grabbing material. As Paul tells it, it is bigger, and wiser, and grander than anything we can possibly imagine.

The story has three movements like a symphony. We have listened to the first movement which highlighted the will of the Father (1:3-6), and the second movement which majored on the work of the Son (1:7-10). In the third movement the focus switches to the Holy Spirit as *a seal* (1:13) and *deposit* (1:14). The underlying emphasis in this section (1:11-14) is on the broad scope of these blessings.

Paul is at pains to point out that they belong equally to Jewish and Gentile believers. God does not make fish of one and flesh of another—he treats everyone the same! God has no favourites.

No one ethnic group has a monopoly on God's blessings.

The structure of the paragraph makes this clear and plain for there is a progressive development in Paul's line of thought. The apostle begins in verse 11 with the pronoun *we* and that refers to himself and his fellow Jewish believers. Then in verse 13 he progresses to *you* and that applies specifically to his believing Gentile readers. Finally, in verse 14, he moves to *our* and that all inclusive term is relevant to both groups.

It would appear that Paul is setting the stage for the next chapter where he elaborates on the theme of Jew and Gentile reconciliation (*cf.* 2:11-22). In paving the way, Paul shares with us a trio of great truths about God's people:

- they are God's possession,
- they depend on God's will, and
- they live for God's glory.

An alphabet of grace

When we look at this chapter and see all the wonderful ways in which God has blessed us, we begin to realise what the writer to the Hebrews meant when he wrote about our 'great salvation' (Hebrews 2:3). We can safely call it 'the ABC of the Christian gospel'. Let me show you what I mean:

- A—we are *adopted* as God's children (*cf.* 1:5),
- B—we have been *blessed* in Christ (*cf.* 1:3),

- C—we have been *chosen* by God (*cf.* 1:4, 5),
- D—we are *delivered* in Christ (*cf.* 1:7),
- E—we have been *enlightened* by Christ (*cf.* 1:8, 9),
- F—we are *forgiven* in and through Christ (*cf.* 1:7),
- G—we are *gathered* in Christ (*cf.* 1:10), and
- H—we are *hallmarked* in Christ (*cf.* 1:13, 14).

No wonder Paul talked in 3:8 about the *unsearchable riches of Christ*. They are out of this world! And yet they are real! They are personal! They are mine! Away back in the dim and distant aeons of eternity past our Father God was thinking about us. Today, we continue to feature prominently in his overall plan. And the future—our future—is as bright as the promises of God.

Treasure heaven

What has he promised us? He has guaranteed to give us an inheritance (*klēros*). It was the apostle Peter who portrayed it as one 'that can never perish, spoil or fade' (1 Peter 1:4). That simply means:

- nothing can destroy it,
- nothing can defile it,
- nothing can diminish it, and
- nothing can displace it.

According to verse 14 it is a cast iron commitment on his part. We have a fabulous future mapped out for us. These are just some of the stunning things God has planned and prepared for those who passionately love him. The potential is awesome! Mind blowing!

1:11

Jesus, I am resting, resting

The opening couple of words underline the security of our foundation. It is *in him*, that is, in the Lord Jesus Christ. You see, apart from him, all a person can expect to receive from God is condemnation. His spiritual blessings are graciously bestowed only on those who are found resting in him.

The words *we were also chosen* can be translated to read: 'we have obtained an inheritance'. Gripping stuff! This phrase of five words in the English actually translates a single compound word in the original, *eklērōthēmen*. When something in the future was so certain that it could not possibly fail to happen, the Greeks would often speak of it as if it had already occurred. That is precisely what Paul does here. A similar tense is used in 2:6 where Paul says that we are *seated with him in the heavenly realms*.

We know we are not there yet, we are still kicking the dust off our shoes down here! We need to remember that nothing can happen in this life to stop us from being there at the end of time. The same is true of our inheritance—nothing and no one can deprive us of claiming it!

I am his. He is mine.

There is a powerful double thought implied here. We are his inheritance. We are the Father's love gift to the Son—he won us at Calvary. We are the spoils of his epic victory over sin, Satan, and death. We are his valued possession.

The other way to look at it is that we receive the inheritance. He is ours. He belongs to us! He rewards us for something we have not done! When we take them both together, it means that our lives should be identified with his life.

- We are to love as he loved,
- we are to help as he helped,
- we are to care as he cared,
- we are to share as he shared, and
- we are to sacrifice for others just as he did.

You see, like our blessed Lord Jesus, we are in the world to lose our lives for the sake of others.

In the words of Jim Elliot, prior to his martyrdom at the hands of the Auca Indians: *'He is no fool who gives what he cannot keep to gain what he cannot lose.'*

God's angle

When we think about that unique inheritance, Paul looks at it from two angles. First, there is the divine perspective when he talks about God's predestination. I think it is best to read verse 11 in close harmony with verse 4. We are what we are because of what God chose to make us before the world was fashioned. From eternity past he declared that every elect sinner—though vile, rebellious, useless, and deserving only of death—who trusted in his Son, would be made as righteous as the one in whom they put their trust.

Divine energy

God's power is also given an incredibly high level of prominence in verse 11b—the word *works* (*energeō*) is the root from which we get such English words as 'energy, energetic, and energise'. It seems to me that energising is an indispensable part of God's creative plan and work. Because in his wondrous grace, God chose us to be his children, citizens of his kingdom, and joint heirs with his Son, he will bring all of that to fruition.

Yes, God has a plan and that plan is up and running, and one day that same plan will be finally completed—it will come to pass. Paul says something similar in Philippians 1:6 where we read: '... he who began a good work in you will carry it on to completion until the day of Christ Jesus.'

In other words, God works out what he has planned and purposed. He energises every believer with all the power necessary for his spiritual completion.

God not only makes the plan, he also makes it work out.

The pre-eminence of our Lord is seen in the reason why he redeemed us. It is that we *might be for the praise of his glory* (1:12). It is for the purpose of restoring the divine image that was seriously marred by sin. Ah, the goal of salvation is the goal of creation! He wants each of us to give him the glory, both by our lives and by our testimony.

Man's perspective

There is a human perspective to all of this. Why do we give our lives to Jesus Christ? There is only one viable reason—because there is *hope in Christ* (1:12). That means we place our simple faith and childlike trust in him, knowing he will not let us down, and he will never let us go.

1:13

Hearing is believing

And you also were included in Christ when you heard the word of truth, the gospel of your salvation. Look again at verse 13 and ask yourself the question: how did we do it? We heard the truth, we heard the gospel, we heard the good news—that is where faith comes from! It comes from hearing the word of God. That is how a sinner becomes a saint.

There is no other way! Nobody can be saved apart from the word of truth. Human cleverness, a high IQ rating, eloquence, persuasive oratory, none of these can save our souls. God has not promised to bless our programmes or even bless our performances, although he may do that, but he always blesses his word. This is the great ministry of the Holy Spirit, he drives home the word as we see in Isaiah 55:11.

'The witness of the Spirit of God is to the Son of God by means of the word of God.' (Warren Wiersbe)

The same God who ordains the end in the salvation of precious souls also ordains the means to the end—the preaching of the gospel in the power of the Spirit.

So there are two sides to the same coin—there is God's side and there is man's side. Faith is man's response to God's elective purpose. Or again, we can look at it like this: God's choice of man is election, man's choice of God is faith—in election God gives his promises, and by faith men receive them.

A gentleman's agreement

The final sentence draws attention to the guarantee of our inheritance. From day one, men have always wanted assurances. They want to see it in black and white before they believe it! The promises of men are often unreliable and because we have been let down at the last minute on different occasions, we demand oaths, sworn affidavits, surety bonds, warranties, and such like.

God's word should be sufficient for us. At least we know where we stand when God speaks. He says what he means, and he means what he says. He is as good as his word, every time, for his word is his bond.

However, in grace, the Lord makes his promises even more certain, if that were possible. He gives us his personal assurance— he underwrites the whole salvation project from start to finish. We read: *having believed, you were marked in him with a seal, the promised Holy Spirit.* Such a statement intimates the proof of our faith.

The divine validation

The *seal* (*sphragizō*) which Paul speaks of refers to an official mark of identification that was placed on a letter. Even today, we often see something similar on a contract or other important document. The seal was usually made from hot wax. It was then placed on the document and impressed with a signet ring.

The document was, therefore, officially identified with the person to whom the signet belonged. It was also under the authority of the person whose seal had been used. The clear implication from what Paul is saying is that the Holy Spirit himself is the guarantor.

That breathes absolute assurance into our hearts—it speaks of eternal security and suggests a finished transaction. We can look at it like this: here is the prime reason for our faith. We are saved because of Calvary, we are born again because of love's redeeming work on the cross, we are made right with God and reconciled to him because of what he accomplished there, it was there that the great work of redemption was completed.

We are where we are ... we are what we are ... we are whose we are, by the amazing grace of God.

Since we are resting on the impregnable rock of a finished work, all is well with our souls. Not only are we baptised in the Spirit, not only do we receive the gift of the Spirit, not only are we indwelt by the Spirit, but our heavenly Father comes along and sets his personal seal upon our salvation—the person of the Holy Spirit. It shows we belong to Jesus.

God's eternity ring

We look at some people and we wonder (rightly or wrongly) about the genuineness of their conversion, we question the sincerity of their profession of faith, we sometimes doubt the reality of their experience of the grace of God. However, the abiding truth is: the Lord knows (*cf.* 2 Timothy 2:19). The genuine article, the real McCoy believer, always bears the seal and that seal can never be broken. It cannot be severed.

Our life in him is everlasting, his life in us is eternal.

And eternity is never ending, it just goes on, and on, and on! That means no matter what life throws at us, we will always belong to the Lord. We will always be kept by his power (*cf.* 1 Peter 1:5). We have the royal crest of heaven indelibly graven upon our hearts.

God's untouchables

So far we have looked at the general idea of our being sealed, let us be a little more specific. The seal of God's Spirit in the believer signifies four primary truths: number one, security.

In ancient times the seal of a king, a prince, or some other dignitary represented security and it spoke of that which could not be violated. When Daniel was thrown into the den of lions, Darius placed his seal on the stone which was placed over the entrance to the den (*cf.* Daniel 6:17). Any person, but the king, who broke or disturbed the seal would likely have forfeited his life. They would have been thrown to the lions.

In a similar way, the tomb where Jesus was buried was sealed (*cf.* Matthew 27:66). Fearing that Jesus' disciples might steal his body and falsely claim his resurrection, the Jewish leaders obtained Pilate's permission to place the seal of the Sanhedrin on the stone and to guard it with soldiers.

In an infinitely greater way, the Holy Spirit secures each individual believer. We are marked with his seal—unbreakable and tamper proof.

A poisoned pen

The seal also spoke of authenticity. For example, when king Ahab tried unsuccessfully to get Naboth to sell or trade his vineyard, his bossy wife Jezebel volunteered to get the vineyard her way. We read that she wrote letters in her husband's name and sealed them with his personal seal (*cf.* 1 Kings 21:6-16).

She mailed the defamatory letters to various high ranking officials who lived in Naboth's city and demanded that they begin a whispering campaign against him. She wanted them to accuse the man of God of blasphemy and treason. These men were like poodles in the hand of Jezebel—they toed the party line and, eventually, Naboth was stoned to death. Ahab then confiscated the vineyard which he wanted so badly.

Even though the letters were crammed full with lies, they were authentic because they were sent with his approval and marked with his seal, his personal signature.

When God gives us his Holy Spirit, it is as if he stamps us with a seal that bears the inscription: '[Sam Gordon] belongs to me and is an authentic citizen of my divine kingdom and accredited member of my divine family.'

The divine proprietor

Security. Authenticity. The seal represents ownership. When Jerusalem was under siege by Nebuchadnezzar and Jeremiah was under arrest, the Lord gave special instructions to his servant. He told him in Jeremiah 32 to buy a plot of land in Anathoth for which he had redemption rights. The contract was agreed and the full amount was paid in the normal way. In the presence of the witnesses, the deed was signed and sealed. That meant Jeremiah was the new owner of the property.

When the Holy Spirit seals us, he marks us out as God's own possession. We are under new ownership. Under new management.

From that moment we belong entirely and eternally to him.

The seal of the Spirit thereby declares the transaction of salvation as divinely official and final.

Divine clout

Finally, the seal signifies authority. Even after Haman had been hanged for his wicked plot to defame and execute Mordecai, Queen Esther was distressed about the decree that Haman had persuaded the king to make (*cf.* Esther 8:8-12). The baseline: it left the floodgates wide open so that anyone could attack and destroy the Jews and expect to get away with it.

The king himself could not even revoke the decree that was marked with his own seal, so he had to issue another one and seal it, thereby overturning the previous statute. In both cases the absolute authority of the decrees was represented in the king's seal. Those who possessed the sealed decree of the king had the king's delegated authority set forth in the decree.

The same principle holds true in our lives. When we are sealed with the Holy Spirit we are delegated to proclaim his gospel, to teach his truth, to defend his word—we are called to minister in his name because we have his authority so to do.

1:14

Playing the end game

The goal of our inheritance is the wonderful theme of this verse. We have a fascinating picture of the Holy Spirit as *a deposit* (*arrabōn*). The general drift of Paul's insight on this aspect of his ministry is that he is a down payment.

- He is not only proof of our position in Christ, he is also the pledge of our possessions in Christ.
- He not only confirms our faith, he also confirms our future.
- He not only guarantees our eternal security, he also guarantees our eternal satisfaction.

A sample of all things nice

What is the meaning behind such an apt description of the Spirit of God? Back in Romans 8:23 we read about the 'firstfruits' of the Holy Spirit. You could be forgiven for thinking, what is the connection between them when it appears as though Paul is talking about two entirely different concepts. The fact is, he isn't! Believe it or not, it is exactly the same idea.

As a deposit, the Holy Spirit is the foretaste of all that is to come. We find this beautifully illustrated in the story of the spies who made a reconnaissance trip into the land of Canaan. Caleb and Joshua brought back with them the luscious fruit of the land of promise—a huge cluster of delicious mouth watering grapes as well as pomegranates and figs (*cf.* Numbers 13:17-25).

That was a glimpse of what the people could expect when they crossed over into Canaan land. Likewise the Holy Spirit brings to us a foretaste of heavenly fulness.

He gives us a little bit of heaven to go to heaven with!

Absence makes the heart grow fonder

Another illustration is that of the engagement ring. When a fella gives the girl he loves such a token for her to wear on her fourth finger, whether he realises it or not, he is making a firm commitment to her. It is a covenant of love between two parties—an agreement which, in the biblical analogy, is binding.

The promise of the forthcoming marriage will one day be honoured. He has given his word and that is all that is needed. He has given his ring and that is his guarantee. Between now and the event we know as the wedding of the Lamb (*cf.* Revelation 19:6-9), we are said to be engaged to the Lord Jesus Christ. What a stunning and special relationship that is—breathtakingly beautiful—a relationship based on mutual love.

At this moment in time we are absent from our Lord. That is true! Nevertheless, our love for him grows stronger and deeper. We look forward with bated breath to the happy day when we shall meet in the glory. We anticipate the joyful hour when we shall see him in all his beauty.

Better on before

The term can also be spoken of as a deposit that has been paid. The Holy Spirit is like a first instalment that has been made—the rest to follow later. What God has already given in part, we know he will bestow at last in perfection. Now we have the initial experience, but we know the best is yet to be. We enjoy him at this point in time, but this is only a pledge of future happiness in glory.

Oh yes, there is some little delay before the final goods are delivered, we have only received the sample copy, as it were—the inheritance is ours right now but we do not enter into it until then. There is a supremely better life waiting for us on the other side of death. Today, we have grace—tomorrow, it may be glory. What is grace? Grace is glory begun in the soul.

It was C H Spurgeon who coined the phrase: *'Little faith will take your soul to heaven, but great faith will bring heaven to your soul.'*

Eavesdropping on eternity

That has to be the singular most important aim of the Holy Spirit in our lives—to give us a foretaste of that which is to come. Soon the new day will break and the shadows will flee away. Then, for the first time, our eyes will see the Lord. A spine tingling moment! To be sure. What a meeting! I often think of the words penned by Charles Butler:

Once heaven seemed a far off place,
Till Jesus showed his smiling face;
Now it's begun within my soul,
It will last while endless ages roll.

Thank God, we have heaven in our hearts. At the end of it all, Paul has shown us exactly where we stand. And he has done it by giving us a vista of the trinity in action on our behalf: we have looked at the will of the Father, the atoning work of the Son, and the affirming witness of the Holy Spirit.

Priorities

I read a story recently which really touched my heart. It was about a distraught wife who could not make any sense of her life—her dreams were shattered, her high hopes had not been realised, her marriage was falling apart. Life for her was little more than broken pieces.

On an emotional level, she was coming apart at the seams. She had come to the point where she was tearing her hair out!

One day, bless her, she plucked up courage and went to a counsellor. It was not long before she opened up and, through her tears, she poured out her heart. Every so often she would punctuate a sentence with the words: '... but we have so much!'

And then she went on: 'Look at this diamond ring on my finger, it's worth thousands. We have a hugely expensive mansion in an exclusive area. We have three cars, and even a cottage in the mountains. Why, we have everything money can buy!'

The wise counsellor listened and after a while he said: 'It's really good to have the things money can buy, provided you don't lose the things money can't buy. What good is there in having a big expansive house, if there's no home? What benefit is there in having an expensive ring on your finger, if there's no love?'

When I reflected on that story, it suddenly dawned on me, it hit me between the eyes, and I began to realise that in Christ we have the things which money cannot buy. These riches which Paul talks about in Ephesians 1 were all planned by the Father in eternity past, they were purchased by the Son on the cross at Calvary, and they were presented to us by the Holy Spirit at the moment of our conversion.

There is really no need for us to live our lives as if we were below the breadline, when all of God's wealth is at our disposal.

For the believer, there is no poverty trap when it comes to the riches we have in Jesus. The apostle has left us breathless with the sheer undiluted wonder of it all. It seems to me we can do nothing more than think big thoughts about God.

Full circle

What is it all for? Why has he done it? Paul provides the answer at the end of the verse when he says, for the third time, it is all *to the praise of his glory* (*doxa*). Before we go any further in our study this delightful phrase needs to be unpacked.

The 'glory of God' is the revelation of God and the 'glory of his grace' (*cf.* 1:6) is when he manifests himself as a gracious God. John Stott says, when we live *to the praise of his glorious grace* it means: 'We are worshipping him ourselves by our words and deeds as the gracious God that he is and, at the same time, we cause others to see and to praise him too.' This was God's will for Israel under the old economy of the law, it remains his purpose today for the international community of the redeemed people of God.

We have almost come full circle—everything we have and all that we are in Christ both comes from God and returns to God!

It begins in his will and it ends in his glory.

Signed. Sealed. Delivered. That is why we lustily sing the cheery words:

To God be the glory,
Great things he hath done!

1:15

Touching the throne

In the previous section (1:3-14), the apostle has been reminding us where we stand. The bottom line: we stand complete in Christ. He is all I need and all that I need is found in him. In the second half of the chapter, Paul goes a logical step further and intimates the reason why we stand, where we stand—it is all down to prayer!

Prayer makes a world of difference because prayer makes all the difference in the world.

Prayer is the baseline. It is the oil that keeps us running. You see, when we pray, God works! When we take a moment and analyse Paul's impassioned prayer for the Ephesian believers, we discover there are two major components to it. For example, it is:

- a church centred prayer (*cf.* 1:15, 16), and
- a Christ centred prayer (*cf.* 1:17-23).

Great prayers

This is marvellous for here we see the great man himself down on his knees. We rarely picture Paul as an outstanding man of prayer, but he was! We normally think of men of the ilk of Moses as a mighty intercessor when he met God on top of the mountain. We think of David with his worshipful and celebratory Psalms. And Elijah who stood alone before an altar drenched with water at Mount Carmel. Then there was Daniel who opened his window toward Jerusalem and prayed three times a day, even though he lived in a hostile and secular environment.

When it comes to storming the gates of heaven, Paul may not have hit the headlines to the same extent that these Old Testament heroes did—but that does not make him any less an intercessor! On a good day, he was more than a match for any of them!

The fly on the wall syndrome

We watch Paul praying the first of two prayers right here (the second is in 3:14-21). We eavesdrop. We hear all that he has to say. Hopefully, we will learn the lessons that we need to learn. If we do, our lives, like theirs in the first century, will be the richer for it.

Why does Paul pray? What is the reason behind it? What is it that drives him to his knees? It seems there are two main contributory factors in verse 15. He talks about *their faith* (*pistis*) *and their love* (*agapē*). By any stretch of the imagination, that has to be seen as a delightful combination.

Sometimes, when Paul was penning an epistle, he warmly commended the believers for their faith (*cf.* Romans 1:8). There were other occasions when he picked up his quill and, writing on the parchment, he drew attention to three influences which he believed are most important in any church—the trusted trio of faith, hope, and love—he highlighted these life enriching qualities when he corresponded with the churches in Thessalonica and Colosse (*cf.* 1

Thessalonians 1:3; Colossians 1:3-5). However, in Ephesians, the apostle, not a stickler for change, broke the mould and only mentioned two of them: *faith and love.*

Their faith reached up and their love reached out. Their faith was toward the Lord and their love was toward the people of God.

The work goes on ...

Paul had spent the best part of three years in the environs of Ephesus and he would know many of the Christians by name. They were buddies. For quite a few of them, he was their father in the Lord—he had personally led them to saving faith in Christ. He had seen them gloriously converted under his anointed ministry.

Even with him well out of the way, the move of God's Spirit was continuing. The faithful preaching and systematic teaching of Scripture was being signally owned and blessed by God. People were responding to Jesus, people were growing in their faith—these are the ones that Paul is talking about in verse 15.

Their faith was not like the man who was attempting to cross the frozen St Lawrence River in Canada. Unsure whether the ice would hold, the man first tested it by laying one hand on it. Then he got down on his knees and gingerly began making his way across. When he got to the middle of the frozen river trembling with fear, he heard a noise behind him. Looking back, to his horror he saw a team of horses pulling a carriage down the road into the river. And upon reaching the river they did not stop, but bolted right onto the ice and past him, while he crouched on all fours, turning a deep crimson. If only he had known how firm the ice really was that day!

The news, especially about them, which has filtered back to Paul through the grapevine, is excellent. Heart warming stuff. We need to keep in mind that Paul finds himself in prison so he cannot pay them a pastoral visit. However, not one to give up easily, Paul knew there was a way to beat the system!

With a 'never say die' attitude, Paul knew he could drop them a line, and he did—he could certainly pray for them, and he did! Take heart, we are never out of work when it comes to serving the Lord Jesus!

The devil had as much reason to fear Paul's prayers as he had to fear his preaching and his pen.

I can't stop loving you

I suppose most of us find it fairly easy to love some of the Lord's people, some of the time. Not much of a problem there. No big deal. However, evangelical churches being what they are, it is not quite so easy to love all of the Lord's people, all of the time. That, it has to be said, is a different ballgame! In situations like that, we are relationally challenged! Believe me, it can be tough!

They managed to buck the trend in Ephesus! They did it! Their love was not just a motto or an adhesive sticker to put on the back window of their flashy car. Their love was real. They wore their heart on their sleeve. It was the badge on the lapel of their lives.

This brand of love is not confined to those we like, nor those who like us, nor even those we would like to have like us.

There is nothing selective about true love. I must say there is one thing I really appreciate and admire about Paul—he does not have the clique mentality. Yes, we can love the lovely, we can love the loveable, and we can love the loving. That is easy! In the congregation in Ephesus, however, their love embraced every member of the church family. In other words, Christian love is indiscriminate.

Turned off

Sometimes we hear well-meaning Christians say: 'I love [so-and-so] in the Lord.' To be honest with you, every time I hear it, I cringe! It implies that they have no personal affection for them, no real heart for them, no sense of commitment to their needs as a person—an individual made, like them, in the image of God. They extend a certain spiritualised kind of love to them only because the other person is a fellow believer. Such love is like drinking skimmed milk—there is nothing of substance to it!

To truly love a person in the Lord is to love them as the Lord loves them—genuinely and sacrificially. No matter who sat down in the fellowship of God's people at Ephesus, they were loved. They knew it! And everyone else knew it! Think about it like this:

- how do we love those who see things differently to us?
- how do we love those in God's family who disagree with us?
- how do we love those whose temperament is the opposite of ours?
- how do we love those whose culture clashes with ours?
- how do we love those who have a different mindset?
- how do we love those with a different set of values?

The key question—a challenging one—how do we love them?

Contagious Christianity

Paul loved the Lord's people with an *agapē* kind of love. John 3:16 love. What thrills me is this, Paul's love was infectious and contagious. The believers at Ephesus caught it, it had rubbed off on their lives, and so too had their converts. It must have been a super fellowship.

In spite of a motley crew of people and the pressures and problems they brought with them, there was a love that was overflowing in their midst. That, in the final analysis, is always the acid test. I often think of the words penned by John in his epistle: 'We know that we have passed from death to life, because we love our brothers' (1 John 3:14).

Sound theology is mega important but sound theology is no substitute for love.

You see, without love, the best doctrine is like a resounding gong or a clashing cymbal (*cf.* 1 Corinthians 13:1). When it came to the church at Ephesus, there was nothing like that! They had a living and vibrant faith toward God and a I-can't-do-enough-for-you, I'll-take-you-the-way-I-find-you love toward each other. We may try from now until the cows come home but we cannot separate the two—they always run in tandem.

1:16

Perseverance in prayer

How does Paul pray for these wonderful people? Is it now and again? No, certainly not! We read that he has *not stopped* (*pauō*) *giving thanks* (*eucharisteō*) for them as he has fondly remembered them in prayer. It was constant. He was always at it. He just kept on praying for them. There was a lot of praise mingled with a lot of prayer. In a word, Paul says, 'thanks Lord' for them.

There was obviously a time when he started praying for them—however, the important thing is, he has not stopped. They mean so much to him. He regularly and frequently thanked God for each of them and for the tremendous joy they have brought to his heart. How encouraging that must have been for them.

Paul writes and tells them that he feels for them in the way that he does—the horizontal component. At the same time, his praise is directed heavenward—the vertical constituent. It works two ways for they would be uplifted and God would be exalted. I am sure that must have boosted their morale and really blessed them.

I reckon the best time to give flowers to people is when they are living, not dead.

So Paul turns to them and says: 'Thanks for the privilege of being with you!' And he turns to God and says: 'Thanks for letting me be there!'

1:17

Hotline to heaven

Paul's opening phrase is a choice one indeed! In fact, it is so good, it conveys more than words can possibly tell. He tells the truth by saying: *I keep asking.* Here is a man who never gives up, who does not know what it is to give in, for whom it is always too soon to quit.

As I mentioned earlier, there was obviously a time when Paul began praying for them and, even with the passing of time, he is still at it, he has not stopped. That is commitment, loyalty, and stickability. That is prayer the way God intended it should be.

Prayer list

When Paul spent time in prayer on their behalf, I wonder, what kind of things did he pray for? This is what we see illustrated in a profound manner in verses 17-23. Basically, he wanted them to get to know God better!

- To know more of the attributes of Christ (*cf.* verse 17).
- To know more of the achievements of Christ (*cf.* verse 18).
- To know more of the ability of Christ (*cf.* verses 19-21).
- To know more of the ascendancy of Christ (*cf.* verses 22, 23).

The chances are that is not the way we pray! Nine times out of ten when we get down on our knees before the Lord, other matters loom large in our prayers. Better health. More money. Ideal job conditions. Family problems. World crises. The reality is that we are quite narrow and insular in our praying.

There is a parochial bent to our intercession—more often than not, it revolves around me, myself, and I.

It is our personal needs and the needs of our close family that we generally focus on and, now and again, we widen the net and zoom in on a handful of national and global matters.

Focused prayer

There is absolutely nothing wrong with praying for these other items—each is important and all are perfectly legitimate. And yet, what amazes me is this, in none of Paul's prison prayers does he request anything of a material nature. The emphasis is always on spiritual perception and the development of real Christian character. He does not ask God to give them what they do not have—he prays that God will reveal to them what they already have.

Paul prayed that people might know God better and, in so doing, become better acquainted with Jesus. They needed to see and know what was on God's heart. It is the *knowing you, Jesus, there is no greater thing* (Graham Kendrick) mindset. He wanted them to have a profound appreciation of who they are in Jesus Christ, and then to appropriate the resources which are available to them. They can begin to answer their own prayers as they personalise all that they have in the Lord.

Be what we are

Warren Wiersbe tells the story of how William Randolph Hearst once read of an extremely valuable piece of art which he decided he must add to his extensive collection. He instructed his agent to scour the galleries of the world to find the masterpiece he was determined to have at any price. After many months of painstaking search, the agent reported that the piece already belonged to Mr Hearst and had been stored in one of his warehouses for many years.

Unfortunately, too many of God's people appear to suffer an identity crisis in relation to who they are and what they have in Christ. The repercussions of their confused outlook are far reaching for it seriously impinges on their lifestyle. You see, it is only when we know who we really are that we can live like who we are. For example, because we are rich in Christ, there is no need for us to live like mendicants!

It is only when we come to understand how our lives are anchored in eternity that we can have the right perspective and motivation for living in time. What we are is reflected in what we do!

It is only when we come to a fuller understanding of our heavenly citizenship that we can even begin to live obedient and productive lives as godly citizens on planet earth. Perhaps we need to pray that prayer for ourselves today: 'Lord, it's really great to know you, but I want to know you more and more.'

Geared for growth

Paul had his head well screwed on for he knew that growth in knowledge is indispensable to growth in holiness. We cannot have one without seeing the benefit in the other. And so, in his first petition in verse 17, Paul longed that they might know more of the attributes of the person of Jesus Christ.

It is interesting to note that when the apostle interceded on their behalf, he directed his prayer in the first instance to the *God of our Lord Jesus Christ*. What a lovely phrase that is. When we go into reverse mode and move back to verse 3, he referred to him there as the *Father of our Lord Jesus Christ*. Why the difference between the two?

It seems to me to be a reminder to us that Jesus became such a real human being that God was his God just as much as he is our God. That means it is only through the Lord Jesus that this God can be fully known and approached. The Lord Jesus is the only one who has spanned the huge gap between God and man. He is the only one who has bridged the gulf.

God of glory, we exalt your name

Paul portrays him in the next phrase as *the glorious Father*. What a marvellous title that is! It can actually be translated to read: *the Father of glory*. Remember, Jesus is spoken of as the 'Lord of glory' in 1 Corinthians 2:8. Then in the following two verses the Holy Spirit is described as the revealer of glory. Invariably, when it comes to glory, it is all wrapped up in the trinity. There we find:

- the origin of glory,
- the source of glory, and
- the King of glory.

And, because of that, he is the one to whom all glory belongs. It is exclusive. Sure, we can know about God—and that is really good. But, says the apostle, we can know God—and that is a million times better.

We can know him in the glory of his person, and we can know him in all the glory of his personality as he reveals himself to us. He has chosen to make himself known to his people in a couple of ways— in the inspired word and in the incarnate word.

'He has said what he is like in the one, and he has shown what he is like in the other.' (John Phillips)

That means the ball is back in our court—the onus is on us to get to know him better. That is the perpetual challenge we face! The key questions: how do we do it, how do we go about it? I think the answer is fairly straightforward: get to know the Scriptures for the more *au fait* we are with them, the more we will know the Saviour of whom they speak. That should not surprise us for we find Christ in all the Scriptures (*cf.* Luke 24:27).

Going on with God

I cannot think of any greater or grander occupation this side of heaven for the pilgrim people of God. To be honest with you, I cannot think of a better way to spend my time. I would encourage each of you right now to make this your personal goal, and go for it.

Make it your ambition to get to know the Lord.

We should not be content with what we know of him today— there is so much more to learn. We should not be satisfied with where we are spiritually at this moment—there is a lot more land to claim. Our experience of God is designed to be a deepening one—it should be growing and developing. It is going from strength to strength as we move on with God and follow through into a more intimate walk with the Lord. Quite simply, it is getting to know God better.

The divine eye opener

That is why Paul prayed that we might have the *Spirit of wisdom (sophia) and revelation (apokalypsis)*. As it were, they are the tools of the trade. It has nothing to do with our attainments in the world of education, nor has it anything to do with our level of intelligence. No matter how clever we think we are, unless the Holy Spirit gives us an understanding of truth, our hearts will remain darkened. We desperately need the light which comes when he shines within. He excels in the art of illumination.

We have been caught up in something so big, so basic, so beautiful, and so far beyond anything we could ask or think, that our tiny minds simply cannot take it all in. No wonder Paul prayed the way that he did. To know God, we cannot go higher than that.

- The atheist tells me: 'There is no God for us to know!'
- The agnostic tells me: 'If there is a God, we cannot know him!'
- Fact: we know there is a God—we have met him and, in the person of Jesus Christ, we know him.

We can look at it like this:

- to know God personally is salvation,
- to know God increasingly is sanctification, and
- to know God perfectly is glorification.

Ah, the better we know God, the better we know ourselves, and the better we know each other! It is not enough to know God only as Saviour. We must get to know him as our heavenly Father, as our faithful friend, as our trusted guide and, the better we know him, the more satisfying and enthralling our relationship will be. We join with Mark Prendergrass and say:

The greatest thing in all my life is knowing you,
The greatest thing in all my life is knowing you,
I want to know you more, I want to know you more,
The greatest thing in all my life is knowing you.

1:18

Where hope is at a premium

When Paul comes to verse 18 he prays, with an inspirational touch, for something totally different. He wants the believers to know more of the splendid achievements of Christ. He prays that the Lord would open our eyes and, when he does, that we would take the blinkers off! His aspiration is that our vision of Christ would not be blurred. Why? It is far too good to miss!

Our hope is in the Lord. He says: *that we may know the hope to which he has called [us].* There are two main thoughts which Paul has successfully linked together—we have a hope and we have been called. There is a connection between them!

When biblical writers employ the word *hope* (*elpis*) in a portion of Scripture, it generally homes in on the unfolding drama of end time events, or it focuses attention on the completion of what has already begun, because hope is faith standing on tiptoe. By linking the idea of the 'call' to the 'hope', Paul is saying that the calling of God is not without a context. In other words, God is not calling to us in a fog!

God has graciously called us *to* something and God has called us *for* something.

The word *called* (*klēsis*) is an extremely important word in the Christian's vocabulary. For example, the word 'church' is a combination of two words, *ekklēsia*, which means 'called out'. When we stop and think about it, that calling was initiated in the council chambers of God in eternity past (*cf.* 1:4). It was more fully implemented in our lives when we came to know Jesus Christ as Lord and Saviour, and the Holy Spirit as Comforter (*cf.* 1:13). Needless to say, it will have its ultimate fulfilment in heaven (*cf.* 1:14).

From eternity to eternity

Our calling is all down to the intention of God. It embraces the wide sweep of God's eternal purposes in Christ.

We have not merely hitched our wagon to a wandering star.

It is entirely focused in Christ from beginning to end. We are the objects of his personal attention and constant affection. He is vitally interested in each one of us now and, at the same time, he is passionately enthused about our eventual destiny. Here is the great God who has turned aside from running the world to concentrate on people like us. We have been called.

On the bandwagon

Paul never tired of testifying that God called him by his sovereign grace (*cf.* Galatians 1:15). He reminded young Timothy that ours is 'a holy calling' (2 Timothy 1:9). Peter, not one to be left behind, said in 1 Peter 2:9 that we have been 'called out of darkness into his marvellous light'. And in 1:3 of his second epistle, Peter goes on to say that we been 'called to glory'.

Charles Hutchinson Gabriel (1856-1932) captured the mood well when he wrote:

> *He called me long before I heard,*
> *Before my sinful heart was stirred,*
> *But when I took him at his word,*
> *Forgiven, he lifted me.*

Keeping your head above water

Because we have been called, we have a wonderful hope. Paul wants us to be occupied with exhilarating thoughts about our hope in Christ. When we do that, it enables us to place the mundane things of time and sense into proper perspective. We see events in our lives through a different lens.

It begs the question: what is the hope that we have? It is not a 'hope so' vague kind of hope—rather, it is a firm watertight assurance for the future. The hope we have is that one day we shall see Jesus and with our eyes we shall behold the King in all his impeccable beauty. It is the hope that one day in God's time we shall be with the Lord, and that promises to be much better than anything we could ever imagine. It is the hope that one day Jesus shall return and that, for the Christian, is the icing on the cake of a fruitful life of walking by faith.

Jesus makes a difference

When we were lost and still in our sin we read in 2:12 that we were a people *without hope.* But when we came to Jesus, he gave us a living, pulsating hope. We gladly sing with John Peterson:

> *I have a hope that will surely endure,*
> *After the passing of time,*
> *I have a future in heaven for sure,*
> *There in those mansions sublime.*
> *And it's because of that wonderful day,*
> *When at the cross I believed,*
> *Riches eternal and blessings supernal,*
> *From his precious hand I received.*

To me that is hope with a capital H. That is what keeps us going when the burdens are heavy and the battle is hard. Such a hope will put a twinkle in our eye, it will add a metre to our every step, it will put the sparkle back into our jaded lives. Yes, thank God, when we know Jesus, we have a hope!

Recently I came across the story of Philip Henry, the father of Matthew Henry, the famous Bible commentator. As one does, he and a young lady had fallen head over heels in love with each other. She belonged to a higher level of society than he did and, although she had become a keen Christian and therefore regarded such things differently, her parents saw the disparity in social status as an obstacle to their proposed marriage.

'*This man, Philip Henry,*' they brusquely said, '*where has he come from?*' To this derogatory question, the future Mrs Henry gave the immortal reply: '*I do not know where he has come from, but I do know where he is going!*'

Primarily, that is what hope is all about—it gives us a distinct edge over the man next door. It gives us an imperial confidence to face the uncertainties of tomorrow, an ability to see beyond the ups and downs of today. We are marching to Zion! Destined for the throne!

Edward Mote (1797-1874) crystallises our thoughts with his hymn:

My hope is built on nothing less
Than Jesus' blood and righteousness;
I dare not trust the sweetest frame,
But wholly lean on Jesus' name.

On Christ, the solid Rock, I stand;
All other ground is sinking sand.

Inheritance with a difference

We discover another wonderful fact in this verse—God has a vested interest in each of us for Paul speaks of *the riches of his glorious inheritance (klēronomia) in the saints.* Wow!

It is worth noting that this is not the same aspect which we talked about when we put the spotlight on verse 11—there we have an inheritance in him. Seven verses later, we find that his inheritance is in us. Breathtaking!

In moneyspeak, God looks upon his people as an asset.

We are an integral part of his phenomenal wealth because we are seen as the dividend he received from his massive investment at Calvary. This surely reminds us that God gets something out of our salvation as well. Incredible! We cannot even begin to understand it.

What we get is him, and that defies description—what he gets is the likes of us, and that transcends comprehension.

A poor bargain for him, or so it would seem. When we stop and think about it for a minute, it is maybe not as bad as it looks on the surface. In his wisdom and grace, God obviously thought we were well worth saving—we are, after all, a bride for his one and only Son.

Heaven's crown jewels

We need to realise that our Father God has no inheritance in the sinner. Absolutely none! It is, exclusively, *in the saints!* It is his redemptive work alone which gives us our value, and that is attributed to his precious blood.

Paul draws attention to the aura of his inheritance. There is a glory associated with it and a gloriousness attached to it. It is the endless theme of seraph song for the angels before the throne sing about it day and night. It is the wonder of all wonders in a land of hope and glory.

Paul talks about the *riches* (*ploutos*) of it. That implies we are a source of untold wealth on the balance sheet of heaven. We really do matter to him in a way that is beyond our comprehension.

We are the brightest jewels in his crown (*cf.* Malachi 3:17).

Great! I cannot explain it, I am out of my depth, but I know it is true. And so, I just rejoice in it, I enjoy it for what it is.

Back to the future

There is another lovely thought in our text which is inextricably linked with this particular truth.

God deals with us on the basis of our future, not on the basis of our past.

One day the Lord spoke to cowardly Gideon and said: 'The Lord is with you, mighty warrior' (Judges 6:12). He said to Andrew's brother: 'You are Simon, son of John. You will be called Cephas' (John 1:42). What happened to each of them?

Well, in God's good time, Gideon did become a mighty man of valour. We can read all about his daring exploits for the Lord in the book of Judges. And Simon did become Peter—he was a rock in the early church in those heady and halcyon days we read about in the Acts of the Apostles.

Something worth living for

The message is: we live in the future tense. Our lives should be controlled by what we shall be when Jesus returns. Exciting! It certainly is. And the more we get to know the Lord, the better it becomes.

Dr Harry Ironside tells of meeting a very godly man early on in his ministry. The poor soul was dying of TB and Ironside had gone to see him on a pastoral visit. His name was Andrew Fraser. He could barely speak above a whisper for his lungs were almost gone.

They chatted together for many hours until Mr Ironside, with tears running down his cheeks, finally said to him: '*Andrew, how come you know the Lord so well? Where did you acquire your depth of knowledge of God and his word?*' Fraser humbly replied: '*I learned these things on my knees on the mud floor of a little thatched cottage in the north of Ireland. There with my open Bible before me, I used to kneel for hours at a time and ask the Spirit of God to reveal Christ to my soul and to open the word to my heart, and he taught me more on my knees on that mud floor than I ever could have learned in all the seminaries or colleges in the world.'*

To me, that is the perennial secret to knowing him—it is quality time spent with the Lord. I believe it is to such people who sit at Jesus' feet that God opens his heart!

1:19

How great thou art!

Someone challenged me recently with the statement: 'Sam, think big thoughts about God!' I think there is a fascinating similarity between this prayer and the benediction recorded at the end of his second prayer. There, Paul commends them to one *who is able to do immeasurably more than all we ask or imagine, according to his power that is at work within us* (3:20, 21).

What we glean from both these statements is that our God is a great God, a God of power, a God who is able, a God who can surprise us, a God who can do absolutely anything for nothing is too hard for the Lord, a God for whom nothing is impossible.

God is working his eternal purpose out in each of our lives for we read in Jeremiah 29:11 that his plans for us are 'to give us hope and a future'. He is patiently shaping our lives and moulding our characters so that Jesus might be seen more and more.

- By making us his inheritance, he has shown us his love.
- By promising us a wonderful future, he has encouraged our hope.
- Now he offers us something to beef up our faith—something to invigorate and stimulate our faith.

If God's call looks back to the very beginning, and God's inheritance looks on to the end, then surely God's power spans the interim period in between. It is on this that the apostle concentrates for he knows full well that the only way it can all be realised is through the power of God.

It's the way he tells it

Paul encourages us to think about the magnitude of the power of God in verses 19-21. The apostle is one hundred percent convinced that God's power is sufficient and he accumulates words to convince us. The no holds barred adjectives really say it all. There is:

- *power,*
- *great* power, and
- *incomparably great* power.

Power. Real power. There is nothing quite like it. We cannot compare it with anything else. Unique. It stands alone. The word, *hyperballō*, tells us that God's power is so unimaginably great that, in the words of Skevington Wood, it belongs in 'another sphere altogether'.

How can we best know the surpassing greatness of the power of God? Because he has given a public demonstration of it in the resurrection and exaltation of Christ. Actually, when we examine the text a little closer, we discover that Paul refers to three successive events—three proofs to pin our confidence on.

- One, he *raised him from the dead* (1:20a).
- Two, he *seated him at his right hand in the heavenly realms* far above all rivals and competitors (1:20b, 21).
- Three, he *appointed him to be head over everything for the church, which is his body* (1:22, 23).

These three events belong together. As John Stott points out: 'It is because of Christ's resurrection from the dead and [his] enthronement over the powers of evil that he has been given headship over the church.' The resurrection and ascension were a decisive demonstration of divine power.

We all know from personal experience that there are two powers which man cannot control and which persistently hold him in bondage—death and evil.

Man is mortal and cannot avoid death. Man is fallen and cannot overcome evil.

The good news, however, is that God in Christ has conquered both and, therefore, can rescue us from both!

Stupendous power

When we begin to unpack the text, we can easily see the direction of this unmatched power in the opening phrase in verse 19—it is channelled to us—*it is [toward] those who believe* (*pisteuō*). When we lift our eyes to the starry heavens and look around us in the world of nature, what do we see? Nothing less than an awesome and stunning exhibition of the power of God.

The Russian hymn (translated by Stuart K Hine, 1899-1989) captures the essence of this majestic display so vividly when it declares:

> *O Lord my God, when I in awesome wonder,*
> *Consider all the works thy hand hath made,*
> *I see the stars, I hear the mighty thunder,*
> *Thy power throughout the universe displayed.*

When we sing it and when we see it with our own two eyes, we cannot help but exclaim: 'My God, how great thou art!' Oh yes, we can behold the exceeding greatness of his power skyward and earthward.

Take another look! In the tremendous work of redemption we see his wonderful power as it reaches out to us. It took as much power to effect our salvation as it did to effect creation. To create, God only had to speak. But to draw us to himself, he had to suffer for our sin on Calvary's cross.

John Phillips confirms that *'an endless universe is the unmistakable demonstration of the one, an empty tomb is the indisputable evidence of the other.'*

Power to live

We hear a lot about power in these vacuous days! For example, we have power lunches, power dressing, power walking, power packs, power healing, power evangelism, people power. The power which Paul is conversing about here says:

* there is no need for us to be defeated in our Christian lives,
* there is no need for us to live our lives on a downer,
* there is no need for us to be disheartened and discouraged.

For, according to Paul, we have the power of God coming our way—it meets us where we are.

We see the many sides of power in verse 19b where the apostle used four different synonyms to describe the incredible greatness of the power of God—the words are: *power, working, mighty, strength.*

Spiritual Semtex

The word for *power* is *dunamis*. We get our English words 'dynamite' and 'dynamo' from it. Something explosive! The potential is phenomenal. Mind blowing. And, says Paul, this is what God has given to us.

When we are saved we receive all of God's grace and all of God's power. There could be no more and it is foolish and presumptuous to ask for more. This breathes assurance into our hearts for it means that one day our hope will be realised. Peter says more or less the same thing when he reminds us that we are kept by the power of God (*cf.* 1 Peter 1:5).

Energy levels

Working (*energeia*) is the word from which we get our English word 'energy' and the thought here is of the energising force of the Holy Spirit. It means effective or active power.

This is what facilitates us to live for the Lord for he is the one who empowers us, equips us, and enables us.

The bottom line: without him we can do nothing (*cf.* John 15:5). This aspect of his power finds an echo in the statement recorded in Acts 1:8.

God's endowment policy

Mighty (*ischus*) has the idea behind it of a power which has been endowed or an ability which has been given. I think this is marvellous for it reminds us that every single one of us in the body of Christ has been gifted. Paul shares with us elsewhere in 1 Corinthians 12 and 14 that every believer has been allocated at least one spiritual gift—it is up to us to find it, then use it.

The divine sway

The word *strength* (*kratos*) can also be translated as 'dominion' and we find this alluded to in 1 Timothy 6:16 and Hebrews 2:14. It is the ability to conquer—a force that overcomes resistance—as when Caesar conquered Cleopatra. This word is used only of God, never of believers.

It seems to me when we put them all together like pieces in a jigsaw that the end result is staggering. It is even more breathtaking when we recognise that this supernatural power is available to every one of us!

- Power to witness and evangelise.
- Power to endure trials and suffering.
- Power to do the will of God.
- Power to be the kind of person that God wants us to be.

Paul is speaking here about the presence of the divine dynamic in the life of the Christian. He is also reminding us of an eternal energy which is accessible and available to us.

1:20

Alive!

Jesus Christ—when men had done their worst to him, when all hell had unleashed its forces against him, when unthinkable anguish had been endured by him, when unbearable pain had been felt by him, when midday was midnight as the Father turned his back upon him, when incredible loneliness and a sense of utter abandonment swept over his soul, when he died and was buried in a borrowed tomb in a beautiful floral garden—they thought, this was it.

Jesus has gone! Good riddance! For his enemies, that was a cause for joyous celebration. It was party time. They were dancing on the streets. To say the least, it was a little premature. We know the thrilling sequel to the story. Thank God!

Three days later—Easter Sunday AM—a great while before dawn had broken and the sun had risen in the east, the stone was miraculously rolled away. Jesus Christ emerged. Up from the grave he arose! He tore the bars of death away. He was alive. He *is* alive!

Resurrection power

How did he do it? We read in Romans 1:4 that Paul attributes it to the power of God. What a manifestation of the energy of God. In a single stroke of sheer brilliance, God did what man could not do and could never do! He *raised* (*egeirō*) Jesus from the dead!

The resurrection of Jesus Christ is an eloquent testimony to the incalculable and immeasurable power of an omnipotent God.

In doing what he did, God arrested the natural process of decay, he refused to allow his Holy One to see corruption (*cf.* Acts 2:31-

33). In all fairness, that is what the prophetic pundits of the Old Testament said would happen, and it did!

Then, he did not just reverse the process in restoring the dead Jesus to this life, he transcended it. He raised the Lord Jesus to an altogether new life which nobody had ever experienced before, and which no one has experienced since—or not yet, at any rate!

We shall rise also

What are the implications of this event for us? It means he can and will do exactly the same for us. The same power that lifted Jesus from the grave to the earth, from the earth to heaven, will ultimately take us home to glory.

We have nothing to dread or fear with regard to the unknown tomorrow, it is all in his capable hands. We have nothing to worry about, he will make sure we reach our final destination.

1:21

Heaven! Here I come!

The power that raised Jesus from the tomb has taken him back to the throne. Can you visualise it in your mind's eye?

Jesus is standing on the summit of Olivet to the east of the golden city of Jerusalem, he is saying a final fond farewell to those he had come to redeem, he would look one last time into the faces of his shell shocked disciples, he gazed for a fleeting moment into the eyes of his loyal and devoted mother Mary—then he raised his hands, summoned an escort of angels, and rose towards the sky.

He ascended, he went on through the clouds, he continued beyond the stars. The earth gradually receded—heaven's gates appeared, and on he went. There were hallelujah's in heaven in a burst of spontaneous praise from the angelic host. Jesus made a beeline for the throne of God where he sat down at his Father's right hand. In his exaltation, his Father promoted him to the place of supreme honour and executive authority. In doing so, he fulfilled the messianic promise of Psalm 110:1. That is where he went, and that is where he is.

All seats of power are beneath him. Around him are twenty four other thrones and those who sit on them cast their crowns before him. At the four corners of his throne are the four living creatures who sing his praise. An innumerable company of angels hang on his every word and rush to do his blessed will.

Majesty. Worship his majesty.

We marvel at his might, sure we do; in this verse, however, we are confronted with his exquisite majesty. Says the writer: 'We see Jesus ... crowned with glory and honour' (Hebrews 2:9). 'Where is he?' is the question on everyone's lips. The answer comes back: 'He is *far above all*.'

- He is far above everyone else.
- He is far above everything else.
- He is above Satan and his world system.
- He is above the holy angels and the fallen angels.
- He is above the saved people and the unsaved people.
- He is above it all for time and eternity.

God has kept his promise of old (*cf.* Isaiah 52:13), and exalted his beloved Son, far above all! In this context, I often think of the words of the song composed by H E Govan (1866-1932) of the Faith Mission:

Far above all, far above all,
Jesus the crucified, far above all.
Low at his footstool, adoring we fall,
God has exalted him, far above all.

Or again, by Thomas Kelly (1769-1855):

The highest place that heaven affords,
Is his by sovereign right.

For Christ, Psalm 24 has become a glorious reality. Enthroned is Jesus now!

Jesus is first!

The apostle speaks of *rule (archē) and authority (exousia), power (dynamis) and dominion (kyriotēs)* for these are the names given to various ranks of angels in the host of heaven. Our Lord has gone beyond them all! He surpasses them. He outshines them. Hebrews 2 concludes in a succinct manner that Christ is greater than angels.

Jesus comes out tops when it comes to secular influence as well— that is the thought behind the phrase: *every title (onoma) that can be given.* It does not matter who they are or what name or title they may assume. They are all subject to Jesus the king.

Earthly kingdoms come and go, empires rise and fall, but the throne of the Lord is for ever and ever. He reigns on high. He overrules them all. He is sovereign. God has set his king on his holy hill of Zion. No power in heaven, no power on earth, no power in hell can alter that. All bow the knee before Jesus. All—no matter where they are in the pecking order of the good and the great—are subservient to him.

The common denominator—in his presence and before his throne, everyone finds themselves on a level playing field.

A God who spans the ages

It is not only true in the present age *but also in the one to come.* Hence Paul's comment at the end of verse 21. Our God is omnipotent. All power belongs to him.

When we see all that is happening in today's world, we sometimes wonder: why does he stay his hand, why does he hold back, why does he not intervene? How true it is, in an age where sin abounds, the grace of God super abounds. Because we live in an age of grace, injustice often seems to triumph and the abuse of power appears to go unchecked. Well, it may look like that, but that is only a short term analysis.

In the light of escalating violence, the pertinent question was asked: *'Why doesn't God stop the trouble?'* The reply was given: *'Why should he? He didn't start it!'*

He could do it! He can do it! However, in his sovereignty, he chooses not to do it. This is not the day of intervention. There is an even greater mystery when we reflect on the cross of Jesus. Think of all that happened there: when he could have called ten thousand angels, he chose not to. Ah, this is the age of grace. Man today has further opportunity to get right with God.

The worst is yet to come

This is not 'the day of vengeance of our God' (Isaiah 61:2). That day will come and, when it does, man will know all about the power of God. Read the Apocalypse and zoom in especially on chapters 6-19—it will make the hair stand on the back of your neck. In that day, it will be patently obvious to a watching world that God has given him a name above all other names and that before him all men must bend the knee.

1:22

Jesus puts his feet on it

The final thought in Paul's prayer is found in verses 22 and 23 where the apostle switches his emphasis to the ascendancy of Christ. There are two facets worth thinking about here. The first one is highly unusual in that it speaks about the *feet* (*pous*) of the Lord Jesus. Strange? Not really!

Those feet which evil men pierced and cruelly nailed to a cross will—when Christ returns to earth—be placed on the necks of his enemies. That is the moment when planet earth will be his footstool.

I often think about the aged apostle John, exiled on the isle of Patmos, in the middle of the Aegean Sea, when he saw the Lord that he deeply loved in all the splendour of his unveiled glory and untarnished majesty—he saw his face shining like the sun, his feet glowing like burnished bronze, his eyes flaming like fire—what did he do? He fell at his feet as if he were dead (*cf.* Revelation 1:12-17).

That was John's immediate reaction. There was no hesitation on his part. None! One glimpse of the glorified Christ and John was prostrate on the floor. He bit the dust. And, remember, he was a close friend of the Lord's. What will be the reaction of his foes?

- Men like Caiaphas, the self seeking high priest?
- And Herod, who scoffed at Jesus?
- Even Pilate, who signed the death warrant of an innocent man?

- What about those who have maltreated him?
- What about those who have cursed his name?
- What about those who have spurned his grace and refused his offer of salvation?

We are left in no doubt, just like the devil, every one of them is under the feet of Jesus. Better believe it, a day of reckoning is coming when he will yet trample on that old serpent and crush his head.

1:23

A full Jesus

Paul has been thrilling our hearts with his gripping account of the sovereign exaltation of Jesus. We have been riveted to the spot as he has recounted the story of his resurrection from the dead, and of his enthronement far above all. The apostle continues to elucidate this theme by relating the meaning of this double triumph for the church (*cf.* 1:22, 23).

As a matter of interest for those of you who are into statistics, this is the first mention of the *church* in the Ephesian letter. The emphasis here is on the Lord's *fulness* (*plērōma*). It is crystal clear from Paul's insights that the church finds its fulness in Christ for he is recognised as the head. The apostle develops this analogy later in the epistle when he portrays the church as a body (*cf.* 4:1-16).

We are blood bought believers—ransomed, healed, restored, forgiven. We are saved by the amazing grace of God, we have been immersed by the Holy Spirit into the body of Christ, we are indwelt by him from day one—that is the ethos and experience of the true church of Jesus Christ.

It knows no labels of denominational ties or of religious affiliations. It has no boundaries of geography. It is not limited by race or creed, colour or class, time or space, for many of its members are now in heaven.

The church is global, mystical, and invincible.

By divine appointment

We see here his appointment in relation to the church for Jesus Christ is the *head* (*kephalē*). I think that is what gives the church her air of dignity combined with a real sense of destiny. Members of the church find their fulness in their relationship to him.

It is worth noting that Jesus is not only head in relation to the church, he is head over *all things*.

Christ rules the world, and he rules the church.

Since *all things* have been put under his feet by God, he is thereby *the head over all things*. The *head* and the *feet*, the *over* and the *under*, are obviously complementary.

But Paul goes further than this and that is what I have touched on already. His point is not just that God made Jesus head over all things, but that he *gave* him as head over all things to the *church which is his body*. You see, the one whom God gave to the church to be its head was already head of the universe. Therefore, both universe and church have in Jesus Christ the same head. That is exceptionally good news.

A full church

That is not the end of the story for we find in verse 23 that Christ finds all his fulness in us. This is a concept which is impossible to fully comprehend and, because of that, it should make us gasp. If we are honest, we have to admit, we cannot really understand it nor can we even begin to exhaust it. We are only scratching the surface as we try to come to terms with the far reaching implications of such a beautiful, rip-roaring relationship.

God says that the Lord Jesus—the one who fills all and the one who is in all, the one who is higher than the heavens, the one who conceived and created the universe through his omnipotent and omniscient power, the one who holds it all together, the one who is the object of angelic worship and the ceaseless theme of seraph song—is incomplete without us (*cf.* 1:23).

I have to say that I have no real problem understanding the fact that we are incomplete without him. But I cannot even begin to visualise for a moment how he can be incomplete without us. And yet the more we allow our minds to meditate upon it, the more it makes spiritual sense.

After all, Jesus is the head and we are the body. The baseline: we need one another! What is the point in having a head if there is no body? What is the point in having a body if there is no head? One complements the other!

Let's get connected!

R. Kent Hughes tells the story that just before World War II, tragedy burned its way through the little town of Itasca, Texas, scorching the hearts of nearly every family who lived there. The local school caught fire and 263 children died in its heat.

Itasca's residents had neither the drive nor the resources to rebuild the school while the war raged on. But the end of the war brought hope and soon the walls went up on a new building. The fire was not forgotten, however. This time, the school installed the finest sprinkler system technology could design.

When the project was complete, the townspeople came out in droves to see the facility. Honour students guided visitors through a tour, the highlight of which was the reassuring sight of sprinkler heads standing guard over the heads of the pupils. Parents sent their children to class with confidence, secure in the knowledge that a school fire would never again claim young lives in Itasca.

Just seven years later, though, the town had grown, and already the school needed to be enlarged. As workmen began construction, they discovered an appalling fact.

The best sprinkler system their money could buy had never been connected!

Incredible! It sends the shivers down the spine. Makes us shudder.

Turned on

What is the link to your life and mine? It is all about being connected! I say it reverently (and change the metaphor)—we need to plug our lives into the socket of his salvation, flick the switch on, and allow his current to flow right through us.

When we go back and read through the four Gospels, we see many stirring manifestations of the power of God at work in the ministry of the Lord Jesus. When we go forward into the Acts of the Apostles, we see the same power working in the lives of ordinary men and women.

Before and after

I suppose Peter, the big fisherman-cum-apostle, is the classic example. What an incredible transformation took place in his life between the end of the Gospels and the beginning of the Acts. What made the difference so that people sat up and took notice? It can only be attributed to one thing—the resurrection power of Jesus Christ!

We can examine it from another angle for there is also a link between knowledge and faith in this entire section. We find it most clearly in verses 18 and 19 where Paul brings together the verbs *to know* and *to believe*. In other words, the very same resurrection power which God exhibited in Christ is now available to us.

First we are to know its surpassing greatness as demonstrated in Christ's resurrection and enthronement, and then we are to lay hold of it personally and experimentally.

John Stott makes the valid point that *'knowledge is the ladder by which faith climbs higher, the springboard from which it leaps further. They need each other. Faith cannot grow without a firm basis of knowledge. Knowledge is sterile if it does not bring forth faith.'*

Horses for courses

I read a comment recently by one respected Bible teacher where he likened the church to a great equestrian statue with massive muscle and lifelike vigour, preparing to take a mighty leap forward. Come back twenty years later, however, and we find it on exactly the same spot. It has not moved!

Sadly, many of us feel that this is the sad and sorry state of the evangelical church. It apparently has enormous potential, but it never moves. Its lifelike features seem to be inextricably set in bronze. How we enable the church to become what it should be is really the problem we wrestle with at this juncture in history. What we can do is to make certain that in the particular part of the body where we worship, we give the head all that is his by right.

In practical terms, this means that we should obey him and submit to his rule in our lives. Part of the crown rights of his kingship is our implicit obedience to all that he commands. We can also start to pray for our fellow church members that they too will truly own him as Saviour and Lord. If we do this, the potential of the church will be realised at long last and our local community and our world will be changed as Jesus lives through his body.

The greatest power shortage at this point in time is not in our generators or fuel tanks. It is in our individual lives.

The enigma is that some of us may be running our lives on an empty tank.

2

Big on Reconciliation

2:1

Spot the difference

The compliments are really flying when we read what God thinks of us in this chapter! There is no way we can afford to walk down the high street with our chests out and our noses up in the air. The bottom line: we were spending all our time with one finger on the self destruct button. We were no better than lemmings—we seemed oblivious to our danger as we rushed pell-mell toward the sea.

Some years ago, Pastor R. Kent Hughes and his group of high schoolers hiked to the top of Mount Whitney in California, the highest spot in the continental United States (14,494 feet). They were exhilarated by the breathtaking panorama of the Sierra Nevada mountains and the Mojave Desert below.

'*What a spot,*' Hughes exulted, '*with its rarefied, crystal clear air, its indigo and turquoise lakes—vista giving way to vista as far as one could see.*'

As the group surveyed the world from the pinnacle, one of the teens mentioned that Death Valley, the lowest point in the United States, lay only eighty miles away. In less than a hundred miles, you could travel from a height of over 14,000 feet to a drop of 282 feet below sea level—from crisp mountain air to a suffocating 134 degrees in the shade.

Hughes remarked: '*What a contrast! One place is the top of the world, the other the bottom. One place is perpetually cool, the other relentlessly hot. From Mount Whitney you look down on all of life. From Death Valley you can only look up to the rest of the world.*'

In all honesty, it is hard to visualise a starker contrast, but one does exist—not in the physical world, but in the spiritual. That is what these opening verses in Ephesians 2 are all about! They highlight our personal pilgrimage from the deepest depths of desolation to the highest heights of jubilation.

Grace timeline

Paul has been talking about a gospel of wealth in an age of recession. The emphasis in chapter one has been on the glorious realities of the Christian life. With that in mind, Paul made out an inventory of our spiritual possessions. In this extensive catalogue, Paul looked at salvation from God's point of view and he gave us a comprehensive rundown on the past, present, and future of God's great plan of redemption.

In chapter two, the apostle underlines the velvet revolution of the Christian life by homing in on our spiritual position in Christ. He talks at length about salvation from the perspective of the individual Christian. In so doing, he brings us up to speed when he gives us the past, present, and future of the persons that Christ saves.

How's that for starters?

We rounded off the previous chapter with a marvellous picture of Christ and the church. They are bound together in grace so that they form a single living organism. They are bonded together inasmuch as Christ is the head and the church is his body. I want to know, where did the Lord get the basic material to start making this church? Basically:

- he starts with those who are rejects,
- those who could be written off,
- those who are worthless, and
- those who are only fit for the scrap heap.

In other words, the Lord gets his building programme off the ground with the most unpromising and unlikely material. An auspicious start!

Finishing on a high note

Did you see how it all ends? He climaxes with a church that shares the exaltation of Christ in the heavenlies (*cf.* 2:6). What a fantastic transformation—a complete 360 degree turnaround—a creditable, gracious revolution. Such is the grace of God.

'The Lord builds his church with the crooked timbers of humanity so that all the glory may be ascribed exclusively to him.'
(Ian Barclay)

We can look at it like this—the Lord sees us not only as we are, he sees the awesome potential through grace in our lives of what we can become. He sees beyond tomorrow! He sees the end product, the finished article. The huge difference comes when we salute Jesus Christ as one *rich in mercy* and, who, *because of his great love for us* has made us alive in Christ.

In a split second, he has taken us out of the great cemetery of sin and placed us in the throne room of glory.

'It is away with the grave clothes and on with the grace clothes.' (Warren Wiersbe)

The pendulum swings

Against the sombre grey backcloth of a troubled and violent world—then and now—the landscape of Ephesians 2 stands out in striking relevance. Paul first plumbs the depths of pessimism about man and then rises to new heights of optimism about God. It is this combination of pessimism and optimism, of despair and faith, which constitutes the refreshing realism of the Bible.

In this passage, Paul sketches a vivid life size portrait of what man is by nature, and what he can become by grace. He effectively singles out a number of appalling truths about unredeemed human beings, which included you and me until God had mercy on us.

Bad grammar. Good theology.

Before we unpack the teaching in this chapter, it is worth noting that Paul ditches the most basic rules of grammar. He begins sentences and never finishes them—he begins with one construction and halfway through he glides into another. 'That,' according to William Barclay, 'is because this is far more a lyric of the love of God than a careful theological exposition.'

The euphonious song of the nightingale is not to be clinically analysed by the rigid laws of musical composition. The lark sings for the pure joy of singing. That is what Paul is doing here.

'Paul is pouring out his heart, and the claims of grammar have to give way to the wonder of grace.' (William Barclay)

As dead as a dodo

Look at what Paul says, rather pointedly, in verse 1: *As for you, you were dead* (*nekros*). For you and me, that is what we were outside of Jesus Christ. We were as dead as dead can be. We were cut off from life because we were cut off from God. What a desperate position to be in. Spiritually speaking, we had no life. Such is the horrendously awful plight of man without God—he is dead!

We need to be clear in our own minds that Paul's devastating thumbnail sketch of man before God is a description of everybody. He is not giving us a portrait of some particularly decadent jungle tribe living in a remote backwater, nor is he pointing the finger at a sybaritic, drugged-out segment of inner city society, or even at the extremely corrupt paganism of his own day. No, this is the biblical diagnosis of fallen man in a fallen society in a fallen world.

From bad to worse

That was surely bad enough but Paul does not end there, he goes on by informing us: *you were dead in your transgressions* (*paraptōma*). We trespassed and that means we stepped out of line. We have fallen aside when we should have been standing upright. We were out of bounds. We have rebelled against God.

And, to make matters much worse, Paul adds: *you were dead in your ... sins* (*hamartia*). Put simply, we completely missed the mark—we failed to reach up to God's high and holy standard. We fell miserably short of the target God set for us. He set the goal and we did not make it.

Paul's clever use of these two words to describe our wrong-doing embraces both sins of commission and omission—namely, things we did do and should not have done, and things we did not do that we should have done! Before God, we hang our heads in remorseful shame, we were both rebels and failures. That was our fundamental problem, that was our condition. We were dead.

Such is the state of every sinner today!

Is there a pathologist in the house?

The unbeliever is not sick, he is dead.

A withering diagnosis, indeed! Accurate, nonetheless! It seems to me, therefore, the sinner does not need resuscitation, he needs a personal resurrection. He does not need the kiss of life to revive him, he needs a brand new life to change him. He needs a change of heart.

We may be tempted to think that we were born with a genetic bias that makes us drift a little off course and, if we pull ourselves together and make a sturdy effort, we can get back on track and arrive at our destination safely. In reality, we do not stand a chance!

Across the board

All lost sinners are dead—the good looking, the good living, the good, the bad, the indifferent—the hardened criminal on skid row, the tramp sleeping in a box under the arches, the man with a million stashed away in a Swiss bank account. All are dead.

The only difference between one sinner and another sinner is the state of decay. One may not be as bad as the other, but one corpse cannot be more dead than another! This means that our world is one vast graveyard.

An Irishman was once asked to define a cemetery. He quipped: *'It's a place where the dead live!'*

Our world is full of people who are dead while they live; in that sense, they are nothing more than spiritual zombies. John Gerstner said they 'are an offence to God's nostrils and these decaying spiritual corpses stink.' It is the 'live human in a morgue' syndrome—modern man in a mobile coffin.

Dead and alive

Paul's statement about the deadness of people who do not know the Lord Jesus raises all sorts of problems for many because it does not seem to square with the facts of every day experience. For example, in our out of town shopping malls, scores of people appear to be very much alive!

One has the vigorous, well honed body of an athlete, another has the lively mind of a bookish intellectual, a third has the vivacious personality of a Hollywood film star. Are we to say that such people, if Christ has not saved them, are dead? Yes, indeed! There is no alternative!

- Such people are blind to the dazzling glory of Christ,
- they are deaf to the dulcet tones of the Holy Spirit,
- they have no heart love for the Lord Jesus,
- they have no sensitive awareness of the personal reality of God,
- the cry for intimacy—Abba, Father—is not in their vocabulary,
- they have no longing for fellowship with the people of God.

At the end of the day, it is like banging your head against a brick wall—they are as unresponsive as a corpse! We have no option but to affirm that a life without God is a living death, and those who live it are dead even while they are living. It is a paradox. However, if it does nothing else, it graphically depicts the monstrous tragedy of fallen human existence—that people who were created by God and for God should now be living without God. You see, that was our condition until the Lord Jesus found us!

2:2

Ignorance is not bliss

We were not only dead—the opening phrase in verse 2 indicates that we were deluded: *in which you used to live when you followed the ways of this world and of the ruler of the kingdom of the air.* Paul says this was the way we used to live—the norm, so far as we were concerned. In golfspeak, it was par for the course.

Ours was not only a living death, it was a walking death.

We did not know any better. The devil pulled the wool over our eyes and then led us down a blind alley. The great deceiver conned us, he hoodwinked us.

Culture shock

We *followed the ways of this world.* That phrase is a telltale one for it speaks of a global social and value system which is alien to God. It permeates and dominates nonChristian society and holds people in captivity. It is a form of cultural bondage. The fact is, we were all on the same sinking boat until Jesus rescued us. We 'drifted along the stream of this world's ideas of living' (J B Phillips).

Before they gave their lives to Jesus Christ, the people at Ephesus were no different to anybody else. Their hopes and their dreams were controlled by all that this *world* (*kosmos*) had to offer, and people today are just the same.

For so many people in our pleasure oriented, narcissistic culture, their aims, ambitions, and aspirations are influenced by the soap opera world of television, or by what their neighbours think, and have, and do. It is a world swayed by the glamour of the showbiz or sports personality, the ideals of the jet set, or the weekend colour supplement in the quality broadsheet. Such influence is both pervasive and invasive.

Paul says, there is the difference. That is what you used to be! Yes, we still live in the real world but it has ceased to be the controlling influence in our lives. No longer is it our guiding light. When we found life in Jesus, we saw through the superficial sham of all that the world had to offer.

The Pied Piper mentality

I was intrigued to read that the devil is depicted as the *ruler* (*archōn*) *of the kingdom* (*exousia*) *of the air*. The word Paul uses for *air* (*aēr*) can be translated 'foggy atmosphere'—a smog. It indicates the depths of inky black darkness which the devil prefers to the white light. He was well named when he was called the 'prince of darkness'.

We were seriously influenced by him in every area of our lives. He was in the same groove as the proverbial Pied Piper—he played the tune, we liked what we heard, and quickly followed behind. To change the metaphor, Paul is talking here about the devil and he more or less says that we were his poodles. He had us eating out of his hand, such was his mastery and control of our lives.

As they say, it takes two to tango. We spent our time dancing in the dark with the devil.

That was until Christ changed us and we saw the light.

The devil made me do it

Dead. Deluded. Disobedient. In the final phrase in verse 2, Paul mentions *the spirit who is now at work in those who are disobedient*. There is really so much more to Paul's comment than initially meets the eye.

Paul was not simply saying that we were *disobedient* (*apeitheia*) children! He is suggesting that we were sons of the disobedient one. That is, we were children of Satan because our father was the devil (*cf.* John 8:44).

If we recall the teaching that emerges from Romans 5:12, we remember it was by one man's disobedience that sin entered the world—consequently, we are heirs to a disobedient spirit. We were on the side of the devil, and he is the sworn enemy of Jesus Christ. Basically, we flatly rejected God's rule over us.

Take, for example, the little girl who was disciplined by her mother for kicking her brother in the shins and then pulling his hair. *'Sally,'* said her mother, *'why did you let the devil make you kick your little brother and pull his hair?'* To which she answered: *'The devil made me kick him, but pulling his hair was my idea!'* It proves the point—people sin under the devil's influence, but they also sin off their own bat.

2:3

Men behaving badly

Paul described us as defiled when he wrote: *All of us also lived among them at one time, gratifying the cravings (epithymia) of our sinful nature and following its desires and thoughts.* Not a pretty picture!

It is worth noting that the NIV has a footnote associated with the word *nature* thereby suggesting an alternative translation by using the word 'flesh' (*sarx*). Either rendering is possible so long as we remember that the 'flesh' does not refer to the living fabric which covers our bony skeleton, but our fallen, self centred human nature.

Paul is certainly not handing out fragrant floral bouquets when it comes to man's innate tendency to go his own way and do his own thing. With a few candid strokes on the canvas of Scripture, we see ourselves as God sees us.

As sophisticated pagans, we were doing what came naturally. We were slaves to sin. We were searching for pleasure. We were always living to gratify our many *desires (thelēma)*. Whatever we wanted, we went after it. We were controlled by natural desire and natural depravity. We were fallen creatures. We were grovelling in the dirt, crawling in the muck and mire of sin. We had sunk to an all-time low in the gutter.

We reached rock bottom only to discover it was nothing more than sinking quicksand.

We got ourselves into it and we could not get ourselves out of it! We have no one else to blame. We cannot blame God—it is not his fault that we found ourselves in such a mess! The problem is compounded because each sin makes the next sin easier. William Wordsworth in the *Intimations of Immortality* wrote:

The youth, who daily from the east
Must travel, still is Nature's priest,
And by the vision splendid
Is on his way attended;
At length the man perceives it die away,
And fade into the light of common day.

As the old saying has it: 'Sow an act and reap a habit; sow a habit and reap a character; sow a character and reap a destiny.'

On a hiding to nothing

Because of the sheer magnitude of our condition, is it any wonder Paul goes on to declare that we were doomed: *Like the rest, we were by nature objects of wrath.* Some do-gooders have a problem here when they consider the wrath of God. However, God's *wrath (orgē)* is not like man's.

When God is angry, it is not a show of bad temper—he does not fly off the handle at a moment's notice. It is neither spite, nor malice, nor animosity, nor revenge. His hackles never rise, his blood never boils. There is nothing resentful about God's displeasure for he never acts in a fit of pique. His indignation is never arbitrary.

There is an air of predictability about the wrath of God for it is never subject to mood swings, whim, or caprice.

It is not easy to describe the wrath of God, but I think John Stott excels when he says it is 'God's personal, righteous, constant hostility to evil, it is his settled refusal to compromise with it, and it is his resolve instead to condemn it.'

Where wrath and mercy meet

So far as Paul is concerned, divine wrath is not incompatible with divine love. As we shall see, the contrast between verses 3 and 4 is notable for Paul moves easily from the wrath of God to the mercy and love of God without any real sense of embarrassment or anomaly. It is a smooth transition from one to the other. We do well to remember that 'the wrath that judges and the grace that saves are both personal—they are the wrath and the grace of God' (John Stott).

Paul is able to hold both traits together in his mind because he believed they were held together in God's character. In that sense, there is nothing schizophrenic about the attributes of God—he does not have a split personality.

Dyed in the wool sinners

I think we can summarise Paul's razor sharp assessment of sinful people like this:

---

by nature, we were children of wrath—*by deed*, we were children of disobedience.

In other words, without a personal knowledge of Jesus as Lord and Saviour, we were destined to spend eternity in hell. The unconverted person is 'condemned already' (*cf.* John 3:18). The sentence has already been passed but God in his mercy has stayed the day of execution so as to give men time and opportunity to get right with God.

Reality bites

Paul is from the old school, he tells it like it is—he never puts a gloss on unpalatable truth. He pulls no punches. He calls a spade, a spade, not a sharp edged gardening implement. He is an old fashioned, straight from the shoulder, give-it-to-them preacher. That is why he did not mince his words when he said that we were without God, without hope, and without Christ. And we had better not forget it!

The eminent evangelical prophet Isaiah would encourage us to 'look to the rock from which you were cut and to the quarry from which you were hewn' (Isaiah 51:1).

* We were sinners by birth,
* sinners by choice, and
* sinners by practice.

Invariably, your lot and mine was cast in a world controlled by the evil one. And our destiny, at the end of the road, was an eternity banished from the immediate presence of the Lord. We were faced with a triple whammy of the world, the flesh, and the devil.

Such was our past condition—moribund, lifeless, and inert. That was yesterday! Thankfully, the Holy Spirit did not end at verse 3! Praise God for providing an escape route out of this nightmare!

2:4

One word makes all the difference

The opening word grabs our immediate attention: *but.* It seems to me this monosyllable makes a world of difference! According to R C Sproul, this is his 'favourite word in all the Bible'.

We were the objects of his severe wrath but God had mercy upon us—we were dead, and dead men do not rise, but God made us alive with Christ—we were slaves, in a dire strait of dishonour and powerlessness, but God has raised us with Christ and exalted us to a position at his right hand of honour and power.

With the advent of Christ, God went into recovery mode and took all the necessary steps to reverse our condition in sin—an axis of grace!

Thank God for that little word—what a blessed *but* it proves to be. There is often something special about the 'buts' of the Bible. Arresting! They stop us in our tracks. As it were, they are the hinges on which great issues turn.

Paul has just painted a dreadfully black and unerringly bleak picture of man's depravity and the anger of a holy and just God. Now he draws attention to God's limitless mercy and unfailing love. God is *rich* (*plousios*) *in mercy* (*eleos*). And more, he is fabulously rich in wisdom, majesty, and glory. He has magnanimously lavished the vast treasures of his mercy upon us. Rest assured, in any situation where God is involved, it is never too little, too late.

In his infinite mercy, he does not give us what we do deserve. In the greatness of his love, he gives us what we do not deserve.

Such love

Did you see the grateful recipients of his love? Yes, you have guessed it, you and me! Hell deserving, devil embracing sinners. God does not just pity us, he loves us! He does not just feel sorry for us, he loves us! There is the wonderful reality of his strong love. He loved us *even when we were dead in transgressions.*

When we were at our most unlovable, he did not turn away from us, he seized the initiative and came towards us. He did not shrink from us even though our condition was wretched and hopeless, he came to save us. Yes, we were far gone, no doubt about that, but in love he reached out to us. He met us individually at the point of our need. It is as personal as that. We can say with Paul that '[he] loved me and gave himself for me' (Galatians 2:20).

Mercy there was great ...

The Lord has shared his love with us, but how has he done it? He plucked us from the tomb! We were dead and, therefore, unable to help ourselves—only mercy could reach us. We were under the sentence of God's judicial wrath—only love could triumph over that.

We deserved nothing at God's hand but judgment on account of our sin—only grace could rescue us from our just desserts.

Mercy is love for the down and out.

Why then did God act in the manner he did? He did it because his is a big heart that oozes with mercy, love, grace, and kindness!

2:5, 6

Easter day, every day

Paul continues to boost our morale by reminding us that *[he] made us alive (syzōopoieō) with Christ ... and raised us up with Christ.* You see, the only thing to do with a dead person is to bury him. So far as I am aware, there is no other realistic and acceptable solution to the problem of death. A corpse can be washed and groomed, all sorts of procedures can be followed to enhance it, nevertheless, it remains a corpse, and the only place suitable for it is six feet under the ground.

However, our living God is not daunted or deterred by death. Our transgressions and our sins brought us to the place of death. Then God swiftly acted in grace and power. He quickened us, he made us alive, he delivered us from the tomb. He did for us what no one else could do. He did for us what we could never do for ourselves for no one can crawl from a casket. The resurrection of Jesus was the key. Easter Sunday! Because all our sins were dealt with on the cross, when Jesus arose, it became possible for us to arise to a new life.

'God raised us from the tomb in which our sins had placed us, just as he raised Christ from the tomb in which our sins had placed him.' (John Phillips)

The debt was cancelled. Sin's penalty was paid. Death's hold was broken. We were made alive in him, and with him. Grace triumphed over guilt and the grave. God reached down into the corruption of death and raised us up. As John Stott says: 'All this talk about solidarity with Christ in his resurrection and exaltation is not a piece of meaningless Christian mysticism.'

It bears witness to a living experience that Christ has given us— on the one hand, a new life and, on the other, a new victory. What Paul is touching upon here, the poet Gerard Manley Hopkins described as letting God, 'Easter in us'.

A royal touch

Quite simply, at one time we were dead, but now we are spiritually alive and alert. For a lengthy period in our lives we were no better than hostages held in captivity, but now we have been set free and enthroned!

See where he has put us—on a throne! Talk about a change in altitude! The wonder of it all. The awesome wonder of it all. We are seated on his glorious throne. In Christ, we are already seated where he is. 'That place, in Christ, at the right hand of God the Father,' writes James Montgomery Boice, 'is the place of intimacy and revelation. It is where God opens up his heart.'

God has enveloped us in Christ so that when he looks at us, he always sees him. No matter how or when God looks at us, he always sees Jesus.

---

* He sees him in all the beauty of his holiness,
* he sees him in all the glory of his grace,
* he sees him in all the splendour of his person.

In the heights of heaven we see a throne where God sits, a throne where Christ sits, and a throne where he has seated us as well. We sit there together. And we are not out of place even though it is out of this world.

The verbs *made us alive, raised, seated* (*synkathizō*) are all in the aorist tense. It signifies that it is already done, it has happened already. Now! It is something we can revel in at this moment of time, we only have to live in the good of it. We look up as we look down!

2:7

The future is bright, the future is …

We have looked into the past and seen what we were in the yesterdays of life. We have viewed the present and seen what is ours to enjoy today. The question is: what are the prospects for the future? What about tomorrow? We read all about it in verses 7-10.

It is incredible to think that the sin of man gave God an ideal opportunity to show a side of his character that might never have been fully revealed.

For example, in creation, he displayed his wisdom and his power; in redemption, however, he has demonstrated not just his grace, not just the riches of his grace, but the *incomparable* (*hyperballō*) *riches of his grace*.

He will continue to do that throughout *the coming ages*. Such monumental grace is best seen in the church. She will be the object of awe and admiration in the aeons of eternity. Every eye will see the throne of God, every eye will see the Lord Jesus, and every eye will see us there as well. Trophies of the grace of God, and he is the one who gets all the pleasure in showing us off.

The story is told about the Rev Paul Gibson when he retired as principal of Ridley Hall, Cambridge, that when a portrait of him was unveiled, he paid a well-deserved compliment to the artist. He said that in future he believed people looking at the picture would ask not: 'Who is that man?' but rather: 'Who painted that portrait?'

That says it all for in our case God has displayed more than an adroit touch or skill. A patient after a major operation is a living testimony to his surgeon's expertise—a condemned man after a reprieve to his sovereign's mercy. We are both!

We are exhibits of God's ingenuity and trophies of God's grace!

Charles Swindoll makes the observation: 'If all the treasures of the sea, if all the gold, silver, diamonds, rubies, and emeralds of the earth could be heaped into one towering pile, they would amount to a speck of dust next to the immense riches of God's grace and kindness. We who are redeemed by Jesus are a shining testimony to the marvellous grace of God to all generations.'

There is an expression: 'When you see a turtle on a fence post, you know he didn't get there by himself!' It is obvious that someone had to put the turtle up there. In a very real sense, Christians are turtles sitting atop fence posts, put there by the grace of God!

2:8, 9

The gospel in miniature

Here is one of the greatest summaries of the gospel message in the entire New Testament. The generous gift is nothing less than salvation, made available to us by the amazing *grace* of God, and received by us through an act of childlike *faith* (*pistis*). It is largesse!

- We cannot purchase it.
- We cannot work for it.
- We cannot earn it.

As a gift, it is totally free. Works do not enter into the equation, full stop! All our efforts, no matter how commendable or charitable, will be no more beneficial than rearranging the deck chairs on the *Titanic*. It is *gratis*. Yes, it cost Jesus everything—it costs us absolutely nothing. In the familiar words of Augustus Toplady (1740-78):

Nothing in my hand I bring,
Simply to thy cross I cling;
Naked, come to thee for dress,
Helpless, look to thee for grace;
Foul, I to the fountain fly;
Wash me, Saviour, or I die.

Rock of ages, cleft for me,
Let me hide myself in thee.

We must never think of salvation as a kind of two way transaction between God and us in which he contributes grace and we
contribute faith. We were dead and had to be quickened before we
could believe. It is clear from such verses as Philippians 1:29 that
saving faith is God's gracious gift. John MacArthur writes that 'faith
is simply breathing the breath that God's grace supplies.' There is
nothing for us to attain. It is not something which we can achieve. It
is not even a reward for living like a model citizen in our local
community.

There is an old story from the Middle East which speaks to this
issue. A man was travelling on his donkey when he came upon a
small fuzzy object lying in the road. He dismounted to look more
closely and found a sparrow lying on its back with its scrawny legs
thrust skyward. At first he thought the bird was dead, but close
investigation proved it to be very much alive. The man asked the
sparrow if he was alright. The sparrow replied: *'Yes.'* The man said:
'What are you doing lying on your back with your legs pointed
toward the sky?' The sparrow responded that he had heard a rumour
that the sky was falling, and so he was holding his legs up in
support. The man replied: *'You surely don't think you're going to*
hold it up with those two scrawny legs, do you?' The sparrow, with
a very solemn look, retorted: *'One does the best he can!'*

Because there is no room for human merit, it naturally follows
that there is no room for human boasting either. We have nothing to

write home about, we have nothing to glory in, we can take no credit whatsoever—it is all of God from start to finish. There is no way that any one of us will be able to strut round heaven like proud peacocks. Heaven will be filled only with the exploits of Christ and the praises of God. We join hands with James M Gray in the sentiments of his hymn:

> *Naught have I gotten, but what I received,*
> *Grace hath bestowed it, since I have believed,*
> *Boasting excluded, pride I abase,*
> *I'm only a sinner, saved by grace.*

2:10

Grace for growth

Paul is concentrating in this verse on growth. Good works are an integral part of God's plan for your life and mine for *we are created* (*ktizō*) *in Christ Jesus to do good works, which God prepared in advance for us to do.* They are not the price of salvation—they are the proof of salvation. We are not saved as the result of good works, but good works are the result of our salvation.

'*We are saved by faith alone, but faith that saves us can never be alone.*' (John Calvin)

They are clear evidence that God is actively at work in our lives. They are the token that we have passed from death to new life in Jesus Christ. You see, God's plan for our lives extends beyond salvation to sanctification, beyond standing in grace to walking in good deeds. It is relatively easy for us to engage in chitchat and talk the talk—he expects us to engage the world and walk the walk!

God's poem

There is a lovely thought here for Paul reminds us that *we are his workmanship.* The word *poiēma* employed here indicates that we are his poem, his literary masterpiece. Each of our lives is the papyrus on which the Master is producing a work of art that will fill the everlasting ages with his praise.

- We are meant to be visual aids to a gawking world.
- We are live exhibits under the glare of staring eyes.
- We are an advertisement of all that the grace of God can do in the lives of ordinary people.

The story is often told of the rowdy, disruptive young boy in a Sunday school class who continually frustrated his teacher. One morning the teacher asked him: *'Why do you act like that? Don't you know who made you?'* To which the boy replied: *'God did, but he ain't through with me yet!'*

Sure, we may be rough uncut diamonds, but he is still working on us and he has not finished with any one of us yet. When he does, that will be eternal ecstasy. And when we think of what we were and look at what we now are, we should get thrilled and excited with what we shall be. In moments like these, I often ponder on the words of the Seth Sykes chorus:

Thank you, Lord, for saving my soul,
Thank you, Lord, for making me whole,
Thank you, Lord, for giving to me,
Thy great salvation, so rich and free.

Moses and me!

Ever wondered: why does God work in us? Surely it is that he might work through us. The Bible provides many fine illustrations of this important principle. Take Moses, for example.

God spent the best part of forty years working in the heart of Moses before he could work through him. At the very outset of his ministry, Moses was impetuous and depended on his own strength. He killed an Egyptian and he had to flee the land of Egypt—not the recommended way to start a new ministry. But during those forty years as a humble shepherd in the desert, Moses experienced God's working in his life—a working that prepared him for forty more years of magnificent service.

Whatever way we choose to look at it, this incident shows the creative side of God's character in that he has made something beautiful out of nothing!

'There is no such a thing as a self made man—it is a contradiction in terms—we are God made!' (Anonymous)

The ins and outs of Christian living

The underlying principle in this verse can be easily summed up in a classic one liner: God works in and we work out! Having said that, God is more concerned about the workman than he is about the work. And we see that in the meticulous way he operates in each of our lives so that we might be at our best for him.

Moses was not the only one in Scripture to experience a personal touch from the Lord. There is a host of prime examples:

- Joseph suffered for thirteen years before God put him on the throne of Egypt, second to Pharaoh.
- David was anointed king when he was a relatively young man, but he did not gain the throne until he had suffered many years as an exile.
- Paul spent three years in Arabia after his conversion where he must have experienced God's deeper work in his heart to prepare him for his future ministry.

The bottom line: God has to work in us before he can effectively work through us.

A will to work

The *works* (*ergon*) which Paul writes about here have two very special characteristics. They are *good* (*agathos*) and they are *prepared* (*proetoimazō*). This is a staggering pronouncement by Paul. It means that God has an overall purpose for our lives—he wants to do something positive with us.

There is nothing airy fairy about it, it is not pie in the sky. Paul is talking about the gracious plan of a loving heavenly Father which he longs to see fully implemented in our lives.

We need to remember that the 'good, pleasing, and perfect' (Romans 12:2) will of God comes from the heart of God.

In the know

A famous actor was once the guest of honour at a social gathering where he received many requests to recite favourite excerpts from various literary works. An old preacher, who just happened to be there, asked the actor to recite the much loved Psalm 23.

The actor agreed, on one condition, that the preacher would say it after him. The actor's recitation was beautifully intoned, the emphasis was dramatic, the effect was stunning. It was a truly cultural experience to listen to him. When he finished, he received lengthy applause from an adoring public.

The old preacher then stood up and his voice was rough and gravelly, his diction was anything but polished. But, when he finished, there was not a dry eye in the room. The impact was so moving, it was unbelievable. Quite uncanny.

When someone asked the professional actor what made the difference, he was heard to reply: 'I know the Psalm—he knows the Shepherd!'

Poles apart

In essence, that is what a Christian is—someone who has a dynamic relationship with the living God. Pulsating, vibrant, heart stopping stuff! We see that in the second half of Ephesians 2 where Paul explores and then expands the twin themes of peace and reconciliation. Before we unpack the teaching, let me give you some background information.

Here were a people who at one time were separated, now they are united. There is the power of the gospel of Jesus. He is the one who breaks down barriers. The world around us is festering with feuds—the fact is the only one who can bring men together who have little or nothing in common is Jesus.

* There is no class or social distinction with him.
* There is no colour or racial prejudice with him.

No Iron or Bamboo Curtain or Berlin Wall divided people so absolutely as the gap that existed between Jew and Gentile in the ancient world. In a sense they were under the same roof, but neither party was talking to the other! Two communities living as if the other one did not exist—two highly visible people groups who were polarised, each one having their own particular identity.

We have the Jew who was proud of his circumcision, and the Gentile who was frowned upon because of his uncircumcision. There was no love lost between them. There was a spirit of alienation rife in both ghettos. There was a deep seated hostility between them. They put up with each other with considerable difficulty.

Toleration was the name of the game—even that did not stretch too far! The Jews said the Gentiles were created by God to be fuel for the fires of hell—that shows the open contempt they had for one another. It was not even lawful for a Jew to help a Gentile girl in her hour of greatest need for that would simply be to bring another Gentile into the world. The barrier between them was an immovable object, it was absolute. Charles Swindoll's assessment is right, if you were a Gentile, '[your] spiritual estrangement was bleaker than a Siberian exile.'

If a Jewish boy married a Gentile girl, or a Jewish girl married a Gentile boy, the funeral of that Jewish boy or girl was carried out.

Such contact with a Gentile was the equivalent of death. That is the way it was until Christ came. When he came, he lived, he died, he shed his precious blood at Calvary and, when he did, he crossed the great divide, he stepped over the line of demarcation, he destroyed the barrier singlehandedly. He opened up the way—the one way, the only way—for men to be united in Christ. That was ultra important!

So far, and no further

The standing symbol of this alienation was the *dividing wall of hostility* (*echthra*) as Paul called it in verse 14. It was a notable feature of the magnificent temple built in Jerusalem by Herod the Great. Let me try and describe it for you.

The temple building itself was constructed on an elevated platform. Round it was the Court of the Priests. East of this was the Court of Israel, and further east the Court of the Women. These three courts were all on the same elevation as the temple itself. From this level, one descended five steps to a walled platform and then, on the other side of the wall, fourteen more steps to another wall, beyond which was the outer court, or Court of the Gentiles.

This was a spacious court running right around the temple and its inner courts. From any part of it, the Gentiles could look up and view the temple, but they were not allowed to approach it. They were cut off from it by the surrounding wall, which was a one-and-a-half metre stone barricade, on which was displayed at intervals warning notices in Greek and Latin. They read, in effect, not 'trespassers will be prosecuted' but 'trespassers will be killed'.

(A couple of these notices have been discovered in archaeological digs in the last hundred years or so—one in 1871 which I saw recently in a museum in Istanbul and the other, unearthed in 1935, is housed in the Rockefeller Museum in Jerusalem.)

Living dangerously

Paul knew all about this from personal experience. In fact, on one occasion, he diced with death. Only about three years previously Paul had nearly been lynched by an angry Jewish mob who thought he had taken a Gentile with him into the temple. Hairy, to say the least!

It is ironic, but the man in question was an Ephesian named Trophimus (*cf.* Acts 21:27-31). In some ways that gives us a back-drop to Ephesians 2, at least we know now where Paul is coming from and what he is talking about.

2:11, 12

- We must never forget what we once were (*cf.* 2:11, 12), and
- we must never forget what we now are (*cf.* 2:13-22).

Mud slinging

In a timely way, we are exhorted to *remember* (*mnēmoneuō*). However, if you are anything like me, you are probably wondering: remember what? Well, there are five unforgettables outlined in this mini section.

Before we go through them one by one, we need to remind ourselves that Paul has waved the red card to the warring factions. He has shown them the senseless fallacy of calling each other derogatory names (*cf.* 2:11). That is what spoilt children do! When all is said and done, names are unimportant and labels do not amount to very much either. They are no big deal!

In verse 12, the apostle drops the business of what Jews and Gentiles called each other and moves on to the serious reality of Gentile alienation. In Romans 9:3-5, Paul listed a significant number of Jewish privileges—here he lists a handful of Gentile disabilities.

- They were Christless for they were *separate* (*chōris*) *from Christ*. That means throughout the whole period BC, the Gentiles were neither 'in Christ' nor 'with Christ' but 'separated from Christ'.
- They were stateless for they were *excluded* (*apallotrioō*) *from citizenship* (*politeia*) *in Israel*. They were without a spiritual home. John MacArthur writes: 'They had no God blessed community or kingdom and no divine benefactor.'
- They were friendless for they were *foreigners* (*xenos*) *to the covenants* (*diathēkē*) *of the promise* (*epangelia*). They were outside the blessings of the covenant and they were on the wrong

side when it came to receiving the many benefits of the kingdom.

- They were hopeless for they were *without hope*. The stark reality is although God planned and promised to include them one day, they did not know it and, therefore, had no hope to sustain them. They were faced with the same conclusion that Satan was in Milton's *Paradise Lost:* 'Our final hope is flat despair.'
- They were Godless for they were *without God in the world*. Even though, in grace, God had revealed himself in the world of nature, they deliberately suppressed the truth they knew and turned instead to idolatry.

That was true of them—it is no less true of you and me! We were in exactly the same plight, hence Paul's bold challenge to us to *remember*. I just wonder, how could we ever forget!

We really were in a terribly bad way, so enormously great was our plight, so devastatingly awful was our predicament. We were on a hiding to nothing. We had no leg to stand on. The system of our lives had crashed around us and all that was left was broken pieces and shattered dreams.

Someone was once talking with John Newton, the converted alcoholic slave trader, whom God brought from a position of utter wretchedness to be a preacher of the gospel. They were talking about despair, and the person asked Newton if he did not despair of the salvation of some person. Newton replied: *'I never did despair since God saved me!'*

2:13

A light at the end of the tunnel

At least there is a light at the end of the tunnel as Paul clearly indicates what made the significant difference in our lives. Then we were *far away*—now we have been *brought near* (*engys*). We were, to quote the poet: *Out on the mountains wild and bare, far from the tender Shepherd's care.* Now we are up close, so close, we are in the fold. We sing with meaning: *Things are different now, something happened to me!* Jesus made the difference!

When the Rabbis spoke about accepting a convert into Judaism, they said that he had been *brought near.* For instance, the Jewish Rabbinic writers tell how a Gentile woman came to Rabbi Eliezer. She confessed that she was a sinner and asked to be admitted to the Jewish faith. 'Rabbi,' she said, 'bring me near.' The Rabbi refused.

The door was shut in her face—but now the door is open! His precious blood shed for us at Calvary has enabled us to come right into the immediate presence of God. We have come out of the dark and into the light. We are there because we are unashamedly depending on the atoning blood of Jesus and, thankfully, as Charles Wesley (1707-1788) wrote: *His blood avails for me.*

See what we were! See where we were! A change for the better and all because of the wonder working power of the blood of Jesus.

We have been brought in from the freezing cold into the warmth of the love of God. That is grace! That is God!

2:14

God's Good Friday agreement

Peace!

- Jesus Christ procured peace for us (*cf.* 2:14-16),
- he proclaimed peace to us (*cf.* 2:17, 18), and
- he personified peace—*he is our peace* (2:14a).

In Jesus Christ, we have peace. Real peace. Peace with God. Peace with one another and peace with ourselves. We have been reconciled to God. The reconciler becomes the one in whom reconciliation can be found.

That spells a successful outcome to the greatest peace mission in world history.

Jesus not only reconciled Jew and Gentile—a huge achievement in itself—but he effectively reconciled both to himself in one body, which is the church (*cf.* 2:15, 16). The words of Neville Chamberlain ring true at this point for here we have 'peace in our time and peace with honour.'

2:15-17

Peace at any price?

How did Jesus Christ do it? The copious and definitive answer is given in these three verses. They are packed tight with theology and need to be carefully unpacked. I think the best way to do it is to follow the well-thought-out sequence of Paul's concept by isolating the three main verbs which he uses: we are told that he *abolished* (*katargeō*) the law of commandments in order to *create* (*ktizō*) a single new humanity and to *reconcile* (*apokatallassō*) both parts of it to God.

The first assertion Paul makes is that Christ broke down the wall of hostility by demolishing the rigid rules and unbending regulations of the old economy. The main thrust of Paul's teaching here is regards the endless demands of the ceremonial law. Having said that, it probably incorporated the moral law to a lesser extent. Jesus certainly did not abolish the moral law as a standard of behaviour, it is still in force and binding on his followers—although he did abolish it as a way of salvation.

During World War II a group of French soldiers lost one of their comrades in battle. They carried his body to the only cemetery in the area, which happened to be Roman Catholic. When the priest was told that was not the dead man's religion, he said: *'I am sorry, but he cannot be buried here.'* The disheartened and discouraged soldiers decided to do what they thought was next best, and during the night they buried their friend just outside the cemetery fence. They returned the next morning to pay their last respects, but they could not find a grave outside the fence. When they told the priest of their quandary, he said: *'The first part of the night I stayed awake sorry for what I told you. And the second part of the night I spent moving the fence!'*

That is what Jesus did—he moved the fence! To sum up in the words of John Stott: 'Jesus abolished both the numerous regulations of the ceremonial law and the condemnation of the moral law. Both of them were divisive and both were put aside by the cross.'

Out with the old, in with the new

Paul changes up a gear in verse 15b when he moves away from the termination of something old to the creation of something new. In both senses which we have been considering, the law had made a deep rift in humanity. Jews and Gentiles were alienated from one another and at enmity with one another. But once the schismatic law had been set aside, there was nothing to keep the two halves of humanity apart.

Instead, the Lord Jesus brought them together by a sovereign act of creation. It is interesting to note that this new unity does much more than merely span the Jew and Gentile divide. It also eliminates sexual and social distinctions. Paul says as much in Colossians 3:11 and Galatians 3:28 for we 'are all one in Christ Jesus'.

Some things do not change—men remain men and women, women—Jews remain Jews and Gentiles, Gentiles. Some things do change—a feeling of inequality and an inferiority complex before God is eradicated for there is a new unity in Christ.

Jesus' success story

The third stage is amplified in verse 16 where Paul highlights the tremendous success of our Lord's redemptive work at Calvary. Jesus not only dealt with the prevailing problem, he quashed it. He stamped it out.

In one fell swoop, Calvary ended the bitter internecine conflict between the opposing forces of Jew and Gentile.

Jesus brought them both together. He removed all the offending labels and dispensed with all the trimmings and trappings of both groups. He did what no one else could do, he made peace between them. In other words, Christ crucified brought into being nothing less than a new, united human race—united in itself and united to its Creator.

Life on the street

We need to keep our feet on the ground and resist the temptation to get too carried away—what Jesus accomplished does not mean that the whole human race is now united and that man is reconciled to his fellow man. We know from observation and experience that that is not the case. It is wishful thinking on our part to think otherwise!

Such a blending of hearts and minds can only take place when men have the peace of God reigning in their lives. There is no other way! It can only happen when sinners bend the knee at Calvary and receive the forgiveness of God. Because of that, Christianity is hailed as an equal opportunity faith.

This can be ours when we come to Christ in simple faith. The fact is, when we are at peace with God, we are at peace within ourselves, and that enables us to live at peace with each other. That is why in our lives and in our churches, there is no place for segregation along ethnic lines and there is no need for racial tensions to simmer under the surface.

The need to repent and seek God's forgiveness puts every one of us on a level playing field at the foot of the cross!

Africa leads the way

A beautiful illustration of this is seen in a section of the contemporary African church, composed of believers from various tribes who had been the bitterest of enemies for countless generations. A missionary who was sharing at a communion service in the church was deeply moved when he looked around him.

He saw the chief of the Ngoni, along with many other members of that tribe. He also saw members of the Senga and Tumbuka tribes—singing, praying, and participating in the Lord's Supper together.

In former years each of these tribes loved to brag about how many men, women, and children of the other tribes they had killed, raped, or maimed. The old chief could remember the days when the young Ngoni warriors had gone out to attack their enemies. They had left behind a trail of burned and devastated villages and had come home with their spears bloodied with the death of Senga and Tumbuka people.

But as they once were divided by the spilling of each other's blood, they were now united by the blood of their common Saviour, the Lord Jesus Christ. In the crisp comments of Eugene Peterson: 'The energy of reconciliation is the dynamo at the heart of the universe.' John Oxenham (1852-1941) writes:

In Christ there is no East or West,
In him no South or North,
But one great fellowship of love
Throughout the whole wide earth.

2:18

Unlimited access

Within the veil, I now would come,
Into the holy place, to look upon thy face.
I see such beauty there, no other can compare,
I worship thee, my Lord, within the veil.

Paul was operating on the same wavelength as Ruth Dryden when he shared with us a lovely thought in verse 18. He reminds us that we *have access to the Father*. The *access* (*prosagōgē*) that we enjoy into the presence of the Lord is instant and immediate.

There is no standing on ceremony, there is no lengthy rigmarole to go through, there is no secret code or password to get in—we simply come and walk on in! This close proximity which we enjoy is a rare privilege which I think we take too frequently for granted.

Thankfully, our God is an amiable and gracious God who does not keep his distance or stand on his dignity like some oriental potentate, nor does he insist on any complicated ritual or protocol.

On the contrary, through Jesus Christ and by the Holy Spirit we can approach him at any time as our Father. That is a wonderful blessing afforded to the people of God and it is something we should probably take advantage of more often than we do!

An audience with the King

We notice the overwhelmingly positive influence of the trinity in this sacred and special environment. Each member of the Godhead has a distinctive role to play—it is through their combined efforts that we are able to touch the throne by faith.

I was intrigued to discover that the word for a 'chamberlain' in the ancient oriental court is the thought behind the word *access*. The chamberlain was the person who had the responsible task of introducing visitors into the presence of the king or emperor. But, unlike the court functionary, Jesus does not simply open the door and announce our names and then disappear. He is also 'the door' and 'the way' so we are not left alone, we are conducted right into the near presence of the Father.

I love the story of the little boy called William who stood wistfully at the gates of Buckingham Palace. He longed to go in and see the king. He had a problem on his hands for between him and the king were heavy iron gates, rigid protocol, armed soldiers, and watchful police. What he wanted was just out of the question, there was no way in!

A corpulent London policeman was telling the boy it was time for him to go back home when suddenly he sprang to attention when another man appeared on the scene. He opened the gates and let the man in but he also took William with him.

They walked and walked for what seemed like quite a distance. The anonymous man showed William the famous ballroom, the stamp rooms that housed the world's most valuable collection, the Belgian suite for the use of state visitors, the royal wardrobe, the music room, the dining room, the dazzling green room.

Finally, they arrived in the king's presence, and the man spoke: *'Hello, father, here's a little boy who wants to meet you. Meet my friend, William. William, this is the king.'*

Unknown to William, he had taken the hand of Edward, Prince of Wales, the king's son. Through him, William gained access to the king. In a similar fashion, we too have taken the hand of the King's Son, his name is Jesus, and he is the Prince of peace. Through him we have direct access into the presence of the King of all the ages.

2:19

Asylum seekers

The ripple effect from this process of reconciliation is felt by every one of us, that is why Paul uses the word *consequently* in verse 19. It is really a link word. I find this quite enthralling for it underlines what we now are in Christ.

Before all this happened, we were like visitors without legal rights, we were aliens in a foreign land. Asylum seekers! Now our status has dramatically changed for we belong in a way that we never did before.

We used to be refugees! At least now we have a home!

Because of what he has done, we enjoy the immense privilege of now belonging to God's people for we read that we are *fellow citizens (sumpolitai) with God's people (hagios)*. We have the same rights as Abraham, Moses, Joshua, David, Elijah, and every follower of the Lord throughout time.

- We are marching to the beat of a different national anthem.
- We are loyal to the flag of another country.

There was a time when we were no more than disenfranchised outsiders, but now we are in the inner circle! We are citizens of this new international, God ruled community which Paul has been talking about—a supreme cosmopolitan community.

D. Martin Lloyd-Jones makes the valid comment that *'we no longer live on a passport, we have our birth certificates, we really do belong.'*

In the family

The metaphor changes and becomes more intimate when Paul says we are members of God's family. We read that we are *members (oikeios) of God's household (oikeios)*. The emphasis here is less on God's fatherhood than on the global brotherhood into which the Father's children are brought.

We are like brothers and sisters who are living under the same roof. It expresses a close relationship of affection, care, and ongoing support. I feel one immediate implication of all this is that we should start to appreciate each other in the family of God.

Committee meetings, social gatherings, the times we spend worshipping in church on a Sunday—all of these should now be approached in a fresh way, we should look at them in a new light. It was C S Lewis (1898-1963) who remarked once in Oxford: 'There are no ordinary people in the kingdom of heaven!'

2:20

More than bricks and mortar

When Paul comes to this point in his epistle, he addresses a theme which is at the very heart of his message. He talks about the identity of the true church.

- We are the *building* (*oikodomē*) of God (*cf.* 2:20, 21), and
- the *temple* (*naos*) of the living God (*cf.* 2:21, 22).

It seems to me that a new dimension is introduced at this point in the proceedings. We saw further up the chapter how Paul likened the people of God to children in a family—we are an integral part of the household of faith, a vital part of the global family of God. So when Paul thinks of a family, he automatically thinks of the house in which they live. In that sense the church is a building for it is the place where God dwells.

The intimacy of our fellowship, the oneness of our association with Christ, the cohesiveness that joins us, the unity that prevails among us, these are all true because, as a building, we are the dwelling place of God.

Team ministry, first century style

There are three people mentioned in this verse: *apostles and prophets and Christ Jesus*. Each has a role to play, each has a part to carry out. They are the foundation. Any construction engineer worth his salt will tell you that if a true building is to stand the test of time it needs a proper foundation. That is where we start. It is vital and central.

The *apostles* is a clear reference to those who had seen the risen Lord, they were witnesses of the resurrection of Christ. They had the honour of being specially commissioned by the Lord and sent out to the ends of the earth to preach the gospel. They were given a special authority to work miracles and establish churches in the regions beyond.

What the apostles taught, they expected the church to believe and preserve—what the apostles commanded, they expected the church to obey.

When we talk about *prophets* (*prophētēs*), some feel this harks back to those who operated in this capacity in the Old Testament era. Others feel that it refers to those who functioned in the context of the early church. For what it is worth, my personal preference is for the second option and that is based on the order of the words used by Paul. He did not speak of the 'prophets and apostles'—it was the other way round!

At the end of the day, a prophet was a person with a message from God which was shared with others. They had a twofold role:

- they were in the business of foretelling because they predicted the future, and
- they were actively engaged in forthtelling because they proclaimed the faith.

Says Paul, the church was *built on* (*epoikodomeō*) them. Not as men though! But upon their teaching, their doctrine, and their message. What was it? It was nothing more and nothing less than the gospel of Jesus Christ (*cf.* 1 Corinthians 15:3, 4). In practical terms, this means that the church is built on the New Testament Scriptures. As it were, they are the church's foundation documents.

Last, not least

The last person in the trio is our Lord Jesus Christ.

- He is the foundation stone—the one on whom we are resting, and

• *the chief cornerstone* (*akrogōniaios*)—the one on whom we are relying.

Such a stone is of crucial importance to the building. It is itself part of and essential to the foundation. Those 'in the know' tell me it helps to hold the building steady—it also sets it and keeps it in line. The temple in Jerusalem had massive corner stones. In fact, one ancient monolith excavated from the southern wall was a little under twelve metres in length.

When it comes to the church, Jesus is the one who holds it up and the one who holds it all together.

If you like, Jesus Christ is indispensable to the church's unity and growth. As William Barclay reminds us: '[The church's] unity is not from organisation, or ritual, or liturgy. Where Christ is, there is the church!'

2:21

First impressions

The truth which Paul wishes to highlight is that of the perfection of this structure for *it rises to become a holy temple in the Lord*. When we walk around the building and look at its foundation, what is our first impression? It is one of holiness!

The size is of minor consequence. It has little to do with its ornate character for there is nothing grand or showy about it. Its great feature should be its holiness—a place suitable for God to live in—as the Psalmist said: 'holiness adorns your house' (Psalm 93:5). It is the sacred place where his honour abides.

This is where God is, where God lives—it is his sanctuary, his home.

Remember the tabernacle in the desert and the temple in Jerusalem. When the presence of the Lord was present, it was obvious because of the shekinah cloud. The people could not miss it! Everyone from the youngest to the oldest was conscious that God was at the centre of their worship.

Surely in a day when standards are declining and when virtually anything goes, it seems to me that holiness should be the hallmark, the landmark, and the benchmark of the church that bears the name of Jesus. As John Stott powerfully indicates: '[God] is not tied to holy buildings but to holy people.'

2:22

Building blocks

Paul advances his premise further by speaking about its preciousness. He says it is *joined together* and *rising*—then he says: *in him you too are being built together to become a dwelling* (*katoikētērion*) *in which God lives by his Spirit.*

The key words are *you too.* We can all take tremendous heart from this breathtaking statement. It is there! And we are there! You and I are a constituent part for this is the church under construction. This is what God is doing in our day by the Holy Spirit. From every kindred, tongue, tribe, and nation, he is gathering a people to worship and praise him.

Progress is being made, the building is going up, the work is going on, it is growing. In some parts of the world he is finding more stones than others but in every generation numerous stones have been added.

To the casual observer, it may seem at times to be at a standstill, it is not! Neither has it ground to a halt, there is one here and one over there. And the work will go on until it is finished—until the last stone is cemented by the Spirit into the framework. This is really dynamic, it is vital. Pulsating. Why? Because these are living stones.

- The stones are related to the foundation of his finished work at Calvary.
- They are related to the cornerstone for we are joined to him.
- They are related to each other for there is a profound sense of harmony, unity, and togetherness among us.

Pick n mix

The question is: how do we get there? By making a choice! Ever watched a stone mason at work? He picks out what he wants and places it in position individually. This is not mass production—on the contrary, it is personal attention and interest. It is a deliberate selection process. Surely this reminds us of our election—we are chosen in Christ.

Another aspect we do well to remember is that all stones are not identical.

We are not bricks! We are stones!

None of us is the same in size, shape, or anything else. We are all different and yet, when we are together, the building forms a magnificent structure. He knows each stone, the great and the small, those at the front and those at the back—he sees the best place for us and that is where he puts us.

There has to be a measure of preparation when the stones are shaped. There will be stones beneath us, above us, and all around us. If we are going to fit in place properly, we need to be chipped away with the hammer and the chisel. For some of us, it may be much, for others, just a little. That is his deeper work of grace in our lives—the sanctifying touch, the chastening influence.

Ah, the church is the building of God, the place where God is pleased to dwell. It just happens to be his home, the place where he spends quality time with his family. When we come into his house, we are his honoured guests.

- He loves to see us at the door,
- he loves to see us at his table,
- he loves to see us listening to his voice,
- he loves to hear us talk to him,
- he loves to watch us talking to others about him.

You see, all this is fine preparation for the glad day when we shall abide in the house of the Lord forever (*cf.* Psalm 23:6).

3

Big on Prayer

Gentilemania

In this chapter, Paul is talking principally about the revelations of the Christian life. It is all about *a mystery*—a sacred secret—where the focus is on God's masterplan as it specifically relates to the Gentiles. He reminds them:

- they were not an afterthought in the plan of God,
- they were not a footnote on God's agenda,
- they were not an addendum on God's charter of global salvation,
- they were not incorporated into God's thinking after some intense lobbying from a few disaffected individuals.

They were part and parcel of God's international plan from day one. There was nothing last minute about their inclusion. I cannot help but get excited when I think about it, because, whether we realise it or not, it includes you and me. Yes, we are in there! Our names are on the list! In actual fact, we are said to be on an equal footing with God's covenant people, the nation of Israel (*cf.* 3:6).

Off the beaten track

At this stage in his complex argument, Paul introduces himself in a totally disarming way as he explains his unique role in God's purpose for the Gentiles. It is not for nothing that he has come to be known as 'the apostle to the Gentiles' (Romans 11:13).

Did you see how Paul commenced in verse 1? Three words say all that needs to be said: *for this reason.* Keep your finger on that spot and travel down the chapter to verse 14. What does he say there? Exactly the same: *for this reason (charin).*

It appears from reading between the lines, therefore, that the apostle has gone off on a slight detour in verses 2-13. To put it mildly, he digressed a little. I suppose we could be forgiven for thinking that he lost his train of thought. Is Paul riding a hobby horse? Not so!

It is a tangent of inspirational genius—Paul merely wrote what God wanted him to write!

The chances are when Paul mentioned the word *Gentiles (ethnos)* that some other related truths entered his mind. It happens to all of us when we engage in conversation with friends and family. As it were, his thoughts were hijacked for a few minutes! Having said that, by the time we come to verse 14, he is back on the right track. It seems to me, therefore, that this section is in parenthesis. Let me share a five point outline with you:

- we have the unabashed prisoner of the mystery (*cf.* 3:1-4),
- we see the unfolding plan of the mystery (*cf.* 3:5, 6),
- we note the unilateral preaching of the mystery (*cf.* 3:7-9),
- we discover the unambiguous purpose of the mystery (*cf.* 3:10, 11), and

• we sense the unique privilege of the mystery (*cf.* 3:12, 13).

I want us to examine and explore these verses from a slightly different perspective. I think it would be immensely helpful to us if we approached them from another angle. You see, the passage before us is an incredibly rich seam of truth and we are in serious danger of missing the wood for the trees. In order (hopefully) to prevent that happening, we will deal with it simply by asking two questions:

---

what kind of man was Paul *and* what kind of message did he preach?

3:1

God is sovereign

The first question: what sort of man was Paul? We find in verse 1 that he was a man with a formidably cogent view of the overruling hand of God. We see that clearly in the choice phrase: *the prisoner* (*desmios*) *of Christ Jesus.* Superb.

Humanly speaking, Paul was not Christ's prisoner, but Nero's. We learn from the historian Luke that he had appealed to the Emperor and, as a consequence, had been committed for trial at some later date (*cf.* Acts 25:11, 12).

True to form, Paul never did speak in purely human terms. He passionately believed in the sovereign providence of God in the affairs of men. He was so convinced that the whole of his life— including his time in prison—was under the Lordship of Jesus. Even there, he sensed in his spirit that he was where God wanted him to be!

Paul knew how to handle himself in the good times as well as in the bad times.

Faith in hard times

When everything seemed to be falling apart, he believed that his God was still very much in control. When all he had was a handful of shattered dreams, Paul was convinced that God would make Romans 8:28 a living reality.

Life for Paul, from a human perspective, had taken a dramatic downturn. Even to a seasoned optimist, it would still appear as though he was destined for a rough ride on the roller coaster of life. He was finding out quickly that life was no joy ride. His life seemed to be collapsing around him like a deck of cards. When he used the phrase that he did, we see his healthy attitude, he smiles through suffering, not with the grin of a Cheshire cat, but with the bright beam of contentment.

Paul's outlook shows us how we can make the best of times out of our worst of times.

I think the terrible throbbing pain was taken out of his adversity because he trusted God implicitly. Paul was not a philosophical theorist. His understanding of providence was not a starry eyed idealism. It was earthed in personal experience. Even though the tapestry of his life seemed to be no more than a collection of twisted knots, he did not start questioning: why? why this? why me? why now?

You see, there he is, under house arrest, chained to a Roman soldier. Times were tough. Incredibly tough. His back was to the wall! He was not going anywhere!

Here was a man who desperately wanted to go to Rome as a preacher, but he found himself in Rome as a prisoner.

At the same time, however, he found peace in accepting this as the perfect will of God for his life. There are no accidents in God's plan for our lives—all that happens in your life and mine is by divine appointment. Somehow I feel if we could grasp that we could save ourselves (and others) a lot of unnecessary heartache. Your life and mine is not a lottery, God has a game plan for our lives.

3:2, 7

Commissioned by God

Paul is a man with a clear sense of commission (*cf.* 3:2, 7). He had no doubts on that score. Absolutely none! He was called by God— if pushed, he could take us to the spot where and when it all happened.

It would appear, however, that he had a lingering doubt in his mind when he wondered if his Gentile readers knew anything of the *administration* (*oikonomia*) of *God's grace* (3:2) that was given to him for them.

He wanted to quietly and quickly reassure them of what the Lord did in his life—all by his generous grace.

God's grace not only saved him, it also put a gift in his hand.

That gift was not for him to enjoy selfishly, it was specially targeted for them and for their eternal benefit and blessing.

The art of delegation

The picture Paul has in mind is that of a manager of a large country estate where it is part of his role to put different responsibilities into the hands of various members of staff. The particular task given to Paul is to preach the gospel to the Gentiles. He is not self appointed. This assignment has been entrusted to him by another who is far greater than he. That is something he cannot possibly forget.

I think verse 7 brings this out with even greater force. The impact of it leaves Paul flummoxed. He humbly acknowledges: *I became a servant* (*diakonos*) *of this gospel by the gift of God's grace given me through the working of his power.*

You see, Paul did not wake up one bright sunny Spring morning and think it was high time to do something about the Gentiles. No! He did not make himself into a gospel minister or evangelistic preacher. It was a function and ministry given to him by the grace of God alone. And the one who sent him into the work is the same one who equipped him for the task in hand. As they say, when God calls us, he enables and equips!

God is attracted to weakness

Paul tells them straight in verse 7 that he was energised by the mighty power of God in all his service for the Lord. They knew that to be gloriously true. They had seen his ministry in action. They were witnesses to how powerful it was, many of them had been converted through it.

How is it that a wee man preaching such a despised message could persuade such a mixed multitude?

There is only one reasonable answer to that question: he was accompanied by the power of God. It was God working through him. The hand of the Lord was upon him for good! We can look at it like this:

- the first gift of God's grace was the mystery itself (*cf.* 3:2, 3),
- the second gift was the ministry entrusted to him which he would share with others.

He received it by God's grace and would exercise it by God's power.

Paul, like some of us, was in the business of communication. He had a message to get across to the man on the street. And with God's help and blessing, he succeeded!

3:8

Bowled over, not bowled out

Paul was a man with an overwhelming sense of privilege. If you cast your mind back to the end of chapter two, you will remember that Paul challenged us never to forget what we once were—he certainly had not. That explains why he says what he does in verse 8.

He was just so glad to be saved. Thrilled! Overawed! He thinks of all those men and women that the Lord has set apart for himself, he recalls the names of the saints who have served the Lord well down through many generations, he remembers with fond affection a long line of worthies, then he thinks of the least and the lowest among them, and he sees himself as being lower still!

This is no false humility. This is no pious claptrap from a man who is proud of his new found lowliness. This man is authentic. Genuine. He has a ring of reality to him. As a servant of God, Paul is perfectly happy to classify himself as *less than the least of all God's people*. He sees himself as the meanest member of the holy people.

A very striking expression. It really is!

Paul takes the superlative (*elachistos*: *least* or 'smallest') and does what is impossible linguistically but possible theologically—he turns it into a comparative (*elachistoteros*: 'leaster' or *less than the least*).

Little is much when God is in it

Maybe the apostle was deliberately playing on the meaning of his name. His Roman surname 'Paulus' is Latin for 'little' or 'small' and, according to tradition, he was not the tallest of men. 'I am little,' he may be saying, 'little by name, little in stature, and morally and spiritually littler than the littlest of all Christians.'

We can be sure when Paul is affirming this that he is neither indulging in hypocrisy nor is he grovelling in self deprecation. He means it! I think a fairly good indication that his modesty was neither sham nor morbid is that it did not hinder him from taking full responsibility as an apostle.

On the contrary, in this very passage he twice used the self conscious apostolic *I* (*egō*) (*cf.* 3:1; 4:1). It seems, therefore, that Paul combined personal humility with apostolic authority. And he meant every word of it!

'While minimising himself he magnified his office.' (E K Simpson)

Unworthy

Had he not been a cruel, rabid, and ruthless persecutor of the Lord's people in those early halcyon days? Had he not thrown many of them into prison? This guy was bad news, big time, among the Christians in the first century. Mention his name and people cringed! If you got wind that he was coming to your town, you did not go out and welcome him—if you had any sense, you made a beeline out of town in the opposite direction. He had the mindset which said: 'The only good Christian is a dead one!'

And now that he was one of their number, he scarcely felt he could lift up his head in their presence. What a priceless privilege he felt it was to belong to an illustrious company of giants. A privilege of which he firmly felt he was not worthy.

If a list were drawn up with the greatest Christian at the top and the least at the bottom, Paul reckoned that his name would trail a long, long way below the last name. This was the man whom Christ called to preach—the Lord took the lowest name on the list and made him his special envoy to the Gentiles. A monumental responsibility. A towering privilege.

Grace ... more than a charming sound

The appointment was not done on the basis of merit, or religious

Brownie points, or academic prowess. It was all of grace. And what could such a man hope to preach? He could not blow his own trumpet for there was nothing for him to make a noise about. He would preach what he was called to preach—he would stand up like a herald and proclaim Christ.

The great Toscanini once gave a concert for which the audience was wildly enthusiastic. There were several encores, and still the audience cheered. Finally, there was a lull in the din, and Toscanini turned his back to the audience and said so the orchestra could hear: 'I am nothing; you are nothing; but Beethoven, he is everything!' Theologically that is where Paul was in his preaching of Christ.

We cannot even begin to imagine with what earnest conviction Paul did that. He had shown Christ nothing but hatred, but Christ had shown him nothing but love.

- His love is without bounds,
- his person is beyond description,
- his work is eternal, and
- his ways are unfathomable.

Paul could never tell all, but he would tell all that he could.

He would share with congregations something of the wonder of the illimitable, inexplorable, and *unsearchable riches of Christ*— the riches that cannot be tracked! It means that the wonders of God's grace exceeds the frontiers of our ability to understand. What these riches are we may judge from Paul's exposition in Ephesians 1 and 2. They are riches freely available to us because of the cross.

Among other things, they include resurrection from the death of sin, victorious enthronement with Christ in the heavenlies, reconciliation with God, incorporation with Jewish believers in a new society, the end of hostility and the beginning of peace, access to the Father through Christ and by the Holy Spirit, membership of his kingdom and family, being an integral part of his dwelling place among men—and all this only a foretaste of yet more riches to come. R. Kent Hughes informs us they are 'saving riches, sanctifying riches, relational riches, practical riches, and eternal riches.' No wonder he called them *unsearchable* (*anexichniastos*).

Like the earth, they are too vast to explore. Like the sea, they are too deep to fathom.

Infinite! Inexhaustible! Incalculable! What is certain about the wealth that Christ has at his disposal is that we shall never come to an end of it.

3:1, 2, 13

Others!

Paul was also a man more concerned with others than he was with himself, this is inferred by his use of the words *you* and *your* (*cf.* 3:1, 2, 13). As we say, he was not born yesterday so he is mature enough to know that he would not be in prison at all if it were not for the Gentiles.

His attitude is exemplary for there is no trace of irritation or hint of bitterness in his carefully chosen words. There are no feeling-sorry-for-himself kind of thoughts playing havoc with his mind—in fact, he does not even talk about his own condition at all (*cf.* 3:1).

Examine the evidence

Anything Paul says he can stand over. No one can challenge the precise details. The documented facts speak for themselves!

The final straw that broke the camel's back and led to his arrest in Jerusalem, his imprisonment there and in Caesarea, his successive trials, and his subsequent appeal to Caesar which brought him all the way to Rome, was fanatical hot headed Jewish opposition to his mission to the Gentiles.

Luke, his friend, medical doctor, and travelling companion, was with him at the time—he kept a diary and meticulously recorded events as and when they happened (*cf.* Acts 21, 22).

Campaigning for the underdog

Paul is suffering in prison on their behalf, no one disputes that. By the same token, he is there as their champion. He is standing firm for their inclusion in God's new society. So convinced is he of the divine origin of his vision that he is prepared to pay any price to see it become a reality. This fella has principle and backbone!

The same is equally true in verse 2 where Paul talks openly of his commission to the gospel ministry. Years after receiving it, he still speaks of the ministry in a totally unselfish way. There was nothing in it for him—he exercised it for the benefit of others.

3:13

Do not lose heart

Paul's comment in this verse is unusually striking for again he has only one thing in mind and it does not concern himself. He prays that they will not be disheartened by what he is going through: *I ask you, therefore, not to be discouraged* (enkakeō) *because of my sufferings* (thlipsis) *for you, which are your glory.* The fact that he is suffering himself is not something he pauses to think about—he is worried about the debilitating and enervating effect his imprisonment may have on others.

In a valiant attempt to encourage and cheer them, he tells them that his time on the sidelines is their *glory* (doxa). He was not there because he had something to be ashamed of—he had not done anything wrong. He was suffering because he had freely preached Christ to the Gentiles. He was there for a worthwhile cause and they ought to be proud of the fact. They should be speaking positively about it.

Here is a man with a big heart for people, ordinary people—a man who is selfless at all times, even when it costs him his freedom.

3:12

Enjoying God

Paul is a man who enjoys sweet fellowship with the Lord for we read: *In him and through faith in him we may approach (prosagōgē) God with freedom (parrēsia) and confidence (pepoithēsis).* Paul does not state it explicitly here, he certainly hints at it—fellowship with God can happen any time, any place!

Paul sees the Lord Jesus as the one by whom we may boldly come to God's throne. The mere mention of his name sets Paul thinking about going to God as confidently as a child skips to his father. The terror has gone! We have nothing to fear, we have access into the holiest of all, and that is our inestimable privilege because of faith.

Outside the box

Remember, Paul was a prisoner at this point! In that locked room and in spite of the duress he was under, Paul enjoyed a warm, open, and relaxed relationship with his God. The prison walls were impregnated with the spirit of believing prayer—two feet thick walls provided no obstacle to his intercession. In a place where fear usually reigned, one man was brave and bold. The reality is— behind closed and bolted doors—Paul had a freedom in his heart and mind to keep in touch with the Lord.

When others in the wider Christian community were asking lots of unnecessary questions and losing confidence, Paul was experiencing it, and revelling in it. With the eye of faith he was looking away from himself to Jesus, his great high priest. In a no win situation where the earthly circumstances were so unfavourable and weighted against him, he was having communion with the King of heaven, the living and true God.

That is a brief sketch of the kind of man Paul was! These verses have provided us with a golden opportunity to look through an open window into his heart and character—we see what made him tick and we see the kind of stuff he was made of.

'Preach it, brother!'

It seems to me that very few men like Paul have ever walked across the stage of world history. It would be difficult to realistically compare him with anyone else and it would not be fair anyway. Paul is a one off in the best sense of the word. The big question: was his message equally unusual, what sort of message did he preach?

There are five points of interest surrounding his message, let me share them with you before we get into the heart of the passage. It was:

- a revealed message (*cf.* 3:3-5),
- a mystery (*cf.* 3:3-7),
- a global message (*cf.* 3:8, 9),
- a message for angels (*cf.* 3:10), and
- a message bringing to pass an eternal purpose (*cf.* 3:11).

3:3-5

A divine message

Paul is at pains to indicate that his proclamation of truth was a revealed message. In other words, there was nothing manmade about the apostolic message—it had not been manufactured in the fertile mind of an eminent scholar like Paul. God himself had drawn back the curtain and revealed it to him. He is the one who in its entirety made it known to him.

At the same time God also enabled him to understand it. He gave him an insight into what it was all about. This was the clearest it had ever been given to the apostles and prophets—it was direct revelation.

This is a specially revealed truth *'of which Christ is both the source and the substance.'* (William Hendricksen)

On a similar note, we notice that Paul refers to it in rapid succession as he speaks of the *mystery* on at least three separate occasions (*cf.* 3:3, 4, 6). They are followed by a fourth instance just three verses later in verse 9.

In today's parlance, when we speak of a mystery we think of an unexplained riddle or something which is puzzling to the human mind—we visualise something which is dark and obscure. What is deemed to be mysterious in our thinking is often inexplicable and incomprehensible.

This is where part of the problem lies for the English and Greek words do not have the same meaning—the word *mystērion* is significantly different! When it uses this word that is not what it envisages. In the Bible it means: here is something which up to this point has been hidden but which is now revealed—it was previously concealed but is now open to view—it was covered but is now unveiled.

God's open secret

The mystery that Paul mentions here is a truth which had never been previously understood. It was kept under wraps. Even though it could be referred to as a secret, it was an open secret! For in God's good time it was revealed to Paul and the other apostles as well as to the New Testament prophets (*cf.* 3:5).

I think Paul's choice of words in this sentence is amazingly breathtaking—he really is a stickler for accuracy. It shows the tremendous importance of what the apostle is saying. It has to be right, first time.

There is no room for error when it comes to documenting the ways of God.

In verse 5 the phrase *has now been revealed* (*apokalyptō*) is in the aorist tense which refers to a specific act or event. Coupled with the word *now* (*nyn*) it indicates the present immediacy of the revelation which was given exclusively to this group of men and not to any other persons before or after them.

These men were the instruments of writing down Scripture—their primary function and unique role within the early church is detailed in 1 John 1:1-3. The last time they met in plenary session was at the infamous Jerusalem Council. The man in the hot seat was James, the half brother of Jesus, and he was not an apostle (*cf.* Acts 15:13).

These leading brethren were soon scattered all over the place. Within a few years they had died, but not before the revelation was complete. These hardy souls are specifically referred to in 2:20 and 4:11, but only here in verse 5 are they called *holy*. This affirms that they were fit for such a revelation from the Lord and it also confirms they were marked with a ring of integrity and authenticity.

Some less, some more

The disclosure made to them was God's masterplan—the big picture. What was it? The Old Testament revealed that the number of believing Jews would get less and less. At the end there would only be a remnant left. It also disclosed that great numbers of Gentiles were going to enter into the full blessing of God's salvation. All this was plain.

But it was never made known that the believing Jews and the believing Gentiles were going to become one body. It was never prophesied that both groups would be batting from the same crease and that they would become one spiritual nation. The barrier between them would be taken away—the middle wall of partition would crumble. This was the mystery.

God has only one people, not two!

- God has only one body,
- he has only one building, and
- he has only one bride.

3:6

A triple together

The Gentiles would become fellow heirs for their blessings would not be second rate or second class. Again, according to verse 6, they would be recognised as members of the same body and equal participants in the promises of God.

'They would share equally in the same legacy, the same life, and the same light.' (John MacArthur)

J B Phillips in his paraphrase of this portion says they are 'equal heirs with his chosen people, equal members in his body, and equal partners in God's promise.' He emphasises the new found equality within the community of God's people. 'For,' according to Matthew Henry, 'when we take God for our God, we take his people for our people.'

The bottom line: we are in it together! *Together* is the 'in' word which is used three times by Paul when he says: *we are heirs together ... members together ... and sharers together.* I think these terms are well worth looking at in detail!

Heirs together

We are *heirs together (synklēronomos) with Israel.* Those who once were kept on the other side of the perimeter fence now have the same legal status before God as his chosen people, the Jews. They have the same marvellous, boundless inheritance in Christ that Paul has already mentioned in chapter 1.

As the apostle told the Galatians, regardless of your racial or other heritage, 'if you belong to Christ, then you are Abraham's seed, and heirs according to the promise' (Galatians 3:29). In other words, the Gentiles are not boarders or strangers, but sons, having the same legal status as all other believers.

There is no inner circle or outer circle when it comes to the family of God.

The Jews are not first rate Christians and the Gentiles second, or vice versa. All those who are in Christ inherit all God's blessing and they inherit it jointly! Charles Swindoll writes that 'human birth may bring racial distinctions, but supernatural birth erases them.'

Members together

The Gentiles are *members together (syssōmos) of one body*. It is worth noting that this word was never used in Greek literature before Paul. They are fully fledged members of the body of Christ and are linked by a common life with every other person in God's global family. They are not second class in-laws or second or third cousins who are begrudgingly acknowledged as distant relatives—they are family! Our family! Because of grace, they are indistinguishable in God's eyes from any other member.

If the Lord does not make a difference between them, why should we? Actually, how dare we!

Every child of God is *only* God's child.

Spiritually, he has no genes but divine genes (*cf.* 1 Corinthians 12:12, 13).

Sharers together

In addition to having the same legal and family status, Gentiles are *sharers together (symmetochos) in the promise in Christ Jesus*. That is not so much a third factor in the grace equation as it is a summary of the other two. It does not make the slightest difference what we were before we were saved—when we gave our lives to Jesus Christ we became 'fellow partakers of the promise in Christ through the gospel'.

In other words, it does not matter who we are, what we have or do not have, where we are from or where we are going, if we know the joy of sins forgiven and have experienced the thrill of being reconciled to God, then we are 'all one in Christ Jesus' (Galatians 3:28).

We are not all the same, but we are all one!

We are different, but we are not divided. We are not uniform, but we are united.

3:8, 9

To the ends of the earth

Paul had one burning, all consuming passion—one compelling desire—to proclaim everything there was to say about Jesus Christ and to do it everywhere! Christ was sending him to preach it to the Gentiles. Its hiding place had been in the heart and mind of God, the Creator of the whole world.

Having now unveiled the mystery to his servant, God's will is that the nations should hear about it. In a nutshell, Paul was to pronounce that men and women can get right with God.

When men are reconciled to God, they are right with each other.

And whatever may have divided them before is now set aside totally. We can know fellowship with each other in the family. You see, fellowship exists where all people stand on the same foundation and enjoy the same privileges and blessings. It is not just that their distinctions are tolerated or put aside for a couple of hours—they do not even exist! And so it is when we are in Christ! That is the thread running through this gem of a letter and it is the message the world around us desperately needs to hear.

The word used for *preach* (*euangelizō*) backs up all that I have just been saying for it means 'to announce good news'. Paul was well aware that his gospel was a message of great good news for the Gentiles.

Incentives to evangelism

It is fascinating to realise that in these verses Paul has given us two of the strongest motivational influences to engage our fellow man with regard to his eternal destiny. Paul started the ball rolling by emphasising that the revelation and the commission which had been given to him belong indissolubly together, for what had been made known to him, he must without fail make known to others. All revealed truth is held in stewardship. We pass the baton down the line!

Biblical truth is given to us to be shared, we are not meant to monopolise it.

A priceless treasure

Paul then went on to emphasise the valuable content of the message itself (*cf.* 2 Corinthians 4:7). He was convinced that Christ never impoverishes those who put their trust in him but always immeasurably enriches them. Here then was the double obligation Paul felt:

- to share God's truth, and
- to share Christ's riches.

What is needed today for a recovery of evangelistic zeal in the church is the same apostolic steely conviction about the gospel. Once we are sure that the gospel is both truth from God and riches for mankind, nobody will be able to silence us!

God's own goal

I was interested to note in verse 9 that Paul refers to God as the one *who created all things.* When we take that concept and link it to what he was saying in the previous verse, it is apparent that Paul brings creation and redemption together in his mind. The old gospel song is right when it paints Christ as *the great Creator who became our Saviour.* The God who created all things in the beginning will recreate all things in the end!

It is good to constantly remind ourselves that the church is not an end in itself but a means to an end—the end of glorifying God.

In this context, the real drama of redemption can only be understood when we realise that the glory of God is the supreme goal of creation. The same thought is developed in the book of Revelation where the angels unite to praise him as the great Creator in chapter 4, and then in chapter 5 they exalt him as the one and only Saviour from all sin.

3:10

Talking to angels

As if proclaiming the good news to the whole world was not enough, Paul's ministry of reconciliation through Christ also impacted another world—the invisible world. In a strange kind of way we find this is a message for angels. Paul says it is God's intention that all of this *should be made known to the rulers and authorities in the heavenly realms.*

The angelic host observes what is going on in the world. They miss nothing! They are *au fait* with events on planet earth.

Angels are keen world watchers and enthusiastic church watchers!

One of the reasons God sends out his life changing message to the far flung corners of the earth is to specifically teach them something.

- They saw the might and power of God in creation,
- they saw the wrath and anger of God at Sinai,
- they saw the kindness and love of God at Calvary, and
- they see the *manifold wisdom of God* in the church.

The word *polypoikilos* translated *manifold* is a very difficult word to translate into English. Some commentators say it means 'many splendoured' or 'many sided'. For example, one diamond can be breathtaking in its beauty—it can sparkle with many colours as its many facets reflect and refract a single light but a diamond is nothing compared with the wisdom of God. It has too many facets that not even the angels have seen them all!

The angels look over the balustrade of heaven and see what is happening—they see God's saving purpose becoming a glorious reality all across the world. They see the church growing and in that church they see Jewish and Gentile believers. Both are redeemed with the precious blood of Christ and both are called by the one gospel of sovereign grace.

Now, angels have been surveying the world since history began but nothing like this ever existed before Calvary. And there is nothing like it anywhere else in the universe. And so the gospel enables them to see a shade of the wisdom of God which they did not even know existed.

Colours on the canvas

We can look at it from another angle for the word *manifold* was used to describe flowers, crowns, embroidered cloth, and woven carpets. In that sense it means 'many coloured'. A simpler form of the word— *poikilos*—was used in the Septuagint (LXX) to describe Joseph's coat of many colours (*cf.* Genesis 37:3).

When we transfer that concept across to the church, we see a multiracial, multicultural community which is like a beautiful tapestry. Each of its members come from a wide range of colourful backgrounds. No other human community resembles it. The church is, quite literally, unique.

Its diversity and harmony are an eloquent testimony to the abundant grace of God. It is God's new society. The 'many coloured' fellowship of the church is a reflection of the 'many coloured' wisdom of God.

A global production

What happens is this: as the gospel of Christ penetrates deeper and deeper into the heartland of the world, this new and variegated Christian community develops. It is as if a great drama is being enacted.

- History is the theatre,
- the world is the stage, and
- church members in every land are the actors.

God himself has written the play—he directs and produces it. Act by act, scene by scene, the story continues to unfold. Who are the audience? Angels! They are privileged spectators of—and occasional participants (*cf.* Hebrews 1:14) in—the fast moving drama of salvation.

The history of the Christian church is the graduate school for angels.

3:11

My Father planned it all

This wonderful message has an eternal dimension to it and this is fully documented in verse 11. The bottom line: God has a plan—a *purpose* (*prothesis*)—as eternal as he is. Its roots go back before time! Jesus Christ is the centre of the plan and it will come to pass through him. It is so certain that Paul sees it as a work already *accomplished* (*poieō*).

The divine aspiration is to see men and women coming to faith in his only Son. His ultimate aim is to see the fruit of Calvary in changed lives (*cf.* Isaiah 53:10-12). His determination in the long haul is to gather to himself a people for his name and a people for his praise. That is the goal, the supreme objective.

With true and genuine humility, Paul sees himself as a small link in a very big chain. And he cannot forget it! Every time he stood on his feet to preach about Jesus he had this thought in the front of his mind—his preaching was bringing to pass *the eternal (aiōn) purpose* of God.

No wonder Paul felt so inadequate and unworthy. No wonder he did what he did with an overwhelming sense of love and compelling urgency. No wonder he spoke with such authority for his words were of eternal significance.

We notice that Paul has spoken about himself but he has not drawn attention to himself.

Paul knew full well that he would have neither message nor ministry if it were not for his Saviour, the Lord Jesus Christ. Grace!

- By grace, Paul made known God's grace to the Gentiles.
- By grace, Christ made Jew and Gentile one in his church.
- By grace, we, Christ's church, declare the riches of God's grace to each new generation.

I love thy kingdom, Lord,
The house of thine abode,
The church our blest Redeemer saved
With his own precious blood.

For her my tears shall fall,
For her my prayers ascend,
To her my cares and toils be given,
Till toils and cares shall end.

For every one of us, in the words of Timothy Dwight (1752-1817), the mystery demands ministry!

3:14

Prison cell to prayer cell

I reckon these verses at the end of chapter 3 are among the most sublime in the entire New Testament. This is a passage of indescribable grandeur. There is a magnificence about it which raises us to new heights for we are taken to a new elevation in our appreciation of who God is—even though the casket which contains such priceless jewels is plain and unadorned. It is wrapped in boring brown paper!

There is almost a tradition that when Christians are put into prison they use their time profitably if they have the opportunity.

That certainly happened in the seventeenth century when John Bunyan's twelve years of isolation gave the world the best selling *Pilgrim's Progress*. And German pastor Dietrich Bonhoeffer's (1906-45) imprisonment in World War II produced his famous *Letters and Papers from Prison*.

When we think of it like that, Paul was a marvellously resilient character for his time in prison was no less fruitful. Even though he drew the short straw and was unceremoniously thrown into a rough prison chamber, he still believed in the providence of God. Even though he found himself chained to a Roman soldier, he knew he was where God wanted him to be.

Doing time. Using time.

It is one thing saying it, it is quite a different matter handling it when the crunch comes. Twenty four hours a day, every day, is a long time to put in when you cannot go anywhere! So I ask myself the question: how did Paul pass the time?

Apart from putting quill to parchment and writing many of his prison epistles, Paul spent many hours witnessing and testifying to those who were guarding him.

Evangelism for the apostle was a way of life (*cf.* Philippians 1:12).

After all, he had a captive congregation and, from Paul's point of view, that was far too good a chance to miss. But that is not all!

When we come to verses 14-19, we notice that his prison cell becomes a prayer cell. Paul turns from exposition to intercession. And what a prayer it proves to be. We all pray about those issues which concern us for prayer expresses desire, it reveals what makes us tick. The old hymn tells us that *prayer is the soul's sincere desire, uttered or unexpressed.*

This is the second of Paul's prayers in this epistle for the believers in Ephesus and beyond.

* In the first, the emphasis was on enlightenment (*cf.* 1:15-23).
* In the second, the accent is on enablement.

It is not so much a matter of knowing as it is of having. It is all about you and me laying our hands on what God has for us and by faith making it a vital part of our daily lives. In other words, we are to personalise all that we have in Christ.

Paul longed that we might be the kind of people God wants us to be. He passionately prayed that we might find our full potential realised in God. In the space of a few verses, he talks about the secret of this dynamic relationship—he also provides us with a clutch of remarkable insights into the wonderful resources which are made freely available to us.

An old Navaho Indian had become very rich because oil had been found on his property. He took all his money and put it in a local bank. His banker became very familiar with the quaint habits of the old gentleman. Every once in a while the Indian would go to the banker and say: 'Grass all gone, sheep all sick, water holes all dry!'

The banker would not say a word because he knew what needed to be done to allay the old man's fears. He would bring him inside and seat him in the vaults. Then he would bring out the several bags of dollars and say: 'These are yours!'

The old Indian would spend about an hour in there looking at his money, stacking up the dollars, and counting them. Then he would come out and say: 'Mr Banker, grass all green, sheep all well, water holes all full!'

What was he doing? Simply reviewing his resources. He was doing what Paul wants us to do in these closing verses of Ephesians 3. At the same time, the old Indian could count his resources but we will never count ours—they are incalculable!

Where verse one is square one

Paul begins with the catchphrase: *for this reason*. That means he is resuming his train of thought where he left it in verse 1. What *reason* is in his mind? What is it that stirs his spiritually sensitive heart? What drives this man of God to his calloused knees? What is it that moves him to spend quality time in intercession? What is it that prompts him to pray?

I think it is a combination of two vitally important ingredients. Based on what we have looked at already, it is both the reconciling work of Christ at Calvary and his unique understanding of it by special revelation. It seems to me these are the solid convictions which undergird his prayer. This being so, an important principle of prayer emerges.

The entire basis of Paul's prayer was his intimate knowledge of God's gracious and eternal purpose.

It was because of what God did in Christ and revealed to Paul that he had the necessary warrant to pray. That is what gave him the impetus he needed for the indispensable prelude to all petition is the revelation of God's sovereign will. In other words, we have no authority to pray for anything which God has not revealed to be his will.

Like Siamese twins, Bible reading and prayer should always go together for one beautifully complements the other. It is in Scripture that God has disclosed his will and it is in prayer that we ask him to do it.

He knelt to conquer

Paul's approach to prayer is graphically detailed for our consideration. Did you notice his posture as he prayed? How did he do it? Paul testified: *I kneel* (*gony*) *before the Father*. He bends the knee in the presence of the Lord.

That was a most unusual position for a man of his pedigree to adopt—the normal posture was standing with outstretched arms slightly raised and palms upwards just as we see pious Jews doing today before the Wailing Wall in Jerusalem, rocking back and forth as they intone their prayers. That attitude showed a readiness to receive whatever God chose to give.

When someone knelt before the Lord it indicated an exceptional degree of earnestness, deep adoration, submissiveness, and urgency. For example, Ezra in his great penitential prayer when he confessed the sins of the people of Israel (*cf.* Ezra 9:5), and Stephen when he faced the unthinkable ordeal of martyrdom (*cf.* Acts 7:60).

Don't just stand there, pray something!

Have you ever wondered how you should pray? What is the best way to go about it? Many times people come to me and that is the problem they are wrestling with. It seems to me if we read the Bible from cover to cover, Genesis to Revelation, we will find that different people do it in different ways at different times! Sounds simple! Sounds confusing! The fact is the Bible lays down no rule for the way we should do it!

- Abraham stood before the Lord when he interceded for the city of Sodom (*cf.* Genesis 18:22).
- David sat before the Lord when he prayed about the future of his kingdom (*cf.* 1 Chronicles 17:16).

- Jesus fell on his face when he prayed beneath the gnarled olive trees in the garden of Gethsemane (*cf.* Mark 14:35).

So there we have it: one man stands, one man sits, one man is prostrate, and the other man kneels—take your pick. What I would say is this:

---

it does not really matter how we do it so long as we do it!

The Nike philosophy—just do it!

It must have been quite an experience for the Roman soldier to whom Paul was chained! Never mind that, the important thing is that we bow our hearts and bend our wills before the Lord.

It is through prayer that we lay hold of God's riches that enable us to behave like a Christian and battle like a Christian.

Father God

To whom is Paul praying? He is addressing *the Father* (*patēr*). When it comes to prayer that is the usual way to do it. In fact I would go a step further and say that this is the biblical way to do it.

We speak *to* the Father, *through* the Son, *in* the Holy Spirit.

Isn't it wonderful to realise that our God is a loving Father—a heavenly Father—and we are his children. Because he is our Father, we do not draw near to him in fear and trembling, afraid that he will rebuff us or be indifferent to us. We do not come to him to appease him as the pagans do to their deities.

He is our Father and like Paul we approach him with confidence and boldness. We know that he is more willing for his children to come to him than they ever are of going to him. He knows that God has been waiting all the while with a Father's heart of love and keen anticipation. He will not turn us away with a scowl nor will he give us a cold shoulder.

The story is told of a little boy whose father was promoted to the exalted rank of brigadier. When the wee fella heard the news, he was silent for a moment, then he said: 'Do you think he will mind if I still call him daddy?'

3:15

Some from earth, from glory some

Paul goes on to say that God's children are found in one of two places. We are sons and daughters in his global *family* (*patria*) but some members of the family are *in heaven* and the remainder are still down here on *earth*. We are either here or there! The impressive fact is this: no matter where we are, we are still an integral part of God's worldwide family.

It means that the church militant on earth and the church triumphant in heaven are two parts of the one great family of God.

Here we have the double barrelled secret to finding total fulfilment in Jesus Christ.

- We have access to the Father! Instant, immediate, and intimate. We can reach him at any time, from any place.
- We are accepted by the Father. He takes us the way that we are for he sees us enveloped in the Lord Jesus.

3:16

Prayer pearls

Paul's prayer for the church contains a minimum of four requests that are interdependent on one another like pearls on a necklace. It is like walking up a flight of stairs—one step at a time—but when we take one it automatically leads us on to the next. Paul's prayer staircase has four steps whose key words are: *strengthen, love, knowledge, and fulness.*

So the apostle prays that the inner man might be strengthened, which leads to a deeper experience of Christ, which enables us to grasp the greatness of the love of God, which results in our being filled with all the fulness of God.

We can look at it like this:

* he prays that they might be *strengthen[ed]* (*krataioō*) with the power of his Spirit,
* that they might be rooted and established in *love*,
* that they might *know* Christ's love in all its dimensions, and
* that they might be *filled* to the brim with the fulness of God.

There is a progression of thought in Paul's prayer ladder:

* he prays for strength,
* he prays for depth,
* he prays for apprehension, and
* he prays for fulness.

When we put each of these together they have to do with the will (*cf.* 3:16), the heart (*cf.* 3:17a), and the mind (*cf.* 3:17b-19). Charles Simeon (1759-1836) of Cambridge, the founder of the evangelical movement in the Church of England, took these 'Four Magnitudes' as his life verse and virtually died with them on his lips.

Praying for the world

When we stop and reflect for a moment on the breadth of Paul's prayer, it is a resounding challenge to us to widen our horizons. When we pray it is hugely beneficial for us to go beyond our own small interests or the concerns of our limited circle of Christian friends and pray intelligently for the church of God at large. It is enormously helpful for them (and us) to ask that it be strengthened throughout the whole world. When we pray like that we will be greatly encouraged by what God is doing through his people everywhere.

The underlying thought in Paul's intercession is that prayer makes a world of difference because prayer makes all the difference in the world!

A people of power

Resource number one in the divine survival kit is the invincible Spirit of God. It does not matter what life throws at us, if we are going to make anything of it and keep our heads above water then we need to appreciate something of his enabling work and his transforming ministry in our lives.

The fact that we know his presence within is a clear indication that we belong to Jesus (*cf.* Romans 8:14-16). However, Paul is not thinking here about his presence, but his revitalising power. The verse that readily springs to mind is a familiar one: 'you will receive power when the Holy Spirit comes on you' (Acts 1:8). You see, without him operating in our lives we can do absolutely nothing.

The wind of God

Whenever Jesus was performing his ministry, he always did it in the unstoppable energy of the Holy Spirit. When we read through the Acts of the Apostles we see the Spirit's dynamic work in the formative years of the primitive church—he is referred to at least fifty nine times. That tells me the Spirit of God was central to their forward march, he was the driving force. That is why the flame spread so rapidly.

It has been said, tongue in cheek: *'If God took the Holy Spirit out of this world, most of what we as Christian's are doing would go right on, and nobody would know the difference.'*

Sad! But there is probably a measure of truth in it!

Power from on high

How is the Holy Spirit given to us? According to Paul, it is *out of his glorious riches.* We receive him by faith at the moment of our conversion. There is no need for us to work anything up, the power has to be sent down. He gives him to us richly for he has lavished his best upon us. There is no need for us to go around in the tattered rags of our own inadequacy when we can live sumptuously in the superabundance of God's unspeakable riches.

As Stuart Briscoe has remarked, we need to be like the little boy who was heard to say when he fell into a barrel of molasses: 'Lord, make my capacity equal to this opportunity!'

And whatever happens to us down here we cannot do without his power in the inward man. The outward man is perishing by the hour, we are wasting away, but the inward man can be renewed on a daily basis. And that only happens when we are a people controlled by the Lord who is the Spirit. We have available to us the third person of the Godhead—the Holy Spirit—and 'he will reinforce us' (J B Phillips).

When the chips are down

This is most interesting and it all makes sense when we remember the context in which Paul is writing. He has been talking about suffering and I imagine that is the reason why he prays the way he does. You see, it is in the place of suffering that the grace of God is manifested in our lives—it is when the going gets tough that people see us as we really are.

We are used to gritting our teeth and putting on a brave face to Joe Public when things go disastrously wrong.

So often we batten down the hatches on our emotions and adopt the anglicised stiff upper lip approach.

Not recommended in the long term!

In all honesty, when the chips are down, how do we really cope? For example, the moment we are put on a hospital trolley and wheeled into an operating theatre, who has the strength for suffering? When our personal world collapses around our feet—perhaps we lose our health, our financial security, our job, or someone we dearly love—how do we handle ourselves in that hour of crisis?

It is not something we naturally choose, it is an experience we tend to shrink from. Even the thought of it gives us jelly legs and we throw a wobbly. We go into panic mode. If faced with a choice, the chances are we would be more inclined to draw back from it or else we would run a mile in the opposite direction.

Strength for today

If we are to show God's wisdom in such diverse times of trauma, trial, and trouble, it must be by God's strength and God's grace. That is why he sends his angels to minister to us. No matter what situation we find ourselves in—good, bad, or ugly—we need strength and that is why Paul prayed the way he did!

'We are frail containers pulsating with divine power.' (R. Kent Hughes)

3:17a

My heart, his home

The second major resource made available to us is the indwelling Son of God. The sentence *so that Christ may dwell* (*katoikeō*) *in your hearts through faith* actually means 'so that Christ may settle down and feel at home in your heart'. If Christ had not been there already he would not have called them *saints* (1:1).

Paul prays for a deeper experience between Christ and his people. He yearns for the Saviour to feel at home in their lives. John MacArthur writes: 'Paul's teaching here does not relate to the *fact* of Christ's presence in the hearts of believers but to the *quality* of his presence' (*cf.* John 14:15-24).

Such a relaxed relationship is powerfully portrayed in the life of the patriarch Abraham (*cf.* Genesis 18:1-10). Remember when God was going to bless him and Sarah with a son, the Lord himself came down and visited him in his Bedouin tent. He did not come alone for there were a couple of angels who accompanied him.

They came to the tent and chatted away with Abraham for a while and they even enjoyed a delicious meal together. It was a moment to savour, something Abraham would never forget. The heavenly visitors felt very much at home with Abraham because he was a man of outstanding faith and obedience.

A foot in both camps

There was, however, another not so pleasurable mission which needed their urgent attention—they had to investigate the heinous sin of Sodom. Unknown to Lot, God planned to destroy the cities of the plain as their sin was proving so reprehensible and obnoxious to him.

There was one big problem in that Lot was a believer who was living smack on the edge of Sodom. God in his grace wanted to warn him to get out before the judgment fell. Who went and told him? Who tipped him off as to what was in the mind of God? Who gave him advance warning? It was not the Lord! He did not go anywhere near Sodom, not even with a ten foot disinfected barge pole. It was the two angels who passed on the divine message—a frightening message of imminent judgment (*cf.* Genesis 19:1-13).

That settled feeling

Why did the Lord opt to visit Abraham and choose not to go near Lot's apartment? It appears from reading between the lines that the

Lord did not feel at home in Lot's house to the same degree that he felt at home in Abraham's tent.

You see, when it comes to your life and mine, Paul is not thinking here of the Lord having a casual acquaintance or a quickie relationship with us! It is permanent! Because:

- he wants to make our hearts his home,
- he wants to commune with us and enjoy fellowship with us,
- he wants to show his love to us, and
- he longs to share his life with us.

It seems to me that Paul is reminding us if we want to be the kind of people God wants us to be, we need to thank God that we have two wonderful resources at our disposal—the Spirit of God and the Son of God.

3:17b-19a

A lifestyle of love

Resource number one is the Spirit of God who is there to strengthen us in our moments of weakness, resource number two is the Son of God for he wants to make our hearts his home, resource number three is the unquenchable love of God. This really thrills me for it is one of those benefits we can all experience and enjoy. 'We are never nearer Christ than when we find ourselves lost in a holy amazement at his unspeakable love' is the conclusion of John Owen.

Paul actually uses two words in the text—a mixed metaphor—that take us into a couple of different realms. Both emphasise depth as opposed to superficiality and in both the unseen cause of their stability is love.

- One word is botanical for it compares the believer to a plant *rooted* (*rhizoō*) in the love of God,
- the other word is architectural for it likens the believer to a building *established* (*themelioō*) on love as a foundation.

Paul, therefore, associates individual believers to a well rooted tree and a well built house.

For obvious reasons, the verb *rooted* ushers us into the plant world. The tree must get its roots down deep into the soil if it is to find nourishment and stability. And so it is with the Christian—our roots must go down deep, deep, deep into the unfathomable depths of the love of God.

Where do we find nourishment for our souls? Where do we find a degree of constancy and tenacity in a topsy turvy world? You see, if there is to be power and stability in the Christian life, then there must be a measure of real depth.

The word *established* or 'grounded' (KJV) is an architectural term which refers to the foundation on which we build our lives. Any person will tell you that the foundation is the most important part of any building. If we do not go down deep, we cannot go up high.

Our foundation is the love of God and we cannot beat that but we can build on it. With such a solid and stable base for our lives we will be able to weather every storm. We will be able to face all that life hurls in our direction because our lives are built on a proper foundation.

Under the microscope

Paul also advises us that the love of God can be examined. When we take a closer look at the text, we discover that this love is extra special in that it has four dimensions associated with it—it is *wide* and *long* and *high* and *deep.*

'The love of Christ is broad enough to encompass all mankind, long enough to last for eternity, deep enough to reach the most degraded sinner, and high enough to exalt him to heaven.' (John Stott)

Or as Leslie Mitton expressed it: 'Whether you go forward to backward, up to the heights or down to the depths, nothing will separate us from the love of Christ' (*cf.* Romans 8:37-39). It reaches every corner of our experience.

Many ancient Bible commentators went further. They saw these dimensions illustrated on the cross—its upright pole reached down into the earth and pointed up to heaven, while its crossbar carried the arms of Jesus stretched out as if to invite and welcome the whole world.

In the nineteenth century, when Napoleon's armies opened a prison that had been used by the Spanish Inquisition they found the remains of a prisoner who had been incarcerated for his faith. The dungeon was underground. The body had long since decayed. Only a chain fastened around an anklebone cried out his confinement. But this prisoner, long since dead, had left a witness.

On the wall of his dismal cell this faithful soldier of Christ had scratched a rough cross with four words surrounding it in Spanish. Above the cross was the Spanish word for 'height'. Below it was the word for 'depth'. To the left the word 'width'. To the right, the word 'length'. Clearly this prisoner wanted to testify to the surpassing greatness of the love of Christ, perceived even in his suffering.

Churches together

There is a choice little phrase tucked away in the text where Paul says: I want you to grasp this *together with all the saints.* Paul is implying that while the isolated Christian can indeed know something of the love of Jesus in his life, his grasp of it is bound to be severely impoverished by his limited experience. John Wesley's saying is true: 'God knows nothing of solitary religion.' 'No man,' he said, 'ever went to heaven alone.'

It needs the whole people of God to understand the whole love of God.

It is *all the saints* together—Jews and Gentiles, men and women, young and old, black and white, with all their varied backgrounds and experiences. Even then, although we may comprehend its dimensions to some extent with our minds, we cannot fully *know* it in our own experience.

It is too broad, too deep, too long, and too high, even for all the saints together to grasp. We are out of our depth! It *surpasses* (*hyperballō*) all else! Paul previously used this word of God's *power* (1:19) and God's *grace* (2:7), now he applies it to his *love*. There are dimensions to it but we cannot measure it. We are so rich in him but the riches of his love can never be estimated or calculated.

Samuel Rutherford (1600-61) wrote from his prison cell in the granite city of Aberdeen: 'Love, love (I mean Christ's love), is the hottest coal that ever I felt. Oh, but the smoke of it be hot! Cast all the salt sea on it, it will flame; hell cannot quench it; many, many waters will not quench love.'

Knowing the unknowable

The love of Christ is as unknowable as his riches are unsearchable.

Having said that, Paul is not deterred. He is not so easily put off! He takes a deep breath and roundly challenges us to *grasp* (*katalambanō*) it, comprehend it, and then make it our own. He more or less says: 'Look, here is the love of God, it is so incredibly vast, it is limitless, it cannot be contained, it cannot be measured, but we can lay hold of it, we can know it operational in our lives!'

It probably goes without saying but we cannot comprehend the fulness of love unless we are totally immersed in love and we have it as the root and foundation of our being.

When someone asked the highly acclaimed, global trumpeter Louis Armstrong to explain jazz, he replied: *'Man, if I've got to explain it, you ain't got it!'*

In some ways that simplistic idea applies to love. The modern song by Graham Kendrick sums it up best when it says:

Such love, springs from eternity,
Such love, streaming through history,
Such love, fountain of life to me,
O Jesus, such love.

Franklin Graham tells the story of being in an African refugee camp one day when he heard a little child singing. She had nothing but the clothes she sat in. She had lost everything in the genocide in her country, including her family. A guard stood by. Franklin asked him what she was singing. He leaned down and listened and replied: 'She is singing, "Yes, Jesus loves me, the Bible tells me so".'

Wide, wide as the ocean!

There is a marvellous breadth to the love of God for it embraces not only the Jew but the Gentile as well. There is a wide open invitation extended to all men to come to faith in Christ. The glorious gospel message is to the ends of the earth.

It is so wide which means there is plenty of room for all who know Jesus personally. Not even all the church put together has yet realised how wide the love of Christ really is for it covers the breadth of our own experience. It embraces all sinners who take advantage of God's offer of mercy for his love is so wide that we can never get around it!

How long is a piece of string?

That is the big question, isn't it!

- When did he start loving us, and
- when will he stop loving us?

The unalterable fact remains that his love stretches from

eternity to eternity. The love of God is as everlasting as he is! The Lord said to his servant Jeremiah on one of the many occasions when he was having the dreaded blues that he was 'loved with an everlasting love' (Jeremiah 31:3).

As C H Spurgeon said: 'It is so long that your old age cannot wear it out, so long your continual tribulation cannot exhaust it, your successive temptations shall not drain it dry; like eternity itself it knows no bounds.'

He loved us before the world began, he loves us right now, and he will still be loving us when time is no more. Who can possibly measure that? The love of God is so long that we never come to the end of it.

O the deep, deep love of Jesus

It was love which brought Jesus down from the awesome heights of heaven. It was love which moved him to sit with sinners when others ran a mile in the opposite direction. It was love which enabled him to effectively minister to those who had sunk to the very depths of sin.

Paul knew more about that than most for he saw himself as the chief of sinners—yet the love of Christ met him where he was. I thank God today for the incredibly deep love of Jesus. Even though I had wandered far away from him, his arm reached out and brought me back. Even though I had fallen low in the gutter of sin, his love reached down and picked me up.

Even now it reaches down to us in the dark depths of discouragement, despair, and even death. His love is so deep that we never get to the bottom of it!

Beyond the highest hill

Think of the heights to which he has already lifted us—we are the adopted sons and daughters of God, we are seated in heavenly places, we know we are going to enter into our inheritance but, says John: 'what we will be has not yet been made known' (1 John 3:2).

We are going to be lifted to heights of glory which the Bible has not even begun to describe. It rises to the heights of our celebration and elation. It blows the mind because the love of God is so high we will never be able to get over it!

It is appropriate for us to meditate on the words of the gospel song composed by F H Lehman which says:

Could we with ink the oceans fill
And were the skies of parchment made,
Were every stalk on earth a quill
And every man a scribe by trade—
To write the love of God above
Would drain the ocean dry;
Nor could the scroll contain the whole
Though stretched from sky to sky.

A cartoon depicted a man chatting with a boat salesman. In the beautiful showroom were yachts and cabin cruisers that glittered with highly polished elegance. In the caption, the salesman is saying to the customer: *'Sir, if you have to ask how much they are, they are too expensive for you!'*

Such is the love of God when we experience it! We cannot do anything to make God love us more and we cannot do anything to make God love us less. If I were a Scotsman I would say: 'It is better felt than telt!' Overwhelmed with the sheer magnitude of the love of God, Mary Shekleton (1827-83) sat down and penned the lovely hymn:

It passeth knowledge, that dear love of thine,
My Saviour, Jesus, yet this soul of mine
Would of thy love, in all its breadth and length,
Its height and depth, its everlasting strength,
Know more and more.

3:19b

Complete in Christ

The last resource that Paul focuses on is the sufficiency we have in God. The apostle's heartfelt longing is that we might *be filled to the measure of all the fulness of God*. This is what God wants us to experience—his fulness (*plērōma*).

* The means of our fulness is the Holy Spirit.
* The measure of our fulness is God himself.

J. Wilbur Chapman often told of the testimony given by a certain man in one of his meetings: *'I got off at the Pennsylvania depot as a tramp, and for a year I begged on the streets for a living. One day I touched a man on the shoulder and said: "Hey, mister, can you give me a dime?" As soon as I saw his face I was shocked to see that it was my own father. I said: "Father, father, do you know me?" Throwing his arms around me and with tears in his eyes, he said: "Oh my son, at last I've found you! I've found you. You want a dime? Everything I have is yours!" Think of it. I was a tramp. I stood begging my own father for ten cents, when for eighteen years he had been looking for me to give me all that he had.'*

That is a capsule of what God wants to do for each of his children. His supreme goal in bringing us to himself is to make us like himself by filling us with himself, with all that he is and has!

A person filled with venomous rage and vitriolic anger is totally dominated by hatred. A person filled with sunlit happiness is totally dominated by joy. A person, therefore, filled with the *fulness of God* is totally dominated by God!

Like for like?

Sometimes, human nature being what it is, we look at people around us and we compare ourselves with them. Now it depends who we do it with as to how good or bad we feel at the end of it! Either way it can give us a totally false picture—a misguided feeling of security. The problem is exacerbated because we end up fooling ourselves as to where we are at spiritually.

When it comes to measuring spirituality in our lives, other people are not the yardstick or plumbline. Christ is the measure. He is the standard. He is the rule.

That means we can boast about nothing! So far as we are concerned, it is the zero option. For when we have reached his fulness, then we have reached the upper limit. It is the top rung of the ladder and that leads on into glory itself.

Our position at this point in time is that we are complete in Christ. But in the rough and tumble of today's world, we enjoy only the grace that we apprehend by faith. The resources are there and, if we want to find our full potential realised in God, then it is a matter of us tapping into what is freely available to us.

From the top down

When we pause and look back down the staircase we have been climbing with Paul, we cannot fail to be struck by his audacity. He prayed that his readers might be given the strength of the Spirit, the ruling presence of Christ, the rooting of their lives in love, the knowledge of Christ's love in its four dimensions, and the fulness of God himself.

Bold petitions. Indeed. I suppose climbers of this staircase become a little short of breath, they may even feel a touch giddy. The good news—Paul does not leave us in suspense—the benediction is coming in a couple of verses!

He has prayed for them and we would do well to echo his rich sentiments for one another.

Higher ground

The net result is they would start to enjoy the paradox of knowing the limitless love of Christ and having the divine attributes flood their personalities. The cup of their lives would be filled to over-flowing as they begin to experience abundant life in Christ—and, invariably, they end up living their lives on a higher plane.

They wave farewell to mediocrity and rise to a spiritual plateau which they never thought imaginable this side of heaven.

Don't push your luck, Paul!

I think it is fairly easy to envisage what could have happened at this point. I can just see the Ephesian believers wanting to drag Paul off his knees and say to him:

'Hey Paul, get real! You can't pray for us like that! You're pushing grace too far, that's too big a prayer to pray!'

Before they get a chance to douse him with a bucket of freezing cold water, he pronounces a benediction that reveals a God so much bigger than they would ever have thought possible. 'A God who,' writes Charles Swindoll, 'is so far ahead of us that his works outrun the farthest stretches of our imaginations!'

3:20

The 'wow' factor

Like an eagle, Paul soars into the air with a final majestic view of the Lord. Here is a benediction which surpasses any other in terms of catching a breathtaking vision of a great big wonderful God. It is a paean of heartfelt praise as the apostle takes flight into another world.

When the shackled Paul thinks of the immeasurable love of God he gets so carried away that he pens an outstandingly brilliant doxology—a doxology packed tight and full with a plethora of superlatives.

His soul is enraptured! He explodes and the lava of worship flows from his fulsome heart. He cannot contain his feelings. He bursts his banks in praise to his God. He is the God whom he knows so well and whom he wants to know even better. It is almost like a man standing on the shore of a vast ocean—it all gets too much!

The benediction is summed up rather eloquently in the words of the familiar song:

Got any rivers you think are uncrossable?
Got any mountains you can't tunnel through?
God specialises in things thought impossible.
He does the things others cannot do!

To me that is the ethos of verses 20 and 21. As Stuart Briscoe said on one occasion: 'It's like putting a 747 in a Volkswagen!'

God can!

The God we bump into in this duo of verses is the infinite God of the impossible—the God who can do anything—the God who can do everything. He is the God who faileth not, who faileth never! The all powerful God whose power is inexhaustible. Omnipotence!

I often think of the words penned by John Newton (1725-1807) which we used to sing back in the Emerald Isle during the course of a prayer meeting:

Thou art coming to a King,
Large petitions with thee bring;
For his grace and power are such,
None can ever ask too much!

God first!

See how the verse begins? It is *now unto him*. That is always the best place to start. Paul's praise is directed to God—the focus is on him from the very first word. He is the one of whom it is rightly said: 'nothing is too difficult for thee'.

When we bear in mind all that Paul has been praying about in the preceding verses, then it all dovetails together in a most unique way.

- When the Holy Spirit has empowered us, and
- Christ has indwelt us, and
- his love has mastered us, and
- God has filled us with his own fulness,

then *he is able to do immeasurably more than all we ask or imagine.*

You see, until those conditions are met, God's working in your life and mine is seriously restricted. When they are met, then his working in us is unlimited (*cf.* John 14:12-14).

As is frequently pointed out, verse 20 is a pyramid progression of God's enablement!

- *He is able to do,*
- he is able to do ... *all we ask,*
- he is able to do ... *more than all we ask,*
- he is able to do *immeasurably more than all we ask,*
- he is able to do *immeasurably more than all we ask or imagine!*

Little people. Big God.

When we hear a benediction like that we cannot help but get the shrinks syndrome. Some serious questions need to be asked: Have we ever limited God? Have we ever posed the question: 'Can God?' Have we ever doubted God's ability? Have we ever sat down and wondered and said to ourselves: 'There's nothing more he can do for me!' If we have, our God is too small.

When we look again, and again, we are staggered with amazement that our God can! He can do it! Nothing is too hard for him. You name it and so long as it tallies with his character and corresponds with his will, he can do it. Surely in these immensely challenging times, we need to think big thoughts about God.

Seven wonders of God's world

The God we meet in this verse is a God of sensationally stupendous power and a God who loves to exercise and display his power in answering the prayers of his people. It seems to me that God's ability to answer prayer is forcefully stated by the apostle in a composite expression of seven stages:

- One, he is able to *do* or to work (*poiēsai*) for he is neither idle, nor active, nor dead.
- Two, he is able to do what we *ask* (*aiteō*) for he hears and answers prayer.
- Three, he is able to do what we ask or *think* (*noeō*) for he reads our thoughts like a book and sometimes we imagine things for which we dare not and, therefore, do not ask.
- Four, he is able to do *all* (*pas*) that we ask or think for he knows it all and can perform it all.
- Five, he is able to do *more than* (*hyper*) all that we ask or think for his expectations are so much higher than ours.
- Six, he is able to do *immeasurably* (*hyperekperissou*) more than all that we ask or think for he does not give his grace by calculated measure.
- Seven, he is able to do very much more—*far more abundantly* (KJV)—than all that we ask or think for he is a God of super-abundance.

In other words, there is no limit to what God can do! Let me try and illustrate it by culling a few stories from the Old Testament.

God of the impassable!

Remember the children of Israel on their last night in the land of Egypt—the Passover lamb has been killed, they have applied the blood to the lintel and door posts, they go inside and they are safe because they are sheltering under the blood (*cf.* Exodus 12:1-10).

During the hours of darkness they are feasting on roast lamb. They know in their hearts that when the morning comes it will be the dawning of a brand new day. For them, the exciting prospect of a bright and better tomorrow—freed from the shackles of bondage, liberated and redeemed, delivered and saved.

The sparkling waters of the Red Sea lay ahead, the advancing armies of Pharaoh were rapidly encroaching from behind, there were mountains on either side—to all intents and purposes, they were hemmed in! There was no way through, they could go no further! They had come to the end of the road, so to speak. To a man, they probably scratched their heads and thought to themselves: 'This is it!' Was it?

God stepped into a dire situation and told Moses exactly what he wanted him to do. When Moses obeyed, God rolled back the waters of the mighty Red Sea and they walked across to the other side on dry land. And when the last person reached the other shore, the waters came tumbling down and every soldier in the army of Pharaoh perished in a watery grave (*cf.* Exodus 14:1-28).

When we look at it from a human perspective, it may have been the last minute, but God was on time.

There appeared to be no way ahead, but they had not counted on God. You see, our God is the God of the impassable. And the same holds true in our lives! When we feel we have come to the end of the road—between the devil and the deep Red Sea—and we have no idea which way to go or which way to turn, then God often comes and opens up a way for us.

It will stretch our faith and test our spiritual stamina, no doubt about that! But we need to remember that even though God is never in a hurry, he is always on schedule. Can God? Oh yes, he certainly can!

God of the impregnable!

Remember the conquest of the city of Jericho (*cf.* Joshua 5:13-6:27). The people have wandered in the wilderness, a generation has gone, Moses has gone, and Joshua is their new leader. The land of promise lies before them as they cross the river Jordan. If they are going to take the land, there will be a battle. If they are intent on claiming their inheritance, they must take Jericho!

It was an awesome sight to the human eye—an extremely heavily fortified town—it seemed untouchable and untakeable. The walls were high, the gates were locked, it presented them with a major difficulty, a massive problem. A challenge that seemed too big and too much!

Then God gave Joshua clear instructions as to what he was to do. Now, they seemed crazy, it just was not the kind of thing you would normally do. It was not text book material when it comes to military strategy. But they did it, and it worked. The walls came crashing down!

Our God brings walls tumbling down, he lifts curtains, he opens doors—he is the God of the impregnable!

In our lives, it does not matter what the problem is, it does not matter what the crisis is, it does not matter what the barrier or obstacle may be, nothing is too big for him, nothing is too much for him. It is a bit like David and Goliath:

- to the ordinary people, he was too big to hit,
- for David, he was too big to miss!

There is always room for optimism when God is on our side.

God of the impossible!

Another wonderful illustration is found in the book of the historian-cum-prophet Daniel where Nebuchadnezzar saw himself as the golden boy of world affairs (*cf.* Daniel 3). In fact he was so enamoured with the sense of his own importance that he had a golden statue erected in the desert.

At its official dedication, he would arrange for a vast contingent of people to gather from all the provinces for the proceedings. When the band played, people would fall down and worship the image.

The orchestra struck up, the moment came, and out of the 300,000 people present, there were only three who stood their ground. They resolutely refused to do it! There was no way they were going to bow down to anything which deified and glorified man.

Lest they misunderstood, the king gave them a second chance and again 299,997 people went down leaving three young Hebrew men standing defiantly to the end. Shadrach, Meshach, and Abednego—a trio of dissidents—were frogmarched before the king. They stood before him unflinching and unyielding.

Their faith is real, their trust is implicit in God.

They know God can perform miracles and deliver them *from* it, or *in* it, or even *out* of it.

You see, Jehovah specialises in rescue missions! He has done it before. He can do it again. At the same time, the three of them are realistic. They know there is the possibility that God may choose not to intervene in their situation. Whatever happens, they are genuinely resigned to the will of God. They know his way is the best way, even though it may not be the easiest route to follow sometimes.

God is sovereign and their loyalty to him is in death as well as in life.

When they stand before Nebuchadnezzar, he changes colour as his contemptuous anger reaches boiling point. If looks could kill they would drop dead. He had been humiliated by three Jews and that was more than he was prepared to take.

The fire raged internally as he signalled to the stoker to switch up the furnace temperature seven times hotter. It would be a cauldron. His elite guards were commanded to bind the infidels and hurl them into the inferno. Without any offer of resistance, the three complied with the death sentence handed down.

The furnace probably resembled a modern day lime kiln with an opening in the top for the flames and smoke and another opening at ground level for stoking the fire. The soldiers carried the three rebels up the incline and tossed them over the top into the searing excessive heat. Before the military personnel could descend, they themselves were burned alive. Cremated. It was like an incinerator for them on the outside as they went up in smoke.

If that is what it was like on the outside, what must it have been like on the inside? The three young men plummeted to the bottom of the furnace. Within a fraction of time they should have been dead—burned alive! But the end is not yet.

The wily old king cannot resist the temptation to get the last laugh, he looks through the keyhole and nearly gives himself a coronary, the shock is almost too much for him. The old boy is baffled and bewildered. He suffered a momentary lapse of concentration as he tried to reconcile what he saw with what he knew to be true.

Three people were thrown in to the flames, but he saw four. Can we identify the fourth person? Nebuchadnezzar said he was like 'a son of the gods'. That was his pagan way of saying that this person looked like a divine or supernatural being. He was rational as he sought to explain this unusual event within the confines of his own religious framework.

We know it was a theophany—a technical and theological term indicating an appearance of Christ in the Old Testament era.

To put it simply, Jesus was in there with them!

They found liberty in the flames as they were unbound. They found freedom in the fire as they were able to walk around. They were miraculously kept by God.

The king shouted through the aperture for them to come out. When they emerged, they were hemmed in by a vast crowd of interested onlookers. It had never happened before. It never happened again. They were spectators to a miracle and they never knew it. The three of them came out triumphant—unmarked and unscathed.

- No scars!
- No sores!
- No smell!
- Nothing was singed!

God had undertaken for them. That is what the Lord did for them, and he can do the same for us.

Man's extremity is often God's hour of opportunity.

It shows beyond any shadow of doubt that when we are at the end of ourselves, we are only then at the beginning of God. Can God? Yes, he definitely can! He can *do immeasurably more than all we ask or even imagine!*

A God of miracles

Three illustrations—real life incidents—and our God has not changed. He is just the same today. All around the world, he is still proving himself as the God who does wonders, the God of miracles, the one who has done it before, the God who can do it again. He is able!

In our lives, God is actively working. That is what Paul means when he refers to the power *that is at work (energeō) in us.* Think of the millions who have felt and known his power! They have! So have we!

- His power is as gentle as the forming of a dew drop,
- as imperceptible as the growth of an oak tree, and
- as lasting as the throne of God.

All that matters to us is that God is working in us!

3:21

Paul's all consuming passion in life and ministry is for the name of the Lord to be magnified. His purpose is summed up in the opening phrase: *to him be glory.* That should be the ultimate goal of every believer. You see, God does everything for his glory.

From our perspective, that is an important key to understanding his ways and interpreting his word. We can spend all day looking at God's grace, God's government, and God's greatness—they are keys that open other doors.

The master key that opens every door is the glory of God.

Personally

We are to glorify him individually for it is *to him be glory*—that is why God enables and empowers us so that we might bring praise to his precious name.

Publicly

We are to extol him publicly for it is *to him be glory in the church*—that is, in our congregational worship, in our times spent together as his people, in our corporate testimony, all of this should combine to bring honour to his peerless name.

Perpetually

We are to exalt him perpetually for it is *throughout all generations* (in history) *for ever and ever* (in eternity). Whether in the ages of time or the aeons of eternity, the greatest occupation for the people of God is to lift high their sovereign Lord.

So Paul brings to a grand finale another section of his marvellous letter. We are out of breath! Speechless! He is the one who makes our dreams come true. And because the power comes from him, the glory must go to him! The best we can do is join our hearts with Paul and say: 'Praise the Lord! To him be all the glory!' The *Amen* confirms that worthy goal.

4

Big on Church

A book of two halves

The first three chapters of Ephesians are doctrinal in nature—they focus on what we believe. They tell us the truth! Paul has given us the credenda, a statement of faith, something we can sink our teeth into and build our lives upon. Woven into the fabric of Paul's declaration of the Faith is the thread of an overall vision—a vision based on the grace of God. He sees:

- an alienated humanity being reconciled,
- a fractured humanity being united, and
- a new humanity being created.

In the final three chapters, Paul shares with the young church a lifestyle agenda—things to do! He moves on from the new society to the new standards which are expected of it.

It is a mega challenge because what we believe influences the way we behave. Input *versus* output!

Paul turns from exposition to exhortation. He moves on from what God has done in the indicative to what we must be and do in the imperative—from mind stretching and heart warming theology to its down to earth, concrete implications in everyday living. We observe the same transitional change in Romans 12:1 and Colossians 3:5.

In chapters 1-3, we discussed:

* the calling,
* construction, and
* constitution of the church.

In chapters 4-6, we will consider:

* the conduct,
* confession, and
* conflict of the church.

Downhill all the way

The fantastic benediction at the end of the previous chapter is the high point of Paul's teaching where the huge emphasis is on the able-to-do-ness of our God (*cf.* 3:20, 21). In this chapter, however, we leave the lofty heights of this theological mountain peak behind us in order to take our first tentative steps down into the real world— a world hostile to God and a world where there is no sympathy vote for those who seek to love and serve him.

We need to recognise that it does not matter where we are for God's innate ability never falters—it continues, it remains constant— and so does his power which is actively at work in our lives. If we are enjoying life on the summit of the highest hill or languishing in the depths of the darkest valley, wherever, God is still the same.

In an evolving postmodern world, he is changeless.

Take heart! The narrowness of our understanding, the limited nature of our personal experience, the faintness of our prayers, none of these can diminish that phenomenal power. We, therefore, hit the trail and 'we walk the path lit by the starlight of God's grace' (Charles Swindoll). As we begin our trek together, we discover that the first half of the chapter divides into three main sections:

* The greatness of the mystical body (*cf.* 4:1-6),
* the gifts of the mystical body (*cf.* 4:7-13), and
* the growth of the mystical body (*cf.* 4:14-16).

4:1

A gentle nudge

Paul sets the tone for the rest of his letter when he writes: *I urge* (*parakaleō*) *you.* In a nutshell, he shares the major concerns on his heart with these wonderful believers. The bottom line: he taught them well, he prayed long and hard for them, now he pleads with them to respond positively and rise to the challenge. In no sense was Paul detached or indifferent to their needs. There was nothing 'take it or leave it' about his message. Quite the opposite—it was an intense appeal straight from his heart.

John Stott reckons that 'instruction, intercession, and exhortation constitute a formidable trio of weapons in any Christian teacher's armoury.' We know from the New Testament narrative that Paul was no ordinary humdrum teacher. There was nothing boringly run-of-the-mill about him!

Paul was in a groove all his own.

It is interesting to note how Paul introduces himself in this verse—it is the same as what he said in 3:1. He underlines his apostolic authority by using the emphatic personal pronoun *I*, not in any bombastic sense, but as a matter of course.

Not backwards in coming forward

Similarly, for a second time, Paul describes himself as *a prisoner* (*desmios*) *for the Lord.*

Paul is both a prisoner *of* Christ and a prisoner *for* Christ.

The apostle is bound to Jesus Christ by the chains of love and he is in custody out of unswerving loyalty to his gospel of grace. It seems to me that the vested authority of one of Christ's apostles combined with the passionate conviction of a man under house arrest because of his vision of a united church gave a lot of street cred to his exhortation. In that sense Paul put his money where his mouth was!

John MacArthur reminds us that, as a prisoner, 'Paul has the ability to see everything in the light of how it affected Christ. He saw everything vertically before he saw it horizontally. Everything he thought, planned, said, and did was in relation to his Lord. He was in the fullest sense a captive of the Lord Jesus Christ.'

- His motives were Christ's.
- His standards were Christ's.
- His objectives were Christ's.
- His vision was Christ's.
- His entire orientation was Christ's.

Lopsided

The punchline appears in the next phrase where Paul entreats them to *live a life worthy of the calling [they] have received.* This is nothing more and nothing less than the practical outworking of the ability of God in our lives. It will be seen as we live a life that is worthy for this is where the message is earthed to reality.

It seems to me that is reasonably plain and straightforward. However, like so much in the word of God, there is a lot more to it than initially meets the eye. Paul's words are actually much stronger in the original language—he encourages them (and us) to walk in a way which is worthy of our calling.

For example, the word *worthy* (*axiōs*) has the root meaning of balancing the scales—what is on one side of the scale should be equal in weight to what is on the other side. The implication is that our daily living should correspond to our high position as a child of God. Our practical living should match our spiritual position. There should be no contradiction between what we are and what we do.

We are to be like the man who said: *'Christ has done so much for me that I want the rest of my life to be a P.S. to his great work!'*

Walk the walk

When we talk about *living* (*peripateō*) or 'walking' (KJV)—the terms are used interchangeably—we need to realise that this is one of the great themes of this final section of the epistle. Not just how we walk but where we walk.

- Walk worthy (*cf.* 4:1).
- Walk in holiness (*cf.* 4:17).
- Walk in love (*cf.* 5:2).
- Walk in the light (*cf.* 5:8).
- Walk in wisdom (*cf.* 5:15).

Practical Christianity begins wherever we put our feet. We need to translate the truths of the mountaintop into shoe leather.

For most of us, walking is not too difficult! It is simply a question of putting one foot in front of the other and then repeating the process several times. So, says Paul, now you have started, keep on going. It is your walk that really counts!

Avoiding a church split

How are we meant to walk? In unity. And united.

What a stirring challenge that is to each of us as we read Paul's epistle two millennia down the road. The disconcerting fact is that many of our churches are riddled with tensions and suspicion and some, inevitably, are coming apart at the seams. An alarming number of evangelical churches are troubled with cliques and a variety of splinter groups. Sadly, there is hardly a week goes by when we do not hear of some church somewhere having a split.

A cynic quipped after a fairly heated church business meeting: *'If you want to find out about politics, join your local church.'*

It is in such a fractious and fractured context that Paul says what he does: *there is one body* (4:4).

There are many denominations spread right across the evangelical spectrum, there is a whole variety of groups around the country each with their own particular party line or sacred cow, there are different emphases in doctrinal stance, there are distinctive forms of worship, there are diverging opinions on church government—that said, at the end of the day: *there is one body!*

The high priestly intercession of the Lord Jesus when he prayed 'that they all may be one' is answered in the unity of the body of Christ (John 17:21). This is an evangelical unity not an ecclesiastical unity—a unity based on an organism not on an organisation.

Paul indicates four influential factors in our quest for a deeper understanding of Christian unity—four truths about the genre of oneness which God intends his people to grasp.

- Unity does not happen with a click of the fingers (*cf.* 4:1-3).
- Unity makes a lot of very good sense (*cf.* 4:4-6).
- Unity has nothing to do with everyone looking the same (*cf.* 4:7-12).
- Unity is coupled to maturity (*cf.* 4:13-16).

To put it very simply, Paul reminds us that unity is there—let us, therefore, pull out all the stops and go for it! First and foremost, authentic biblical unity is all about the right hand of fellowship, not the right fist of fellowship.

Unity is linking hearts, not banging heads!

A public display of unity

I believe this plea from the heart of Paul is based on the nature of the divine call which we have in faith responded to. The new international community which God is calling into being has two notable features:

- it is *one* people—composed equally of Jews and Gentiles—the single family of God, and
- it is a *holy* people—distinct from the secular world—a company of believers set apart to belong to God.

Here is the crunch!

- Because God's people are called to be *one* people they must manifest their unity, and
- because they are called to be a *holy* people they must manifest their purity.

Unity and purity are two fundamental features of a life worthy of the church's divine calling. In the course of his inspirational comments, the apostle deals with the unity of the church in 4:1-16 and the purity of the church from 4:17-5:21.

4:2

Getting going

Unity! It is one thing knowing all about it on paper, how do we take the first steps to really get moving? Paul solves the problem by strumming five strings on his bow—he lists five attractive qualities which should characterise our lives (*cf.* 4:2, 3).

He earlier prayed that we might be *rooted and established in love* (3:17), now he addresses his appeal to us to see to it that we live a life of love. This is where Paul begins! As the punters say: 'Good enough for Paul, good enough for me!'

In the real world, too many people put the cart before the horse— they begin by changing structures and implementing systems of one kind or another while the apostle starts the ball rolling by introducing a rich texture of moral qualities. Uppermost in his mind is what we are!

Humility

Paul goes for the jugular by immediately challenging us to *be completely humble*. Tall order! The word *humble* (*tapeinophrosyne*) was a much despised word in the ancient world. For example, the Greeks never used it in a context of approval, still less of admiration. Instead, they meant by it an abject, servile, subservient attitude—to them 'it was the crouching submissiveness of a slave' (F F Bruce).

It was not until Jesus Christ came that a true humility was recognised, for he humbled himself (*cf.* Philippians 2:5-8). Jesus led by example! And only he among the world's religious and ethical teachers has set before us as our model, a little child.

We recall Paul's honest appraisal where he saw himself as *less than the least of all God's people* (3:8). In a word, that is how we should regard ourselves—as nobodies with a sense of nothingness before the Lord. Humility is not about drive, energy, or ability, but about valuing. Genuine humility means:

- knowing ourselves,
- accepting ourselves, and
- being ourselves to the glory of God.

'Humility is the grace that when we think we have it, we've lost it!' (Andrew Murray)

Humility means putting Christ first, others second, and self last. The humble person is someone who is grateful to God for all that he has done for him by rightly assessing the value of the gifts which the Holy Spirit has given to him. He will not overestimate himself and fall into the snare of pride, nor will he underestimate himself and be caught in the trap of a false humility. His will be a balanced outlook.

Anonymous saints

It is interesting to note that the King James Version translates this phrase 'with all lowliness' meaning 'I am laid low'—a play on the word. The word 'humility' has a fascinating origin. It comes from the word 'humus'—that is, decaying organic matter. And when we stop and think about it, that is precisely what we are! When we talk about humus we tend to think of the rich compost we dig into the flower beds in our gardens—something not very noticeable but extremely fertile. According to Paul, this is the flagship of all Christian virtues.

Humility is best seen in someone with a servant heart who is willing to remain anonymous.

During the days of slavery in the West Indies, a group of Moravian Christians found it impossible to witness to the slaves because they were almost totally separated from the ruling class—many of whom felt it beneath them even to speak to a slave.

Two young missionaries, however, were determined to reach those oppressed peoples at any cost. In order to fulfil God's calling they joined the slaves. They worked and lived beside the slaves, becoming totally identified with them—sharing their overwork, their beatings, and their abuse. It is not strange that the two missionaries soon won the hearts of those slaves, many of whom accepted for themselves the God who could move men to such loving selflessness.

Humility. In a no punches pulled statement, Paul says that is what we should be. Because everything in God's store is on the bottom shelf, we have to get on our knees to get it!

No place for pride

It goes without saying that humility is essential to unity. Pride lurks behind all discord while the greatest secret of concord is humility. A former Archbishop of Canterbury, William Temple (1881-1944), noted: 'Pride is always the root of spiritual failure.' The solution is an intentional sense of God's grace for grace prevents the ego from inflating its own significance. I have discovered that truly humble people rarely come to blows! It is not a difficult concept to prove in real life experience.

Nine times out of ten, the people we immediately, instinctively click with are the people who give us the respect we feel we deserve, while the people we immediately, instinctively dislike are those who treat us like dirt.

John Stott argues: 'If, however, instead of manoeuvring for the respect of others (which is pride) we give them our respect by recognising their intrinsic God given worth (which is humility), we shall be promoting harmony in God's new society.'

The first jewel in the crown of Christian unity is the rare jewel of humility.

A soft touch

Believe it or not, the rich seam of *gentle*[ness] (*prautēs*) was warmly applauded by no less a philosopher than Aristotle (384-322 BC). Because he hated extremes and loved the golden mean, he saw in gentleness the rare quality of moderation—to him it was the balance between being too angry and never being angry at all. The *gentle* man is the man who is always angry at the right time and never angry at the wrong time.

Having said that, this is one of the sterling qualities which marked the earthly life of the Lord Jesus. He had his life under perfect control (*cf.* Matthew 11:29). We are not thinking especially here of self control, important as that is. The picture here is of a person who is God controlled—when someone is on the tiller of a life which is already in the hands of God (*cf.* Moses in Numbers 12:3).

In the Greek language the word was used for a soothing medicine, a colt that had been broken, and a soft wind. In each case we have ample evidence of power—strength under control. There is nothing spineless or timid about it for gentleness is not a sign of weakness. It means being spiritually and morally strong without being self assertive, pushy, or heavy handed.

'To be gentle means you have finished with yourself altogether.' (D. Martyn Lloyd-Jones)

Patience is a virtue

Be patient (*makrothymia*) is the middle string on Paul's bow. Many of the older translations use the word 'longsuffering' which means 'suffering long'. It is what God does with us! He suffers long with us—if he did not, there would be no Christianity.

We talk a lot today about people having a short fuse. Paul is thinking here of people who have such a long fuse that their temper never gets to the point of exploding. Such patience is:

- not short tempered,
- not quick tempered,
- not ill tempered, but
- long tempered!

Someone has said that 'our temper is such a valuable asset, we should never lose it!'

It talks about people who know what it is to be hurt and walked on like door mats, and still they never complain. Patience in this mould means we will show longsuffering towards people who get under our skin, it means we will react in a restrained manner when people pester, aggravate, and hassle us.

Chrysostom (AD 347-407), Bishop of Constantinople, defined it as 'the spirit which has the power to take revenge but never does so.'

The not so politically correct ditty says: 'Patience is a virtue, possess it if you can, seldom in a woman, never in a man!' For obvious reasons, I have no desire to get sucked into the politics of patience—what I do know, however, is that most of us need a wee bit more of it! And we need it now!

Hugs and bugs!

Then we are to *bear (anechomai) with one another in love.* It is not just a matter of putting up with each other but of getting along with each other. It is refusing to strike back or be bitter. It is when we set our own feelings to one side because the welfare of others is more important.

How can we possibly do that? By tolerant love. The love of God—*agapē*—flowing through us is the only way. Not easy! However, as has been said: 'Be careful of standing on your rights, for then God may stand on his!'

People are funny. Sometimes odd! As they say in South Yorkshire where Lois and I live: 'There's nowt so queer as folk!'

I appreciate the sting in the tail humour of the Peanuts cartoon where Lucy said to Snoopy: *'There are times when you really bug me but I must admit there are times when I feel like giving you a big hug.'* Snoopy replied: *'That's the way I am, Lucy. I'm huggable and I'm buggable!'*

And so it is with our relationships in the wider church family. In Paul's day there were tensions in the church and people were beginning to take sides. Fragmentation. Polarisation. Back then, in the first century, when life was relatively simple and everyone's pace was so much slower, there were childish squabbles—people getting on one another's nerves.

It is awfully sad but some people seem to have nothing better to do with their time than waste it nitpicking and majoring on minors— they specialise in making mountains out of molehills! To an outsider looking on and listening in, it is so embarrassing and incredibly petty.

People can be adults in age and height but terribly childish in their attitudes.

That is why Paul says what he does! In a sense, these are the foundation stones of Christian unity and love is the bonding agent which glues them all together. I think we can be fairly sure that no unity is pleasing to God which is not the child of love—'unconquerable benevolence' (William Barclay).

4:3

Prickly saints

The story is told of two porcupines who were huddled close together on a bitterly cold night in northern Canada. The closer they got to stay warm, the more their quills pricked each other, making it virtually impossible for them to remain side by side.

Silently they moved apart. Before long they were shivering in the wintry gale, so they came back together again. Soon both of them were poking and jabbing each other, so they separated again. Same story, same result. All night long, back and forth, back and forth.

That is what some of God's people are like—hence Paul's incisive comment in verse 2.

They are just like porcupines—they need each other but they keep needling one another.

Yes, our worship is important, our evangelism is important, our prayer life is important, but those things are a million miles away from what the apostle is talking about in this chapter—real

Christian unity. And, according to Paul, it is something we have to work at, we have to pull out all the stops, we have to endeavour with every ounce of energy to *keep the unity.*

Maintenance mode

Make every effort to keep the unity of the Spirit through the bond of peace—in some ways a strange exhortation. Paul first describes the church's unity as the *unity of the Spirit*—a unity which the Holy Spirit creates. And then in the next few verses (*cf.* 4:4-6) he argues that this *unity* (*henotēs*) is as indestructible as God himself. Yet, in the same breath, he also tells us that we have to maintain or *keep* (*tēreō*) it!

What does the apostle mean? Paul is encouraging us to keep the church's unity in a visible sense. He is desperately keen for the world to see a united front! He wants Joe Public to recognise that unity is more than just a theological nicety, he wants him to see it working out in a warring, wounding world. Charles Swindoll reminds us that this 'reflects the reality of God like nothing else on earth.'

The sad fact that it does not always appear like this is no excuse for us becoming complacent and accepting the *status quo.*

There is no room on God's agenda for an acquiescing believer. We cannot afford to sit back and rest on theoretical laurels.

Go for it!

The word which Paul uses in the text is emphatic—it means we are to give it all we have got in zealous bursts of continuous, diligent activity. When we pull out all the stops to preserve this unity we are to do it *through the bond* (*syndesmos*) *of peace*—'the spiritual belt that surrounds and binds God's holy people together' (John MacArthur). It is like a piece of string or twine. St Francis of Assisi (1182-1226) understood this call to the active pursuit of unity via peace, as his prayer so beautifully recalls:

Lord, make me an instrument of thy peace.
Where there is hate, may I bring love;
Where offence, may I bring pardon;
May I bring union in place of discord.

The formula of Rupert Meldenius popularised by the Puritan divine, Richard Baxter (1615-91), is still good guidance: *'Unity in essentials, liberty in incidentals, and in all things charity [love].'*

Suppose for a moment that by a miracle we could bring some of the great Christians of the centuries together under one roof. From the fourth century there would come the great intellect Augustine of Hippo; from the tenth century, Bernard of Clairvaux; from the sixteenth, the peerless reformer John Calvin. From the eighteenth century would come John Wesley, the great Methodist advocate of free will, and along with him George Whitefield, the outstanding evangelist. From the nineteenth century comes the Baptist C H Spurgeon and D L Moody. And finally from the twentieth century the world famous Billy Graham and Luis Palau.

R. Kent Hughes makes the valid point that 'if we gathered all these men under one steeple we would be unable to get a unanimous vote on many matters. But underneath it all would be *unity*. And the more these men lifted up Christ and focused on him, the greater their unity would be.'

Holding hands

It could be argued that Paul is widening the net when it comes to unity in the family of God. Not only is authentic unity most desirable in any church fellowship, it is also a tremendous benefit and blessing when it is shared between like minded church and mission groups as well.

We are not in the business of empire building! Our prime call and our principal reason for ministry is to extend the kingdom of God! The fact is we can do more together to realise that than we can when we go solo and operate on our own. Partnership is the name of the game!

Partnership is God working through people who are working together!

4:4

United we stand

Paul sets before us seven common denominators in the next three verses. I was intrigued to discover that many New Testament scholars believe this was an early Christian confessional hymn, and it may well have been (*cf.* 1 Corinthians 8:6; 12:4-6). Paul is more or less saying: this is what we have, therefore, this is what we should be!

Yes, we may have our differences, but we do have a lot in common. To emphasise the unity of the Spirit, Paul recites the features of oneness that are germane to our doctrine and life. We share each of these seven realities with every member of the international family of God. When we put them all together they pay a silver tongued testimony to the greatness of the mystical body of Christ. What are they?

Global and local

One body—the church is a body whose head is the Lord Jesus Christ.

Each local gathering of God's people is a microcosm or a miniature representation of the whole church.

The *one body* (*sōma*) is the model for the many local bodies that God has established across the world. The fact that a person is a member of the global church does not excuse him from belonging to a local entity—that is where he exercises his spiritual gifts and helps others to grow, where he can be discipled, and where he can be accountable to those in spiritual leadership.

Interdependent

Paul reminds us in 1 Corinthians 12:12-27 that each member of the body is like an organ—he may be an ear, an eye, or a foot. Each of those organs are members of one another in the sense that they belong to one another, they depend on one another. It would be the height of folly and madness to start chopping up the body into separate pieces. The bottom line: unity is incontrovertible.

A spiritual encounter

One Spirit is the next common trait on Paul's list. I believe the third person of the trinity is envisaged here—the Spirit (*pneuma*) of the living God. He is the one who opened our eyes that we might believe in Jesus and, if anyone else believes, the explanation for their change of life remains the same.

There are not several spirits bringing people from darkness to light—there is only one. He is the one who gives us the family feeling we have towards each other. He is the one who integrates us into one body (*cf.* 1 Corinthians 12:13).

'The Holy Spirit creates, fills, coordinates, orchestrates, and empowers the body of Christ.' (R. Kent Hughes)

We happily affirm that the one body is the church, the body of Christ, and that body is comprised of Jewish and Gentile believers—its unity or cohesion is due exclusively to the one Holy Spirit who indwells and animates it. When we look at it from that perspective, unity is coherent.

One hope

One hope (*elpis*) is item three on Paul's register (*cf.* 1:18). The same God calls us to the same privileges and the same destination. We share the same blessed hope that one day Christ will return (*cf.* Titus

2:13). The advent hope is burning brightly on the altar of our hearts. We cannot behave as if we were on different roads bound for different places. That is why unity is tenable.

By the same token, hope brightens our day. It gives a spring to our step, it puts a twinkle in our eye. It gives us an air of expectancy. It refuels our lives after a bad decision. Let us face it: without hope, no student would finish a university course, no artist would finish his painting, no entrepreneur would complete his business deal, no marriage would last. In spiritual matters, hope is the fresh air of survival.

4:5

Jesus is Lord

One Lord (*kyrios*) is the central figure in Paul's thinking and that Lord can be none other than our Saviour, Jesus Christ (*cf.* 1 Corinthians 8:6). All who believe were chosen in him and redeemed by him in order to follow him. It is under his Lordship and his alone that we live. We are going to be with him forever. With Nicolaus Ludwig von Zinzendorf (1700-60) we sing:

> *Jesus, thy blood and righteousness*
> *My beauty are, my glorious dress;*
> *Midst flaming worlds, in these arrayed,*
> *With joy shall I lift up my head.*

> *Bold shall I stand in that great day,*
> *For who aught to my charge shall lay?*
> *Fully absolved through thee I am,*
> *From sin and fear, from guilt and shame.*

When we read those words, on what basis then can we think of disowning each other? We cannot and that is precisely why unity is perfectly reasonable.

Same old story

One faith (*pistis*): we heard the same truths, we believed the same truths, and we relied upon the same truths for our eternal salvation. We are all as different as chalk and cheese, but there is only one gospel.

Saving faith is found in many different kinds of people, but that faith is the same in them all.

We come to faith from different starting points, but the faith we arrive at is identical. I have discovered over the years that true faith does not scatter people, it joins them together, for we have an affinity of heart and mind and purpose. That explains why unity is incontestable.

Immersed in Christ

One baptism (*baptisma*) is the next item on Paul's list. The emphasis here is on the baptism in the Holy Spirit for that is what places us into the body of Christ (*cf.* 1 Corinthians 12:13). It happens to every believing sinner—none are left out, none are excluded. It is for each of us and all of us. We are immersed into the body of Christ at the moment of our conversion.

Allied to that, baptism in water is an outward and visible sign of an inward experience of the saving grace of God. It is a public testimony of an individual's allegiance to Jesus Christ. Water baptism is a symbol of the immersion of believers into the body of Christ. That surely underlines that unity makes a lot of very good sense.

4:6

One in, all in

The final factor—*one God and Father of all*. We gather around the same throne and whisper the sweet name of *Father* to the one who sits there. He is our king and he is *over all*. We are his temple so he is *through all*. The heart of each individual Christian is his shrine, so by his Spirit he is *in all*.

In the light of all this, how can we keep apart from each other, how can we behave as if we belonged more to some of his children than to others? You see, unity is the credible thing to have.

Spiritual innuendo

Here is our noble confession: *one Lord, one faith, one baptism.*

- *One Lord*—therefore, I am saved!
- *One faith*—therefore, I am sure!
- *One baptism*—therefore, I am separated!

Over ... through ... in

And the one who has made a huge difference in your life and mine is the *one God and Father*. Here is a God who is absolute in his power for he is declared to be *over all*. That means no foe can daunt us and no fear need haunt us. No power in heaven, earth, or hell can triumph over him.

He rules the galaxies from planet earth to the uttermost star in the heavens. He is the one who sets the stars in orbit and keeps the planets on track and in line. No government on earth can overrule his decrees.

There is no *coup d'état* when it comes to the throne of God.

We also discover that he is absorbed in his purpose for he is *through all*. In other words, God knows precisely what he is doing, he knows exactly where he is going, he knows how he will accomplish his eternal purposes.

And he is abiding in his presence for he is *in all*. I think most of us are familiar with the concept of the Holy Spirit indwelling the believer and of the Lord Jesus indwelling the believer. Here we learn that the Father also indwells individual believers. God the Father, God the Son, God the Holy Spirit—they are all at home in our hearts.

Here is a God famed for his transcendence and, at the same time, renowned for his immanence.

We are God created, God loved, God saved, God Fathered, God controlled, God sustained, God filled, and God blessed. And the icing on the cake is that this God is our God for ever and ever. John MacArthur writes: 'We are one people under one sovereign (*over all*), omnipotent (*through all*), and omnipresent (*in all*) God.'

Back to front, front to back

This is absolutely thrilling for we are now in a position to repeat the three affirmations—this time the other way round and in the order in which the persons of the trinity are normally mentioned.

- The one Father creates the one family.
- The one Lord creates the one faith, hope, and baptism.
- The one Spirit creates the one body!

Indeed, we can go even further for there can be only one Christian family, one Christian faith, one Christian hope and baptism, one Christian body, because there is only one God— Father, Son, and Holy Spirit.

All one body we

We can no more multiply churches than we can multiply God.

Is there only one God? Then he has only one church! Is the unity of God inviolable? Then so is the unity of the church. The implication is that the unity of the church is as inexpungible and shatter proof as the unity of God himself. 'It is no more possible to split the church than it is possible to split the Godhead' (John Stott). We may split an atom, but we can never split the church! Our unity is more solid than the Andes and more enduring than Venus or Mars.

So, says Paul, do not be like the porcupines we talked about earlier, they have many good points, but they are hard to get close to. We have so much in common, but we are not spiritual clones, we are not meant to be. We are different. But we are on the same team, going for the same goals, for the benefit of one another.

We should be like clocks that strike at the same moment for unity is available and attainable.

Having said that, unity is not automatic, it did not just happen, it is something which has to be worked at. At the end of the day though, unity is justifiable, it makes a lot of incredibly good sense. And therein lies the wonder of it all.

A technicolored church

The main theme woven into the fabric of Paul's incisive comments in verses 7-11 is that unity is not a lifeless or colourless uniformity. We are all one but we are not all the same! There is no standard uniform for God's people to wear—it would spell disaster and it would be wrong if there was.

We are not to imagine that every Christian is an exact replica of every other as if we had all been mass produced in some celestial factory.

On the contrary, the unity of the church, far from being dull and boringly monotonous, is exciting in its rich diversity. We are all very different and we are meant to be—God made us that way and God wants it that way. No two of us are identical. We are not photocopies or carbon copies of one another. We are not meant to be cookie cutter Christians!

No identical twins

We live in God's global family—we come from different backgrounds, we are from different cultures, we have attained different standards, we have different temperaments, we have a different outlook on life, we have a different perception on current affairs, we have different interests, and what is a source of enormous pleasure to me may be pure pain to the person sitting beside me. Point made! We are all different.

Bishop J C Ryle of Liverpool said: 'The church of Christ needs servants of all kinds, and instruments of every sort—penknives as well as swords, axes as well as hammers, chisels as well as saws, Martha's as well as Mary's, Peter's as well as John's.'

The fact that we are all different should not and need not affect the unity of the church. There is so much more to unite us, to hold us together, to bind us together. Unity, there is. Thank God, there is! Uniformity, there never will be.

4:7

Different gifts

Did you notice what Paul wrote: *but to each one of us grace has been given as Christ apportioned* (*metron*) *it.* We have all received different gifts! We are not stereotyped nor have we been mass produced on some kind of assembly line conveyor belt. You see, every one of us has received a minimum of one spiritual gift—the gifts are all different—but the one who allocates them remains the same, Jesus Christ. I think Henriette Auber (1773-1862) was batting from the same crease when she wrote:

And every virtue we possess,
And every victory won,
And every thought of holiness,
Are his alone.

Question: how does the believer discover and develop his gifts? Answer: by fellowshipping with other Christians in the local assembly.

There is a real need for us to be well informed as we ask ourselves the question: 'Which gift do I have?' Study each of the gifts which are mentioned in the various lists (*cf.* Romans 12:6-8; 1 Corinthians 12:8-10, 28-30; Ephesians 4:11; 1 Peter 4:11) in the New Testament and, if the shoe fits, wear it. Our gifting is unique— and we never get the wrong gift, or too much or too little of it!

The next step is for us to be wide open before the Lord for our gift may be different than we think it is. We should allow the Lord and other mature believers whom we trust to help us discover our gift. It is also essential that we make ourselves available to the Lord so that he can use us as a round peg in a round hole.

If we fit easily into position, then our gifting will be confirmed— if we have big problems fitting into the hole then we need to go back to the drawing board and do a radical rethink. 'Not to use our gift is an affront to God's wisdom, a rebuff of his love and grace, and a loss to his church,' writes John MacArthur.

In my genes

We must make a clear distinction between spiritual gifts and natural abilities. When we were born into this world, God gave us certain natural abilities, perhaps in mechanics, art, athletics, or music.

In this regard, all men are not created equal, because some are smarter, or stronger, or more talented than others.

But in the spiritual realm, each believer has at least one spiritual gift, no matter what natural abilities he may or may not possess.

Body ministry

You see, what we have in this verse is the Lord teaching us how the body is meant to function. When we do it God's way, then there will be fruitfulness (*cf.* 1 Peter 4:10). The Lord has provided all that the body needs—he has given us grace so that we can get along with each other, he has given us gifts so that the body can develop and demonstrate that God is with us.

Paul speaks of *grace*—this is undoubtedly one of the apostle's favourite words: *charis*. It occurs numerous times in the New Testament but two out of every three references are from the pen of Paul. It simply means a favour that is free and undeserved. That is what God has given to us! He has gifted us and he has done it in grace.

'The unity of the church is due to *charis*, God's grace having reconciled us to himself—the diversity of the church is due to *charismata*, God's gifts freely distributed to church members.' (John Stott)

In actual fact, we learn from Paul's insightful comments to the church in Corinth that the more gifts we have, the more grace we need.

Use it or lose it

The various gifts which the Lord has given to us are not toys to play around with, they are not given primarily for our personal amusement, neither are they given to boost an already seriously inflated ego.

'They are tools to build with and, if they are not used according to grace, they become weapons to fight with.' (Warren Wiersbe)

That was the big problem which was tearing the heart out of the church at Corinth. I think it is fair and reasonable to assume from Paul's no punches pulled instruction in 1 Corinthians 12 that:

- no gift should be sought,

- no gift should be unused, and
- no gift should be exalted.

It does not matter who we are in the family of God, we have all been gifted personally by the Lord Jesus—those gifts should never be misused or abused. They should only be used, well used, with the grace that accompanies them.

4:8

A blast from the past

Paul begins with a rather unusual phrase when he writes: *this is why it says*. In other words, the gifts which have been allocated to us are a fulfilment of the Lord's promise found away back in Psalm 68:18— *when he ascended* (*anabainō*) *on high, he led captives in his train* (*aichmalōteuō*) *and gave gifts* (*doma*) *to men*—as it were, they are his love gifts to his church.

It is interesting to note that the Jews actually used this particular Psalm in connection with the annual springtime Feast of Pentecost celebrations in the synagogue. And further back in time, this Psalm was a victory hymn composed by David to celebrate God's conquest of the Jebusite city and the triumphant ascent of God (represented by the Ark of the Covenant) up Mount Zion (*cf.* 2 Samuel 6, 7; 1 Chronicles 13).

Ticker tape welcome

No matter what angle we view it from, this is very vivid imagery. The picture Paul has in mind is one which is full of drama. When he thinks of the ascension and exaltation of our Lord Jesus Christ, he links it to a well known practice in his time.

When a Roman general was successful on the field of battle, there would be a kind of ticker tape welcome arranged for him on his return, he would be given a hero's welcome, the flags would be out and flying high, the people would be lining both sides of the main street, the bands would be playing, the atmosphere was electric, all of this to greet the victorious conqueror.

He has the spoils of war with him for he is laden with gifts and booty. At the rear of the long procession, he is attended by a long train of captives in chains. In that unique sense, he would lead captivity captive. He would then sit on an elevated chair and give out the spoils to those who had fought with him and for him— different gifts to different people.

The grace of giving

See the victories of Christ—his enemies have all been roundly defeated, his overthrow of the enemy is total, his conquest is complete, he has returned to his throne in glorious triumph and, when he did, he showered gifts upon his people. It has come from the highest heights down to the deepest depths and back again—grace.

Who are the captives in his triumphal procession? People like you and me! Ah, the all conquering Christ takes us not in chains, but in bonds of love to sit in heavenly places alongside him. It is to you and me that the *gifts* are given, such is the generosity of grace.

4:9, 10

The highs and lows

When we put the spotlight on these verses, we see in the NIV translation that they are enclosed in brackets. I think it is probably fair to say that a lot of ink has been spilt by a lot of people over a lot of years as they have tried to come to terms with the ramifications of all that Paul is saying. These are probably two of the most difficult verses in his whole epistle—mind you, there is a serious danger that we could read into the text much more than is actually there.

Many Bible commentators feel it refers to the incident Peter talked about in 1 Peter 3:18-20 when Christ went and 'preached to the spirits in prison'. I do not think so for the simple reason that it does not sit comfortably alongside the quote from Psalm 68.

Surely what we have here is set against the words of David in plain contrast. There is nothing more sinister to it than that! The one who *ascended higher than all the heavens*—that is, the one who went *far above all* (*cf.* 1:21)—is exactly the same one who *descended* (*katabainō*) *to the lower, earthly regions* in his hour of humiliation (*cf.* Philippians 2:5-11). He is the one who became man, the servant king, and who in degradation went to the cross to purchase our redemption.

Such are the depths to which he stooped and the heights to which he rose.

This twin track approach is summed up beautifully in Graham Kendrick's acclaimed song:

Meekness and majesty, manhood and deity,
In perfect harmony, the man who is God:
Lord of eternity dwells in humanity,
Kneels in humility and washes our feet.

He went on to a cross, he suffered to give us life, he conquered through sacrifice, and the net result is:

Lord of infinity, stooping so tenderly,
Lifts our humanity to the heights of his throne.

When we think of the gifts he has given to us and the grace he has lavished upon us, what can we say?

In God moments like that, all we can do is bow down and worship.

4:11

The big four

Paul makes us aware of the four support gifts which the victorious Christ has given to the church:

- *apostles* (*apostolos*),
- *prophets* (*prophētēs*),
- *evangelists* (*euangelistēs*), and
- *pastors* (*poimēn*) *and teachers* (*didaskalos*).

The various gifts listed here are different from most of those mentioned in 1 Corinthians 12. There, for the most part, the gifts are given to individual believers—however, in the Ephesian context, gifted believers are given to the church. In 1 Corinthians, the gifts are viewed primarily from the standpoint of the local church—in Ephesians, they are viewed from the standpoint of the universal church.

One liner job description

When we think of the first two on Paul's list, *apostles and prophets*, they were gifted primarily to deal with situations as and when they arose. The apostles were specially equipped to guide and mobilise the infant church for ministry, the prophets were uniquely equipped to guard the infant church in relation to doctrine and biblical truth.

The two of them differ in that apostles were sent forth, while prophets spoke forth. Generally speaking, apostles had the gift of a word of wisdom, while prophets tended to have the gift of a word of knowledge (*cf.* 1 Corinthians 12:8).

The third one named is that of *evangelist*—someone who is uniquely equipped to deal with sinners. The fourth one is that of *pastor teacher* whose ministry is supremely with the people of God— he is called by God to tend and teach the flock as an undershepherd.

Reaching the unchurched

Apostles are the first group mentioned on Paul's list. The word means 'one who is sent' or 'one who is commissioned'.

We remember that Jesus had many disciples during the course of his ministry, but only twelve apostles.

We can differentiate like this: a disciple is a follower or a learner whilst an apostle is a divinely appointed representative. They were a relatively small and distinctive group which consisted of the Twelve, including Matthias who replaced Judas, Paul, James the Lord's brother, and possibly a few others such as Barnabas (*cf.* Acts 14:14), Andronicus and Junias (*cf.* Romans 16:7), Apollos (*cf.* 1 Corinth-ians 4:6, 9), and Silas and Timothy (*cf.* 1 Thessalonians 1:1; 2:6, 7). Each of these was personally chosen and authorised by Jesus.

The apostles were the pioneers of the early church, men who went into the unchurched regions beyond. To be a member of this illustrious group, one had to be a personal witness of the resurrection (*cf.* 1 Corinthians 9:1; 15:8, 9). It must be in this sense that Paul is using the word *apostles* here for he puts them at the top of his list (*cf.* 1 Corinthians 12:28).

Apostolic succession?

There are no apostles today in the strictest New Testament sense for they were not self perpetuating. Their ministry was foundational (*cf.* 2:20). They were there in the early days, and that was it! To me that simply underlines what Paul is saying:

---

the sovereign Lord gives different gifts to different people at different times to meet different needs.

As it happens, in many parts of the world today, there are missionaries who are blazing a trail for the Lord—such wonderful people are apostles at heart as they engage in a pioneer ministry for God, but that does not make them an apostle in the sense that Paul is talking about.

God's voice

When we think of a *prophet* we immediately think of people who predict the future—that was part of what they did, but it was only a small part of their total ministry. The main thrust of their work was to proclaim the faith, to forth tell the word of God.

In the primary sense in which the Bible uses the word, a prophet was a person who 'stood in the council of God', someone who 'heard' and even 'saw' his word and who, in consequence, 'spoke from the mouth of the Lord' and did so 'faithfully' (*cf.* Jeremiah 23:16-32).

A prophet was, therefore, a mouthpiece or spokesman of God—a vehicle of his direct revelation.

Like an oil well

I find it interesting to note that the most important Old Testament word for *prophet* (*nābî*) pictures people who are like oil wells gushing out God's truth! Back in the first century, they did not have the New Testament as we have it today—that was the primary role of a prophet—he was God's man to plug the gap. He stepped into the situation and it was his role to impart the word of God.

Apostles and prophets are different, yet both of them are sent by the Lord and both of them are equally necessary. Both groups were unique to the early church. I believe those twin gifts were temporary and transitional as they were intended to help the church become established (*cf.* 2:20).

Get the gist of what Paul is saying? He says: 'Look, there can be unity even in diversity!' There is no mention of the latter two gifted offices of evangelist and pastor teacher replacing the first two offices of apostle and prophet because in New Testament times all were operative.

The fact is, however, as they continued to serve the church, the evangelists and pastor teachers did pick up the baton from the first generation apostles and prophets.

Spiritual obstetricians

An evangelist is someone who heralds good news. He shares the evangel or the message of the gospel with others—that 'Christ Jesus came into the world to save sinners' (1 Timothy 1:15). These itinerant preachers were in the business of communication—they had a message and, thankfully, they knew how to get it across.

Philip, who is the only man in the early church described in this capacity, demonstrates that an evangelist is not a man with ten suits and ten sermons who runs a gospel road show (*cf.* Acts 21:8).

When we read through the Acts, it is clear that New Testament evangelists were missionaries and church planters who went where Christ was not named, their goal was to lead people to faith in the Lord Jesus. When that happened, they then taught the new believers the fundamentals of the word of God—building them up in their new found faith—and then they moved on to new territory.

An evangelist always warns people about Jesus, at the same time, they always warm people to Jesus.

Leave it to the experts?

If Paul's exhortation to young Timothy is anything to go by, every one of us should seek to do the work of an evangelist (*cf.* 2 Timothy 4:5) even though we do not all have the special gifting of an evangelist.

That beefs up my honest conviction that there is an ongoing need for regular evangelistic outreach in a church with a man gifted by God for the job. I really do believe that every local church should consider this strategic ministry as high priority, it should be well up the agenda at every church business meeting. If it is not, it says something about the spiritual health of that congregation. The baseline:

- all believers can be soul winners, but

- not all believers can be evangelists.

We thank God for those who have this special gift from the Lord and for the many around the world who have come to a personal faith in Christ under their anointed ministry. We thank the Lord for those who are gifted in the work of evangelism for 'he who wins souls is wise' (Proverbs 11:30).

As John Stott says: 'There is a great need for gifted evangelists today who will pioneer new ways of exercising and developing their gift so as to penetrate the vast unreached segments of society for Christ.'

Paediatricians of the church

When we think of the important role of a pastor teacher, the writer has in mind someone with a heart for people, who teaches and shepherds the people of God. Their main responsibility is to lead the flock, tend to the flock, instruct the flock, protect the flock, and mobilise the flock—their role is to see and to share the word of God with a people who will then go out into the real world and put into practice what the Bible teaches.

I read recently that there are four checkpoints anyone with this gift must pass:

- They need to be faithful, staying committed to the flock in good times and bad.
- They need to be practical, not afraid to address the seemingly insurmountable problems of daily life.
- They need to be discerning, able to spot danger before it is obvious, able to distinguish the phoney from the real, and sense the struggles of the flock.
- They need to be able to take criticism for people have a tendency to throw darts at their leaders and pastor teachers are not exempt—they must have thick skins to protect themselves emotionally.

It appears to me that it is sound scriptural teaching which builds up the church—it is *sine qua non* of the pastoral ministry, the greatest need of the church worldwide—and, therefore, in every congregation of God's people, it is teachers who are needed most (*cf.* John 21:15-17).

A work for Jesus, none but you can do

The local church is not a one man ministry, it is an every man ministry.

That way, unity can be maintained and diversity is not destroyed. If the truth be told, our unity is enhanced by our variety, not threatened by it. We need to get real because we cannot expect everybody to be the same—one of me is enough! We are what we are because that is the way God has made us. We have what we have because that is what Christ has given to us.

Therefore, says Paul, we should not flatter ourselves, we should not be jealous of anyone else. We can all do something to help build up the body, we all have a vital role to play, we all have a special job to do, we all have a gift which has to be exercised.

Definition: A spiritual gift is a skill or an ability that enables each Christian to perform a function in the body of Christ with ease and effectiveness.

So, your gift and mine, is something which is given to us by the Lord, it is spiritual in kind, and something which comes easily. It is a bit like adding the missing piece to a jigsaw puzzle—when we put our gift into action, the whole body of believers in the church reaps the benefit and blessing.

That means our greatest and most effective and lasting contribution to other believers is for us to exercise our gifts. That is the road to blessing and the path to quality Christian living.

4:12, 13

Maturity matters

The key thought in these verses is that unity is happily married to maturity. God has a pattern for his church to function and we can clearly see the progression of that pattern. The distinctive role of these two groups is to equip people for effective service so that the church will be strengthened (*cf.* 4:12).

The divine rationale is that all the people of God might become increasingly more like the Son of God. The power for such a growth experience is our love for each other, with the final phrase in verse 16 saying all that needs to be said: *as each part does its work.*

There is the timeless secret to growth—it is every person doing what God has gifted them to do.

The perennial problem is that so many believers tend to do little or nothing, or at best they exercise their tongues as armchair generals, leaving a committed few to pick up the slack and carry the load. Such a mindset invariably leads to fractured relationships and a breakdown of mutual trust. Generally speaking, it brings in its wake a people who are frustrated and stressed out and, tragically, it results in a work not being able to develop to its fullest potential. Stunted growth.

What a tremendous difference there would be if every one in the congregation was pulling their weight and pulling in the same direction!

Ministry matters

How does Paul develop his operational strategy further? I think this section offers to us incontrovertible evidence that the New Testament envisages ministry not as the prerogative of a clerical elite but as the privileged calling of all the people of God. It would appear that in our generation this biblical vision of an every member ministry is taking a firm hold in a growing number of our church fellowships.

The New Testament concept of a pastor is not that of a reverend gentleman looking over his shoulder, jealously guarding all ministry in his own hands, and successfully squashing all initiatives from the people in the pew.

The pastor or minister was never intended to be a third millennium Protestant pope!

He is supposed to be a person who helps and encourages all God's people to discover and develop and exercise their gifts. By and large, his teaching and training are directed to this end—to enable the people of God to be a servant people, ministering actively but humbly according to their gifts in a world of alienation and pain. To teach is to touch a life for ever!

Instead of monopolising all ministry himself and seeing himself as God's answer to the local church, he actually multiplies ministries.

It is the pebble in the lake syndrome for the consequences of such a mindset for ministry are far reaching.

Church: structure or stricture?

If this is what we believe to be the ideal pattern for all ministry, maybe we need to ask a simple question: How do we see the church?

Over the years the traditional model of the church is that of a pyramid—the minister perched precariously on its pinnacle while the ordinary members are arrayed beneath him in serried ranks of inferiority. I can assure you that is a totally unbiblical image because the New Testament envisages not a single pastor with a docile flock but both a plural oversight and an every member ministry.

Not much better is the model of the bus which we sometimes see. In that model the pastor does all the driving while the congregation are passengers slumbering in peaceful security behind him.

Quite different from either the pyramid or the bus is the biblical, Pauline model of the body. The church is the body of Christ in which every member has a distinctive and meaningful role to play. Although the body metaphor can certainly accommodate the concept of a distinct pastorate, in terms of one ministry among many, there is simply no room in it, either for a hierarchy, or for that kind of bossy clericalism which concentrates all ministry in the hands of one man, and denies the people of God their own rightful ministries.

Truth recovered

If the sixteenth century recovered the liberating truth of the priesthood of all believers—where every Christian enjoys through Christ a direct access to God, perhaps the twenty first century will herald a total recovery of the ministry of all believers—where every Christian receives from Christ a privileged ministry to men.

Purpose statement

What is the real purpose of ministry? It is *to prepare God's people for works of service, so that the body of Christ may be built up.* The word *prepare* (*katartismos*) is a very interesting word which means 'to equip'.

As a medical term, the word is used in surgery for setting a broken bone or for putting a dislocated joint back into its place. It also means to fit out a ship for a voyage. It can be used in the context of equipping an army for battle. In politics it is used for bringing together opposing factions so that government can go on. Similarly we read of it in Matthew 4:21 and Mark 1:19 where it is translated 'preparing their nets'.

It would appear conclusive then that the thought behind the word is of making something ready, of perfectly equipping someone, of fully preparing something. When we stop and think about it, that is what the spiritual gifts are for—they are specially given to bring the body of Christ to her full potential.

Tools for the job

God in his wisdom and grace has given us four basic tools to get on with the task of equipping the saints. Tool number one is the Bible. The pastor teacher is to feed himself, to feed his people, and to lead them to feed themselves on the word of God (*cf.* 2 Timothy 3:16, 17).

Tool number two is prayer. We recall the example of the apostles in the early church where they gave themselves continually to 'prayer and the ministry of the word' (*cf.* Acts 6:4). That means the pastor teacher is responsible to prepare himself before the Lord and to lead his people to prepare themselves in prayer—the kind of role Epaphras filled so admirably.

Paul knew that he was a good brother committed to building up the Lord's people by these two means. He gave him a glowing testimonial when he wrote: 'He is always wrestling in prayer for you, that you may stand firm in all the will of God, mature and fully assured' (Colossians 4:12).

Tool number three is testing. Trials come into our lives so that we may develop perseverance, and perseverance works within us in such a way that it leads to our maturity and completeness in Christ (*cf.* James 1:2-5). A strange way of working? Maybe! But God knows what he is doing and as a result our spiritual muscles are strengthened and effective service for him is broadened.

Tool number four is suffering. Peter says as much in the closing comments of his first epistle—a manual for displaced persons (*cf.* 1 Peter 5:10). To know the Lord and to follow the Lord will mean a deep sense of fellowship with him in his sufferings (*cf.* Philippians 3:10). It is through suffering and trials that we are refined and better equipped to serve the Lord from a heart overflowing with love and devotion.

Attainable and measurable

It is a tremendous blessing to have each of these tools at our disposal, but what is the goal of our equipping the people of God? Paul says it is for *works of service* (*diakonia*). That means all of us, not just a few of us! Every member involvement! People participation right across the whole spectrum.

Christian ministry is not the labour of one man nor is it the work of a select elitist group of people! It has to be seen as the domain of every child of God for God will enable us and equip us. Otherwise the church would begin to look like a typical Saturday afternoon Premier League football game—50,000 spectators in the stands desperately in need of exercise, watching twenty two people on the field desperately in need of rest!

Since that is, hopefully, not the case, the ball is back in our court. The onus is on us to get our act together and stop playing church. We need to commit ourselves to getting seriously involved by getting our feet wet and our hands dirty. Commitment is the name of the game.

Ministry is serving the Lord Jesus, and serving one another.

It is all about God's people being released into a ministry that they can best do for the Lord and the leadership giving them the tools and letting them get on with it.

On the up and up

The Lord equips us through a variety of means to serve him, but for what reason? It is *so that the body of Christ may be built up*. This is a fascinating word, *oikodomē*, which was used in the construction of a house. When the foundation was laid and the bricks were added, it was said to be *built up*.

It is obvious that with God's blessing the church will be built up numerically through evangelism.

Sometimes we spend so much time trying to keep the sheep in the pen when we should be targeting those who are still out on the hills.

The emphasis here, however, is on internal growth. It is a nurturing in the word of God, an engagement in fruitful service for the Lord Jesus. Paul's farewell words to the elders in the church at Ephesus encapsulate his thinking on this issue: 'I commit you to God and to the word of his grace, which can build you up' (Acts 20:32).

4:13

Vision statement

Paul spells it out when he writes, it is *until we all reach unity in the faith and in the knowledge of the Son of God and become mature, attaining to the whole measure of the fulness of Christ.*

So far as God is concerned, this is the big picture. The phrase *whole measure (metron)* is most intriguing—it is similar to the one that was used of Zacchaeus who was 'a short man' (Luke 19:3) signifying that he was little of stature. In today's speak, he was a wee fella who was vertically challenged!

It can also be translated 'age' as in the story of the man who was born blind whose parents were interrogated by the right wing religious authorities. They responded in John 9:21 by saying: 'Ask him! He is of age.' In a nutshell, they were really saying: 'Look, he's old enough, he has grown up, he can speak for himself!'

That is the wonderful goal the Holy Spirit has for every one of us. He wants us to grow up, to *mature (teleios)*, and he wants all of this to happen so that we might display something of the colossal stature of Christ in our lives. 'In other words,' writes John Stott, 'the church's goal is not Christ but its own maturity in unity which comes from knowing, trusting, and growing up into Christ.'

Ideally, this should happen on two fronts—individually and corporately. There is no doubt about it, it is hugely appropriate in the context of a local church fellowship, hence the phrase: *until we all reach unity in the faith.*

There will be a growth in grace and in resemblance to Jesus when we have a common ground on which to stand together. The bedrock for our unity is the fundamentals of the 'faith that was once for all entrusted to the saints' (Jude 3), and the aim for our unity is to reflect Jesus in every circumstance of life.

During the Crimean War, Florence Nightingale was passing one night down a hospital ward. She paused to bend over the bed of a sorely wounded soldier. As she looked down, the wounded lad looked up and said: *'Nurse, you're Christ to me!'*

The road to unity

We noted earlier that this unity is something which needs to be maintained (*cf.* 4:3), ten verses later, it needs to be attained! In some ways Paul's choice of verbs is a little surprising! If unity already exists as a gift, the question is: how can it be attained as a goal?

Just as *unity* (*henotēs*) needs to be maintained visibly, so it needs to be attained fully, for there are degrees of unity, just as there are degrees of sanctity. And the unity, to which we are to come one day, is that full unity, which a *knowledge* (*epignōsis*) of the Son of God will make gloriously possible. What an aspiration! What anticipation!

4:14

Benefits in kind

Growth is uppermost in Paul's mind when he outlines some of the bonuses which are ours when unity is achieved. By the same token, Paul is a realist and he knows there are certain pitfalls to be avoided. Growth, if we are not alert, can suffer some major setbacks!

What a mighty verse! How wonderfully descriptive! It is packed full of interesting words. For example, the word translated *infants* (*nēpios*) means 'one who is not old enough to speak'—it is a cameo of a little child who is helpless, someone who is picked up and put down by others.

Children are delightful little people to have around us in the home, but they do have their limitations. Two are instability and naïveté. They are notoriously fickle. Paul reminds us that the gifts of Christ to the church are designed to get us well past this stage of infancy in our spiritual development.

Take a brand new convert, for example: they know something life changing has happened to them, but they do not know the theology behind it. A young believer's theology embraces little beyond the bare bones of his salvation. Most likely his views on the person and work of Christ, the Holy Spirit, Scripture, and many important matters, are what he has picked up from other people. Paul, therefore, shows us how incredibly vulnerable we are if we fail to progress and grow.

Spiritual butterflies

There will be no doctrinal stability for he is *tossed* (*klydōnizomai*) *back and forth by the waves*. That literally means 'surging like the sea'. In other words, his opinions are constantly changing as he flits from one thing to another—he espouses one idea for a while, then drops it, and goes enthusiastically after something else. Every new religious fad, every novel interpretation of Scripture, it does not matter what it is, the brand new convert jumps on the gravy train and swallows it hook, line, and sinker.

He has not yet mastered principles of hermeneutics and applied them to the word of God. He has not yet formed convictions of his own regarding the cardinal truths surrounding the gospel.

Taken for a ride

It is a vivid picture of a person who finds themselves in a state of flux. The words *blown here and there* (*peripherō*) are similar to what we read in Mark 6:55 where the sick were 'carried about'. The picture Paul is painting here is of a person who is helpless in the hands of others.

He has not finished yet for Paul goes on to show how some smooth talking predators take advantage of those in the rank and file who are spiritually immature. People who are not well established and anchored in the eternal truths of Scripture are easily swayed. To all intents and purposes they are gullible, they are easily taken for a ride, they are carried about all over the place with *every wind of teaching*.

Religious roulette

It is bad enough when the teachers are saved men, how much worse it is when they are peddling error. It does not come out just as clear in the NIV but there is a phrase which is found in the KJV which reads: 'by the sleight of men'. That means 'a cube' and it refers to a dice whose origins are found in a gambling casino. The underlying thought in using this metaphor is of slyness or trickery.

False teachers play tricks with the truth.

Is it any wonder Paul says we should watch them!

Up the garden path

Paul also talks about their *cunning (kybeia) and craftiness (panourgia)*. Their devious subtlety. Paul uses the same word when he speaks of the devil pulling the wool over the eyes of Eve (*cf.* 2 Corinthians 11:3). She was no match for the devil on her own, but she had the word of God. She only had to use it and, because she failed to use it, she fell flat on her face. The devil tripped her up!

Smooth talking, smarmy false teachers do exactly the same— they deceive innocent people, they con people, they lie in wait and then snare unsuspecting people when their guard is down. When we are least expecting it, then they pounce.

Then and now

In Paul's day growth was being held back and inhibited because Satan was attacking the church with all his craft and power. That is precisely why they needed *apostles, prophets, evangelists, and pastor teachers.*

How much more, two thousand years down the road, when Satan is trying every trick of his trade, do we need sound Bible teaching. We need plain truth spoken in our pulpits so that people like us might know where we stand and what we believe.

4:15, 16

Two spiritual laws

There is the law of love where Paul encourages us to *speak the truth in love*. These words do not fully translate the verb Paul uses, *alētheuō*, because the English language has no comparable verb. A better rendering might be 'truthing in love' which includes all we think and do, as well as what we say. I suppose we can push the pendulum to either extreme when we look at what Paul is advocating in this verse when all of the time Paul is calling for a balanced combination of the two.

- We can speak the truth and not do it in love—when we do that we are being ungracious.

Truth spoken with that attitude often offends and it does very little lasting good. More often than not, it succeeds in getting people's backs up, it alienates the people we are trying to win.

- We can speak in love and suppress the truth—if we go down that road we are being unfaithful.

People who do not want to hurt someone else's feelings may opt to play safe and say nothing. They do not want to rock the boat! By choosing to suffer in silence, they may allow a sinful situation to continue.

True love always speaks at the right time, uses the right words, in the right spirit, and never fails to use the right approach.

Truth without love is brutality but love without truth is hypocrisy.

Striking a balance

There are those in the contemporary church who are determined at all costs to defend and uphold God's revealed truth. Sometimes, sadly, they are conspicuously lacking in love. When they think they smell a heresy rat or spot a flaw in a person's theological wardrobe, their nose begins to twitch, their muscles ripple, and the light of battle enters their eye. They seem to enjoy nothing more than a fight.

Others make the opposite mistake. They are determined at all costs to maintain and exhibit brotherly love but in order to do so are prepared even to sacrifice the central truths of revelation. It seems to me that both these tendencies are unbalanced and unbiblical.

'Truth becomes hard if it is not softened by love and love becomes soft if it is not strengthened by truth.' (John Stott)

The apostle calls us to hold the two together which should not be difficult for Spirit filled believers since the Holy Spirit is himself the Spirit of truth (*cf.* John 16:13) and his first fruit is love (*cf.* Galatians 5:22).

Paul has left us an example worth emulating for he spoke the truth in love to the church at Ephesus. He gets down to some very practical issues in the next few verses—he talks about lying and anger, he addresses the issues of stealing and dirty conversation, he tackles the thorny problem of our interpersonal relationships.

Body works

The second law is the law of life. I hasten to point out that we must not look in these verses for inspired instruction on human anatomy and physiology. The apostle's intention is not to teach how the human body works but rather how the body of Christ functions.

True, Paul did use some terms employed by ancient Greek medical writers like Hippocrates and Galen. That is no problem for Paul had Luke the medical doctor with him on many of his travels— no doubt, he would keep him right when it came to the accuracy of such statements!

A Head start

The emphasis Paul appears to be making is on *the Head* (*kephalē*) into whom we are to *grow up* and from whom the body grows when each part is working properly. The controlling influence of the Head is ably depicted by Paul when he harks back to one of his favourite illustrations—the church is compared to a body and Christ is the Head.

Paul talked at some considerable length in 1 Corinthians 12-14 along similar lines, he showed our interdependence—we need each other, we cannot go it alone—it is being together in our moments of elation and joy as well as sharing together in our darkest hours of deepest sorrow.

Go for growth

Here the theme is our mutual development for we are to *grow up* as individuals and as a body. Watching something grow is a captivating experience for there are so many influences which contribute to it.

Not all parts of the body grow at the same speed, not all parts of the body grow to the same size.

Nevertheless, I think when we understand that, it makes Paul's comment and challenge all the more relevant. The measure of our individual and personal growth is Jesus. The question is: how much more like him have we become? To what extent is his life being reproduced in us? Paul pulls no punches when he says: grow up, look at Jesus, live like Jesus, be like Jesus!

In love

We also find in this verse that we are to *grow* (*auxanō*) and *build* (*oikodomē*) ourselves up *in love*. Two times in two verses the apostle mentions love. Why? Here is the most important ingredient in spiritual life and growth. We see it in the lives of children in the human realm, how apt and appropriate it is therefore in the spiritual dimension—love is the circulatory system of the body.

In recent days, it has been discovered that isolated, neglected babies do not grow properly and are especially susceptible to disease, while babies who are loved and cuddled and handled, grow normally and are stronger.

Love is the pulsating energy which activates every nerve.

Where this happens, the body grows. It becomes more like its Head and operates in a fuller submission to him.

Well oiled

As the body grows and develops, so does its coordination for it is *joined and held together by every supporting* (*epichorēgia*) *ligament* (*haphē*). The organs are running smoothly in sync, they are working better and better together. You see, unity and maturity are vitally linked to each other and can never be separated, they are wedded together and should never be driven apart.

It was John Bunyan (1628-88) who said of the Lord's people: *'When all their garments are white the world will count them his.'* A rather sceptical German poet, Heinrich Heine, said to Christians on one occasion: *'You show me your redeemed life and I might be inclined to believe in your Redeemer.'*

In other words, the authentic life that speaks the gospel with a spirit of loving sacrifice will be eminently convincing. The combination of truth and love in this context counteracts the two great threats to powerful ministry—the lack of truth and the lack of compassion.

Fast forward

How wonderfully inspired, therefore, was Paul's timely message to the church at Ephesus! Within a few years, Jesus would walk back into that fellowship on his tour of seven churches in Asia Minor (*cf.* Revelation 2:2-4).

The Lord would say to them: 'I know all about you, I know you are standing up for the truth, I know you are running an excellent programme to cater for all ages, week in, week out. I know how incredibly busy you are. I know how doctrinally sound you are, but I have something against you. You have all this, you do all this and more, but you don't love me anymore!'

Basically, they were insolvent. Love for Jesus was lacking. And without such real love, everything else was spurious. What a turn of events. Maybe we need to ask ourselves: How is my love for Jesus today? How is my love for his people today?

'Everyone has some gift, therefore all should be encouraged; no one has all the gifts, therefore all should be humble; all gifts are for the one body, therefore all should be harmonious; all gifts are from the Lord, therefore all should be contented; all gifts are mutually helpful and needful, therefore all should be studiously faithful; all gifts promote the health and strength of the whole body, therefore

none can be safely dispensed with; and all gifts depend on his fulness
for power, therefore all should keep in close touch with him.' (A T
Pierson)

Being what God wants us to be

I believe the more we share Paul's perspective on these matters, the
deeper will be our discontent with the ecclesiastical *status quo*. Some
of us are too conservative, some of us are too complacent, some of
us are too ready to acquiesce in the present situation and resist change.
Others are far too radical and want to throw the baby out with the
bath water.

Instead we need to grasp more clearly the kind of new
community God wants his church to be. The verses we have just
been studying give us Paul's vision for the church. God's global
fellowship is to display:

- a warm love in a cold loveless environment,
- unity in a divided and fractured society,
- diversity in a monochrome and stereotyped culture, and
- growing maturity in a childish and pampered world.

4:17-19

Whiter than white

Paul takes a deep breath before launching into what he sees as one
of the most important messages he will ever give on the standards
which are expected of God's people. He focuses on the life which is
worthy of God's call.

Paul argues further up the chapter that we are called to be one
people, therefore, we must nurture unity. By the same token, we are
called to be a holy people, therefore, we must also promote purity.

Purity is as indispensable a trait of the church of God as unity.

Straight from the shoulder

Paul reminds the Ephesian believers of his apostolic authority when he says: *I tell you this, and insist (martyromai) on it in the Lord.* Strong words! It means he is writing to them with the authority the Lord Jesus invested in him.

The gist of his message is unmistakably clear and plain—*you must no longer live as the Gentiles do.* In other words, when a person becomes a real follower of Jesus there has to be a break with the past, a burning of the bridges, a fresh start. It is, after all, a new life in Christ which comes complete with a new wardrobe!

Away with the old clothes, on with the new clothes!

Past put behind us

These first century believers knew exactly what Paul was talking about. They knew from personal experience what he was saying for they had been pagans themselves, and they were still living in a hostile heathen environment.

Just as there is a typical Christian life, so there is a stereotyped pagan life. Paul's punchline: they must live that way no longer. Once they were pagans and so lived like pagans—now they were Christians, they must live like Christians. They had become different people, therefore, they must behave differently.

John Stott hit the nail on the head when he wrote that 'their new status as God's new society involved new standards, and their new life in Christ a new lifestyle.'

Before and after

The skilful way Paul handles his theme is to begin with the doctrinal basis of the new life (*cf.* 4:17-24), and then move on to its practical outworking in everyday behaviour (*cf.* 4:25-5:4).

Paul knows it is essential and desirable for his readers to grasp the contrast between what they had been as pagans and what they now were as Christians. He knows they have to come to terms with the huge gaping difference between their old life and their brand new life. He knows, in the longer term, it would be immensely beneficial to them if they can grasp the underlying theological basis of this radical change.

They had gone through a personal revolution and he wanted to explain to them in plain Greek what had happened to them and in them!

What we have here is an easy read, layman's guide to a profoundly deep work of grace in the heart of a sinner.

Mind games

The first thing which strikes me is the emphasis which Paul lays on the intellectual factor in everybody's way of life. Paul is in the process of describing pagans and he does it in a colourful way. He draws attention in 4:17 to the *futility* (*mataiotēs*) *of their thinking* (*nous*), then he adds that they are *darkened* (*skotoō*) *in their under-standing* (*dianoia*), and then he attributes their alienation from God to *the ignorance* (*agnoia*) *that is in them* (4:18).

Basically, he refers to their empty minds, their darkened under-standing, and their inward ignorance, as a result of which they had become callous, licentious, and insatiably unclean (*cf.* 4:19). This is one of those moments when ignorance is far from bliss.

In stark contrast to them, the believers had *come to know Christ*, they *heard* of him, they were *taught* in him, all according to the *truth that is in Jesus* (4:20, 21). Over against the backdrop of the inky black darkness and blind ignorance of the heathen, Paul sets the liberating truth of Christ which the Christians had learned.

John Stott makes the point that 'the Bible bears an unwavering testimony to the power of ignorance and error to corrupt, and the power of truth to liberate, ennoble, and refine.'

From bad to worse to ...

Externals do matter! They matter a whole lot—our relationships, our work, our circumstances, our body—Jesus Christ wants to be Lord of them all. But the internals are also of ultra importance. In fact, the real key to having Jesus as Lord of our externals is to first enthrone him over what goes on inside us—our mind, our emotions, and our will. With that in vogue, notice the harsh terms Paul uses to describe a person rebelling against the Lord Jesus (*cf.* 4:17-19). What a withering list!

Paul says that their problem stems from the *hardening* (*pōrōsis*) *of their hearts* (4:18). That is fundamental and it is that which exacerbates the issue in a massive way. We can see the logic in Paul's thinking in the way the text flows so easily from one key thought to another. Paul is tracking the terrible downward spiral of evil which starts with an obstinate rejection of God's known truth (*cf.* 4:18, 19).

The dominos are falling

That is how and where it begins—with their *hardening of heart.* Before long, the dominos are falling for it leads to their *ignorance* being *darkened in their understanding*—consequently, they are *separated* (*apallotrioō*) *from the life of God* since he turns away from them—until, finally, *having lost all sensitivity* (*apalgeō*), *they have given* (*paradidōmi*) *themselves over to sensuality* (*aselgeia*) *so as to indulge* (*ergasia*) *in every kind of impurity* (*akatharsia*), *with a continual lust* (*pleonexia*) *for more.*

The parting shot of one translation is: 'They stop at nothing to satisfy their foul desire.' We can put it like this: hardness of heart leads first to darkness of mind, then to deadness of soul under the judgment of God, and finally to recklessness of life. Such is the alarming condition of every sinner on the face of the earth. I think what we have here is not dissimilar from the sequence which Paul elaborates on in the closing half of Romans 1 and neither portion makes for pleasant reading!

The bottom line: having lost all sensitivity, people lose all self control.

Stage one

When we look carefully at the text, there are three features that marked their old behaviour. There is, first, a *hardening of their hearts* that ultimately made them reject anything to do with God. It was a petrifying, fossilising process which had slowly taken over their thinking and decision making. Eventually they would seize up altogether.

Paul's word describes a process which would conclude with their hearts being harder than granite. In a medical sense, it describes the callus that forms after a bone is broken and which, once the healing is complete, is harder than the original bone.

The Bard of Scotland, Robert Burns, in the *Epistle to a Young Friend*, wrote about sin:

I waive the quantum o' the sin,
The hazard of concealing;
But och! it hardens a' within,
And petrifies the feeling!

This *hardening* resulted in the *ignorance* that separated them from *the life of God*. It starved them of divine enlightenment which meant that they would remain *in the futility of their thinking* and *darkened in their understanding*. They have a different set of values because they have suppressed the truth (*cf.* Romans 1:18).

They hold down the truth much like the little boy who smuggled his dog into his room to spend the night. When he heard his mum and dad approaching, he put the dog in his toy box, sat on the lid, and talked with his parents, ignoring the repeated thumps of the poor pet. Paul is talking about an aggressive suppression of the truth—when we turn a blind eye and a deaf ear to all the promptings of the Spirit of God. They blocked out God's light!

Stage two

Their lives were marked by an unquenchable lust that made them *give themselves over to sensuality.* This they did without any thought for anybody else. There was no sense of shame, or regret, or even red faced embarrassment. Actually, the word indicates that they were happy to parade it with their heads held high. No chagrin.

They abandon themselves to a life of sin, sin, and more sin, to a life where indecency and perversion runs wild. Ultimately they come to a point where even their conscience is cauterised.

According to an ancient Greek story, a Spartan youth stole a fox but then inadvertently came upon the man from whom he had stolen it. To keep his theft from being discovered, the boy stuck the fox inside his clothes and stood without moving a muscle while the frightened fox tore out his vital organs. Even at the cost of his own painful death he would not own up to his wrong.

Such individuals are desensitised to that which is killing them and are, slowly but surely, being robbed of the vitality of life.

Like a rampant cancer, it is eating away at them and, apparently, they are oblivious to it. They think they are having a real good time.

Stage three

There was greed for an endless series of horrendously detestable acts. As they say, one thing leads to another and it does not produce a garden of delights! They needed to *indulge in every kind of impurity, with a continual lust for more.* Their depraved desire was fired by a deeper craving for an ongoing experience of even grosser things.

It is the mindset which says: 'If we paint the town red tonight, we have to have a bigger bucket and a bigger brush for tomorrow night!' In other words, sin never satisfies, it just leads to more sin! Their minds are so warped and they are so crooked in their thinking, they could hide behind a cork screw—that is how far sin will take a man.

When sin has ravaged and ruined a man, it will leave him lying naked in a smelly sewer.

4:20-24

Making the right connection

A totally different atmosphere emerges when Paul moves away from the seamy, murky world of the pagan to the fresh and invigorating world of the new Christian. The choice expressions which Paul employs are quite remarkable for they set in motion a whole process of Christian moral education.

In another flash of inspiration, Paul did not link Christian belief and behaviour to a creed or code of conduct (*cf.* 4:20). He links them to Christ. He did not connect them to a precept or a principle, but to a person—Jesus. Christianity is Christ.

Paul is not encouraging the impossible here, nor is he engaged in wishful thinking. For him, the mind was the centre of the personal life. You see, what truly captivates the mind will in the end control the life. And so, according to Paul, it is all down to the mind. Attitudes really do matter.

It is not what we think we are! It is what we think, we are!

Back to school

Paul uses three pedagogical terms which centre on three verbs—all in the aorist tense—meaning to learn, to hear, and to be taught, with a final reference to the *truth that is in Jesus*. Each turn of phrase evokes the image of a school and probably refers to the sound instruction these new converts have all received.

According to the first, Christ is himself the quintessence of Christian teaching. In other words, the Christ whom they had learned was calling them to standards and values totally at variance with their former idolatrous life.

Second, Christ who is the nub of the teaching is himself also the teacher. Paul assumes that through the voice of their biblical teachers, they had actually *heard* (*akouō*) Christ's voice (4:21). That means when sound biblical instruction is imparted, it may be said that Christ is teaching about Christ.

Third, they had been *taught* (*didaskō*) *in him* (4:21). That is to say, Jesus Christ, in addition to being the teacher and the teaching, was also the context, even the atmosphere within which the teaching was given. When he is the personification of all of these, we may have total confidence that what is being taught is unashamedly Christian.

'When true preaching takes place, Jesus is invisibly in the pulpit and walking the aisles personally teaching his own.' (R. Kent Hughes)

In Jesus—this is the Christian experience as the patron saint of Ireland, St Patrick, so beautifully expressed it in the fifth century:

> *Christ be with me, Christ within me,*
> *Christ behind me, Christ before me,*
> *Christ beside me, Christ to win me,*
> *Christ to comfort and restore me.*
> *Christ beneath me, Christ above me,*
> *Christ in quiet, Christ in danger,*
> *Christ in hearts of all that love me,*
> *Christ is mouth of friend and stranger.*

Spiritual makeover

The simple question lurking in the front of my mind is: what does it really mean to *know* Christ? I think that is what happens when we grasp the new creation which the Lord Jesus has made possible and the entirely new life which results from it. It is nothing less than discarding our old humanity like a rotten garment and putting on like clean clothing the new humanity recreated in God's image (*cf.* 4:22-24).

Paul tells us that our old life is like a filthy shirt—it reeks with sweat, it is so badly stained and saturated with grime. The best thing we can do with that is to take it off and dump it in the waste basket. Then with a renewed mind, showered and clean, we are to put on the fresh pure garments of the new life.

This is the genius of the gospel of Christ for it takes a man the way he is and changes him into the kind of person God wants him to be. It is not a classic case of business as usual, it is more that of a life which is now under new management. *Sola gratia,* grace alone!

It is not a matter of us sending our old clothes to the cleaners, we bin them and get rid of them! God has something better for us—he wants to kit us out in garments which bear his designer label.

Bespoke garments

You see, the kind of clothes we wear depends on the kind of role we are fulfilling. For example, when we go to a wedding we wear one kind of clothing—something bright and cheery, when we go to a funeral we tend to wear something different—something darker and more sombre toned.

For many people, their dress is also determined by their 9 to 5 job or the set in concrete bylaws of their chosen profession. Soldiers and sailors and law enforcement officers have different uniforms. Members of the legal profession have special robes which they wear when they appear in a court of law. So do some clergy, and prisoners.

But when we change our role, we automatically change our dress. When a prisoner is released he changes his prison gear and dons his normal clothing. The same holds true of military personnel when they return to Civvy Street.

We borrow the analogy for the same is true in our lives—since by a new creation we have stripped off the tattered rags of our old humanity and put on the new, we must also jettison the old standards and take on board new ones—*true righteousness (dikaiosynē) and holiness (hosiotēs)*. Back on day six, just as God made Adam from the dust of the ground, so he formed our new selves from the raw material of righteousness, holiness, and truth—intrinsic qualities that best reflect the likeness of our Creator.

'Our new role will mean new clothing—our new life a new ethical lifestyle.' (John Stott)

4:25

Fighting subversive influences

Paul specifically shows how the bold decision to lay aside the old life and put on the new life affects every area of our lives, including our emotions. If we are not careful, our hearts can rule our heads and our feelings end up taking us hostage. Notice the four terrorists which Paul unmasks:

- *falsehood (pseudos, 4:25),*
- *anger (orgizō, 4:26),*
- *stealing (kleptō, 4:28), and*
- *unwholesome talk (sapros logos, 4:29).*

Each of these are ruthless and have no scruples whatsoever. Each of them is a potential killer. If we let them loose, they will assassinate our character and torch our testimony. When backed against a wall, we are tempted to react with the comments:

- 'I'm in a tight corner, so it's ok for me to tell a lie.'
- 'I'm staying angry until she says sorry.'
- 'It's not really stealing, I've got it coming to me anyway.'

- 'They needed a dressing down and everybody talks like that, so why shouldn't I give them back some of their own lip.'

However, when Jesus is reigning in our lives, it means all of those victimised feelings will be dealt with promptly.

- 'I must tell the truth, even when it's more convenient for me to tell a lie.'
- 'I must control my temper, even when I feel enraged or wronged.'
- 'I must do my best and be honest in all I do, even when it would ease my situation if I took it.'
- 'I must zip my mouth and train my tongue to lick wounds not inflict them, even when I have been badly bitten first.'

Things are different now!

We sometimes sing Rufus McDaniel's (1850-1940) hymn: *What a wonderful change in my life has been wrought, since Jesus came into my heart.* Tremendous stuff. It is really exciting to look into our hearts and see what the Lord has done for us. Only he could have done so much. We met the Lord on our personal Damascus Road and we have not been the same since! Different. Significantly different! And we are meant to be.

So, says Paul, in these closing verses (*cf.* 4:25-32), the proof of the pudding is in the eating. Whether we realise it or not, people are looking at us—watching our every move, analysing our lifestyle, sussing out our decision making process.

People can see right through us, they can read us like a book—so, because we are different, let us be different.

Live your life like a person who has been transformed. Stand up and be counted. Be seen! Be noticed! Stand out in the crowd! And do it for all the right reasons.

Because we are different! And because there is something attractive about our lifestyle. There is a magnetism that draws men to Jesus when they see the upbeat way we choose to live. How can we show today's generation that Jesus is real in our lives? By the difference in our walk, and talk.

Straight talk

Paul has moved away from the principles of the faith to the practice of the faith. He spells it out. He gives riveting examples of what happens when we take off the rags of the old life and put on the new clothes of abundant life in Christ.

I am amazed how easily Paul can descend from lofty theological talk about the old man and the new man, about the Christ we have learned and the brand new creation we have experienced, to the nitty gritty of Christian behaviour—telling the truth, controlling our anger, honesty at work, kindness of speech, forgiveness, true love, and sexual control. It all sounds extremely down to earth stuff to me.

A threefold cord

Before we cast an eagle eye over Paul's six concrete examples, we need to notice three features common to them all:

- They zoom in with laser accuracy on our relationships.

Holiness is not a mystical condition experienced in relation to God but in isolation from flesh and blood human beings. We cannot be good and godly in a vacuum—only in the real world of real people.

- A negative 'do not do this' is balanced by a positive 'do this'.

It is not enough to tear off the old rags—we have to put on the best of new clothes. It is not enough to call an end to lying and stealing and losing our temper, unless we start speaking the truth, working hard, and being kind to people.

- A reason for the command is either given or implied.

In the teaching of Jesus and his apostles, doctrine and ethics—belief and behaviour—are always dovetailed into one another. They are interlinked. It revolves around our core values and how they relate to life in the fast lane of the third millennium.

Economical with the truth

Paul starts the ball rolling when he says: *therefore each of you must put off falsehood and speak truthfully to his neighbour, for we are all members of one body.* Paul is obviously talking in this verse about lying.

- We lie when we fail to tell the truth, the whole truth, and nothing but the truth.
- We lie when we mislead or deceive someone.
- We lie when we set out to deliberately give someone a false impression.
- We lie when we exaggerate and engage in hyperbole.
- We lie when we only tell part of a story.

Some years ago a Christian man became widely known for his powerful and moving testimony. But after several years he stopped. When asked why, he replied with some degree of integrity: *'Over the years I embellished the story so much that I no longer knew what was true and what was not.'*

We live in a culture where lying is almost encouraged, where deception and falsehood is rewarded. For instance, take the case of the baker who suspected that the farmer who was supplying his butter was giving him short weight. His suspicions were confirmed when he carefully checked the weight of the butter for several days. Incensed, he had the farmer arrested. But the judge threw the case out of court when the farmer explained that he had no scales, so he used a 200 grams loaf of bread purchased from the baker as his counterbalance! In the words of R. Kent Hughes: 'Whether on Main Street or Wall Street, our culture is in an ethical crisis.'

Contrary to public opinion, there is no such a thing as a wee lie or a big lie. The irrefutable fact remains that a lie is a lie, is a lie! There is also the lie of silence—a lie that speaks volumes. André Maurois in a memorable phrase speaks of 'the menace of things unsaid.'

To tell you the truth

Truth should be the hallmark of our lives. God is truth (*cf.* Isaiah 65:16). Jesus said: 'I am the truth' (John 14:6). The Holy Spirit is the 'Spirit of truth' (John 16:13). The timeless and dateless word of God is truth unchanged and truth unchanging (*cf.* John 17:17).

A terminological inexactitude is the idiom of Satan's language—lies are the common currency of the devil, 'the father of lies' (John 8:44).

Zero in on Zechariah

I often think of the words of the prophet Zechariah where he writes that we should 'speak the truth to each other' (Zechariah 8:16). These are the words the apostle Paul is quoting from.

Zechariah came on to the scene after the people returned from living in exile in Babylon. One of his great burdens was that Israel should not repeat the sins of bygone days—he hoped they would have learned the lesson, and learned it well. All the way through Zechariah 8 we have the phrase: 'this is what the Lord says'. Why? Because the post-exilic prophet is making a comparison between what God did before with what God is doing now.

Then the focus was on the government of God, now it is on the grace of God. One of the key points relative to them was that they should be a people who tell the truth. Paul picks up that dynamic phrase and passes it on to the church. As they say, good enough for them, good enough for us!

Bite your tongue

Our tongues should be tamed and transformed—what we say affects us, and it also influences others for *we are all members of one body.*

Honesty is not the best policy for the Christian, it is the only one!

The plaintive chorus to Billy Joel's song *Honesty* expresses a universal feeling:

Honesty is such a lonely word
Everyone is so untrue
Honesty is hardly ever heard
And mostly what I need from you.

One day a parish minister spotted a large group of boys out in the church car park gathered around an irresistibly cute little puppy. They were making quite a commotion when the minister walked over to them and asked: 'Well, boys, what's going on here?'

'We found this puppy,' said one of the boys, 'and all of us want to keep it, so we're having a contest. The one who tells the biggest lie wins the puppy.'

'Shame on you,' said the minister. 'I can't believe you would do such a thing, deliberately telling lies. Why? When I was your age I never told a lie.'

The boys fidgeted and looked at each other rather nervously. Finally, one of the boys said: 'Okay, Mister, you win the dog!'

In a world where lying is endemic, we should be known in our communities as honest, reliable people whose word can be trusted. If we are not, it is a stab into the very heart of the body of Christ. When all is said and done, fellowship is built on trust, and trust is built on truth. Falsehood seriously undermines fellowship, while truth strengthens it.

4:26

Flying off the handle

Paul is batting on the front foot when he instructs us: *'In your anger do not sin': Do not let the sun go down while you are still angry.* This is one of the things I really like about Paul—he has no backdoors, we know exactly where we stand with him, he does not beat about the bush. He goes straight for the jugular when he tells us that we are to get rid of sinful anger. These words are an echo of Psalm 4:4.

By all means, if the situation demands it, be angry, but never, never, never in a sinful way, and never for long.

How Jesus handled anger

I think it has to be said that anger in and of itself is not wrong. Look at the exemplary life and ministry of the Lord Jesus. He was furiously angry on a number of occasions during the course of his public ministry—for example, when he drove the money changers out of the temple (*cf.* Matthew 21:12, 13), when he denounced the Scribes and Pharisees for their blatant hypocrisy calling them 'a generation of vipers' (Matthew 12:34).

Believe me, that was not the most complimentary phrase to use. Neither was it meant to be! Jesus was definitely not impressed with their scandalous activity and he was certainly not amused when he saw their shenanigans in the house of the Lord.

It is fair to say that the Lord was incredibly angry on each of these auspicious occasions—we do not deny that, we make no attempt to rewrite the story. Jesus was angry! But he did not sin.

Angry ... for all the right reasons

To bring it closer to home, we can be angry when it is a righteous cause and, when we are, it will be a wholesome anger. Yes, there are times when we should be angry. We need the anger of a Wilberforce or a Shaftesbury at personal or societal sins, or of a Martin Luther at doctrinal aberration. It is the anger of which the great English preacher F W Robertson of Brighton wrote in one of his pastoral letters. When he once met a certain man who was trying to lure a beautiful young girl into prostitution, he became so angry that he bit his lip until it bled.

Our anger should be kindled by the fire from the altar of God.

An excellent rule of thumb: be angry at the things with which God is angry and only for the same reasons. What are they? I can suggest a couple:

- be angry when his unsullied holiness has been outraged, and
- be angry when his universe has been spoiled.

In the face of evil, we should be indignant not tolerant, we should be angry not apathetic. If God hates sin, his people should hate it too. If evil arouses his anger, it should arouse ours also. Indeed, when we fail to feel it or express it, we deny the Lord, we damage ourselves, and we encourage the spread of evil.

'Give me a hundred men who fear nothing but God, and *who hate nothing but sin*, and who know nothing but Jesus Christ and him crucified, and I will shake the world.' (John Wesley)

Sort it out before sundown

Pure anger is an exceedingly rare commodity. It is thin on the ground! Even our hottest emotions and words are spoiled by sin. When we are angry, we have to make sure that our anger is free from injured pride, spite, malice, animosity, and the spirit of revenge.

Even when anger is justified, it is not to last for long. We are not to go to bed and brood (a good principle for married couples). Paul's time honoured counsel warns us against nursing anger. Basically, it is seldom safe to allow the embers to smoulder. If we keep our anger overnight it will be like the manna from heaven, it will breed all sorts of worms (*cf.* 4:31; Exodus 16:20).

Plutarch tells us that the disciples of Pythagoras had a rule of their society, that if, during the day, anger had made them speak insultingly to each other, before the sun set they shook hands and kissed each other and were reconciled. There was a Jewish Rabbi whose prayer it was that he might never go to sleep with any bitter thought against a brother man within his mind.

We are to rise each morning and face each new day with no feelings of hurt lingering from the day before. I know and you know that is easier said than done. But God can help us and he will help us if we ask him. If we fail, the devil will exploit the situation to the full and he will make hay when the sun is shining.

4:27

Give the devil an inch, he'll take a ...

Do not give the devil (*diabolos*) *a foothold* (*topos*). Bearing in mind what Paul has just been talking about, this all makes a lot of good common sense.

If our tongues and our temper are not transformed, we leave ourselves wide open to the devil.

If we string out our conflicts, we are easy meat for him. If we give him a foothold he will use it to drive a wedge between us and other believers—if we give him an inch, he will not be content until he has taken a mile or two.

Satan does not like people, he certainly has little or no time for the people of God. He hates us with a hatred that beggars description. His avowed aim is to deceive us and lead us up a blind alley. He wants to degrade us and cause us enormous distress and then he will do all in his power to ultimately destroy us. He will do anything to distort the lovely image of Christ in our hearts.

He will trip us up, he will pull us down—name it and he will have a go! That is why Paul says quite firmly: do not drop your guard, do not play around with the devil, do not play into his hands.

4:28

Waving goodbye to crime

He who has been stealing must steal no longer, but must work (kopiaō), doing something useful (agathos) with his own hands, that he may have something to share (metadidōmi) with those in need (chreia). These words are an echo of the eighth commandment which is enshrined in the law of Moses (*cf.* Exodus 20:15).

When a man becomes a Christian there should be a radical difference in his behaviour—we do not keep on doing the things we did before! Therefore, in this context, stealing must stop. In fact the apostle goes a step further by implying that it should never happen again.

Dealing with kleptomania

It is not enough to stop doing something bad, we must start doing something which is good. In other words, we need to redirect our energy and get to work. Do an honest day's work, stop looking for the proverbial easy life.

God expects us to not only meet our own need but also to look for ways in which we can share what we have with others—'a new idea and a new ideal' (William Barclay).

The English preacher Rowland Hill astounded the mourners at his favourite employee's funeral when he told a story in his funeral oration which he had kept secret for thirty years: his first meeting with the man had been when the man attempted to hold Dr Hill up. Hill had argued with him, offering the highwayman an honest job if he would visit him later. And this the robber did, becoming a devout Christian and devoted worker. This man lived out the standard Paul calls the church to in verse 28.

The church should be a family of givers and takers.

Stealing is forbidden! Banned outright! It is a no go area for the Christian. Do not rob yourself, do not rob others, do not rob the Lord Jesus.

With these incisive comments, Paul extols the magnificent virtue of the old Protestant work ethic. In today's couch potato society, some people do not know how to work, some people could not spell work. Here Paul lifts it to a higher level when he says: 'You're a Christian, don't be afraid to do it!' It will do us good and we can be a blessing to others in the process.

Men God called

When we look through the Bible at a random selection of those whom God called, they were all engaged in some form of useful work:

- Moses was caring for his father in law's sheep,
- Gideon was out in the field threshing wheat,
- David was minding his father's flock,
- the first disciples were either casting nets or mending them.

Principle: God calls those to follow and serve him who are already doing all that they possibly can do.

To put it simply, instead of sponging on the community as thieves do, the converted person will start contributing to it, and none but Christ can transform a burglar into a benefactor!

4:29

The chattering classes

Paul lifts the lid on a lot of what happens in everyday life when he says: *Do not let any unwholesome talk come out of your mouths* (*stoma*), *but only what is helpful* (*agathos*) *for building* (*oikodomē*) *others up according to their needs* (*chreia*), *that it may benefit* (*didōmi*) *those who listen* (*akouō*). The apostle turns from the use of our hands to the use of our mouths.

Whether we realise it or not, the ability to communicate with each other via speech is a wonderful gift of God. It is one of our human capacities which reflect our likeness to God. God speaks and like him we also speak. Speech distinguishes us from the animal creation.

Cows moo, dogs bark, donkeys bray, pigs grunt, lambs bleat, lions roar, monkeys squeal, birds sing—only human beings speak!

One bad apple

Paul goes right back to the fountain head in this verse. If the heart is right, the character will be right, and if they are right, so too will our conduct, and our conversation. *Unwholesome talk* will not flow from our lips. The word Paul uses here is the word 'corrupt' or 'evil' meaning that which is 'bad, rotten, or putrid'.

It was often used of rotten trees and rotting fruit. The word is used to describe decaying animal or vegetable matter. When applied to verbal communication—whether dishonest, unkind, or vulgar—we may be sure that in some way it hurts the hearers. A person who engages in this is like the fabled slave who took poison into her system a little at a time, and then more and more, until at last her whole being was so full of poison that her very breath would wither the flowers.

What a graphic picture Paul painted! Such language is unbecoming for the Christian, such words should be unthinkable from a Christian. Nothing will destroy a testimony more swiftly than idle words. Perhaps the finest and saddest illustration of that is seen in the life of Peter when Jesus was on trial (*cf.* John 18:15-18, 25-27).

Augustine, in recognition of this principle, hung this motto on his dining room wall: *'He who speaks evil of an absent man or woman is not welcome at this table.'*

Raising the stakes

What we say should always edify and encourage people, it should build people up and not damage or destroy them. People should feel as if their lives are richer for having spent time with us, they should be elevated and better for having shared with us. Paul says in a parallel passage that our speech should be generously seasoned with salt and always liberally sprinkled with grace (*cf.* Colossians 4:6). We are to be like Alexander Whyte, of whom it was said: 'All of his geese became swans.'

I believe that holds true in every situation—it ranges from the factory floor, to the office telephone, it stretches from the kitchen sink through to the dinner table, it goes from the email that we send to where we sit in church on a Sunday—it is our talk!

When we read through the gospel narrative, it emerges that Jesus taught the great significance of speech. He was an avid believer in communication.

Jesus saw the awesome potential of every conversation, at the same time, he was wide open to the destructive forces of the evil one.

Jesus says that our words reveal what is in our hearts and we shall have to give an account on that final day of every careless word we have uttered (*cf.* Matthew 12:36). When we fast forward to James, he says pretty much the same thing when he emphasises the immense power of the human tongue for good and evil (*cf.* James 3:1-12). As Moffat translates it, Eliphaz the Temanite paid Job a marvellous compliment. 'Your words,' he said, 'have kept men on their feet' (Job 4:4).

Think before we talk

When we assimilate all of this in the unique context of Ephesians 4, it means if we are what we say we are, we will think twice about what we say and how we say it. Instead of hurting people with our words and lampooning people with our harsh ill-timed comments, we will seek to be a blessing to them by stimulating them and doing all in our power to gladden their hearts.

Words are like bullets—once fired, we cannot take them back!

4:30

In step with the Spirit

When I take time out and reflect on what Paul has been saying in this chapter, there are three things which impress me:

- I can see where he is coming from,
- I can see where he is at, and
- I can see where he is going.

All that has been said up to this point begins to come together very potently when we see what follows hard on its heels. Paul almost pulls the carpet from under their feet when he says: *And do not grieve the Holy Spirit of God, with whom you were sealed for the day of redemption.*

Why should we think twice before we open our big mouths and put two size ten feet in? Why should we change our lifestyle to one that brings credit to the grace of God, rather than disgrace to his name? Here is the answer. Because we do not want to *grieve (lypeō)* the Holy Spirit. It seems to me that Paul introduces the Holy Spirit at a strategic time in his thinking. He has just warned us not to give the devil an inch, now he urges us *not to grieve the Spirit of God.*

The Holy Spirit is not a phantom in some divine opera—he is a real person with real feelings.

Consequently, we should do nothing in our power to hurt him or pain him. We must ensure that we never cause him any form of distress. In the light of Paul's earlier comments—our tongue, our temper, our talk, our thieving—all of these can grieve him. Paul is laying it on the line when he tells us not to do it!

A soft heart

The word *grieve* is a word which speaks of tender love. The bottom line: we cannot grieve someone who does not love us. We may annoy them, upset them, disappoint them, and even infuriate them, but we cannot grieve them.

We can only grieve someone who has a heart for us and really loves us—we can grieve God, the Holy Spirit.

It means we can cause him immense pain and enormous sorrow. And that is the last thing we should ever do! We should be different! Why hurt him when he deserves more than that from each of us?

On our behalf

We discovered earlier that the seal of the Holy Spirit is the earnest of our inheritance (*cf.* 1:13, 14). The seal speaks of ownership and possession. John MacArthur reminds us that 'the Holy Spirit is God's personal mark of authenticity on us, his stamp of divine approval.' One of the Spirit's ministries in our lives is to keep us safe and secure from the wiles of the devil, from the weaknesses of the flesh, from the wickedness of the world, until we are saved to sin no more, until *the day of redemption.*

That glorious day is coming when the sons of God will come into their own, when we will be displayed to the universe as an exhibit of God's marvellous grace (*cf.* Romans 8:17; 2 Thessalonians

1:10). It is interesting to note that the 'sealing' and the 'redemption' refer respectively to the beginning and the end of the salvation process. And, in between these two termini, we are to grow in Christlikeness and to take care not to hurt the feelings of the Holy Spirit.

He is a sensitive Spirit. He hates sin, discord, and falsehood—he shrinks away from them. Therefore, if we wish to avoid hurting him, we shall shrink from them too! The fact is that every Spirit filled believer desires to bring him pleasure, not pain!

4:31

Getting rid of the rot

We are tramping down a familiar path as Paul gives us a list of six ticking bombs which we need to dispense with in our lives: *Get rid of all bitterness, rage and anger, brawling and slander, along with every form of malice.* These things should not have any place at all in the heart of the Christian.

What an ugly accumulation of human characteristics. They sour our lives, they scald our brethren, they stain our characters, they spoil our testimonies, and they sadden the Holy Spirit. They are six unpleasant attitudes and actions that should be eradicated—exterminated—from the heart and mind of every believer.

Acerbic saints

Bitterness (pikria) reflects a smouldering resentment, a brooding attitude, and 'a spirit that refuses reconciliation' (Aristotle, 384-322 BC). A bitter person is someone with a grudge, a chip on both shoulders (*cf.* Acts 8:23; Hebrews 12:15). When someone is irritable, they are sour and venomous and they have lost their smile. People often speak of it as a sour spirit and sour speech.

We sometimes talk about a 'sour puss' and I suppose there are sour tomcats too!

Little is sadder in people than a negative and cynical outlook on life.

Rant and rave

Rage (*thymos*) is the 'in' word these days—we talk about road rage, air rage, and every other form of rage that is possible. The Greeks defined *thymos* as the kind of anger which is like the flame which comes from straw—it quickly blazes up and just as quickly subsides. In this context it has to do with wild rage, the passion of the moment resulting in an explosion from within. It is when we boil up and boil over. When people blow it big time—it is over in a moment but they leave a lasting legacy of scars.

Venting your spleen

Anger (*orgē*) is when everything is left on the back burner to simmer. It is a nurtured feeling of hatred that stems from deep within. On the outside, all may seem relatively calm—on the inside, the tempest is beginning to rage. It is a settled and sullen hostility. A touch of pique! We need to know that a hostile Christian is an oxymoron!

Kicking up a shindy

Brawling (*kraugē*) is a shout or an outcry of strife. It happens when we lose control of ourselves in public. It describes people who get excited and so wound up that they raise their voices in an argument and start shouting, even screaming, at each other. When we go down that road, we not only let ourselves down, worse than that, we let our Lord down.

Smear tactics

Slander is an unusual word in that it comes from the word *blasphēmia* from which we get our English word 'blasphemy'. It is when we defame someone's character, when we write them off to other people, and when we undermine what they are doing. It is when we spread malicious rumours and juicy stories about people. It is when we pour petrol on a fire and then walk away holding the fire extinguisher. It is the kind of thing we tend to do behind people's backs because we want to destroy their reputation.

Bad blood

Every form of malice (*kakia*) is a general term for evil. It means we scheme up ways and means whereby we injure or hurt others. It has the thought of venomous ill will about it and it happens when we wish something bad against other people. Animosity. Rancour. Spitefulness.

When I look at that list, I cringe in the Lord's presence, it does not make for pleasant reading. I feel uncomfortable for I know in my own heart that any and all of these sins are possible. There is no place for any of these horrid things in the Christian community. They have to be totally rejected.

Facing the facts

These things happen between real people in the real world. Take it from me, it is not confined to the twilight zone. More often than not, it happens between believers and unbelievers and, sadly, it also rears its ugly head in the family of God—the church of God—where we should know better.

Inevitably, sins like these have disastrous consequences: they break fellowship and destroy relationships, they weaken a church and mar and blight our testimony before the eyes of the world. That is why we should be different!

4:32

Buck the trend

Alright, there have been times in our lives:

- when we have been badly hurt,

- when we have been framed,
- when we have been treated like doormats and people have walked all over us,
- when we have been ripped off,
- when we have been the butt of rumour and the topic of malicious gossip,
- when we have been talked about behind our backs,
- when we have seen our work and our ministry undermined!

Sure. 'Well,' says God, 'I know all that, and I have missed nothing! Be different!'

- Be *kind* (*chrēstos*) to one another.
- Be *compassionate* (*eusplanchnos*) to one another.
- Be *forgiving* (*charizomai*) toward each other.

Follow the golden rule

So they might not do it to us, they might not do it for us, that does not matter, we set the example by showing the reality of our love for the Lord Jesus. Remember, Christ has forgiven us—freely, fully, forever—he made the first move when he even initiated forgiveness before we wanted it! Jesus came to rub it out not rub it in!

Of all people, we are the ones who should be able to do it! It does not come naturally, it is not easy, it is tough, it is a struggle, but when we do it, we are wonderfully blessed. Nothing is achieved by harbouring a bad spirit against a brother or a sister. Even if forgiveness is granted, we sometimes keep the offence available to use in future battles. As a country song puts it: 'We bury the hatchet, but leave the handle sticking out!'

If we refuse to forgive, we live in the devil's playground.

We should treat others the way our Lord has treated us, not the way the devil treats us. What kind of an example is he to follow!

People of integrity

Forgiveness. Not just for our own sake, and for their sake, but for
the sake of the Lord Jesus. 'By this all men will know that you are
my disciples, if you love one another,' said Jesus (John 13:35).
Christian character is a very down to earth affair.

The new man or the new woman whom God has made does not
have a shining face and walk around with a goldfish bowl over his
head. He does not send a tingle down the spine of those who meet
him. He is not known for his sweet smile and marvellous charm.
His hallmark is integrity—and that is what God is looking for in
your life and mine. It is as if Paul is saying: 'Act like Christians, *for
God's sake.* And by God's power as well.'

5

Big on Marriage

5:1, 2

Walking with God

The emphasis in this chapter is on our daily walk with the Lord. We sometimes sing William Cowper's (1731-1800) hymn: *O for a closer walk with God*—that really is an impassioned heartfelt cry for a deeper and more meaningful relationship with the Lord Jesus. That should always be our goal, a life walking hand in hand with God.

The bottom line so far as Paul is concerned is that we need to get up out of our seats and step out in faith. Well, the question is: how are we meant to do it? Again Paul leaves us in no doubt as to what is expected of us as the people of God.

Divine adhesive

In verse 1, the only place in the Bible where these words occur, the apostle says quite clearly that we are to *be imitators* (*mimētēs*) *of*

God. The new birth places us in a new family where we are called God's *dearly loved* (*agapētos*) *children* (*teknon*)—quite humbling, isn't it! To think that God loves us is sublimely wonderful, but he goes a step further—he *dearly* loves us.

The world knows nothing of this intimate relationship we have with the Lord Jesus. It does not have this kind of bond, it is not the kind of thing we find in the local garden centre nor do we find it when teeing off at the first hole or watering ourselves at the infamously called nineteenth. However, we can find it—and do find it—in the family of God.

- We are cemented together in love,
- we are welded together in love,
- we are glued together in love.

God mimics

And because we are members of the global family of God, we are meant to be followers of the Lord. Later, Clement of Alexandria (c.155-c.220) was to say daringly: 'The true Christian wise man practises being God.' Just as children in a human family often imitate their parents, so in God's family we are to imitate him. 'Like Father, like son'—in the spiritual framework, that is the way it should be for he is our role model. We are to mimic him, we are to copy him.

When Alexander the Great discovered a coward in his army who also was named Alexander, he told the yellow-bellied soldier: *'Renounce your cowardice or renounce your name!'*

Those who carry God's name are to reflect his character.

When we think about that for a moment, we soon begin to realise it is a tall order. There are not too many possibilities open to us! The chances of any one of us creating something out of nothing are virtually nil. And so far as upholding and running a universe, that beggars belief, it is a non starter! So what is there about him that we can imitate? We have the answer in the final verse of the previous chapter (*cf.* 4:32).

Forgive and forget

We would do well to emulate his love in our attitude to others and the way most of us experience that is through forgiveness. You see, God is able to forgive us completely because our sins have been taken away by the death of Jesus and God chooses to remember them no more.

It is this ability to forgive and forget that most of us find immensely difficult in our interpersonal relationships. The extent of our love is the extent of our ability to forgive. We need to be so forgiving in our love towards others that we forget about what happened in the past, instead of constantly raking it up.

Ironically, of all people, it was Peter who said: 'Above all, love each other deeply, because love covers a multitude of sins' (1 Peter 4:8). Without sporting the tee shirt, he has been there, done that! The word *ektenēs* ('deeply') refers to a muscle stretched to the limit. Our love is to stretch to the absolute limit as we seek to show the heart of Jesus to those around us.

Where would we be if God continually held our past against us? Thank God, he chooses not to for he is the God of the second chance. Exemplary grace!

- The exhortation: *be imitators of God.*
- The example: *just as Christ loved us.*

A beautiful example is set before us when Paul writes: *and live a life of love, just as Christ loved us and gave himself up for us as a fragrant offering (prosphora) and sacrifice (thysia) to God.* Here is the pattern we are to embrace!

Robert Falconer tells the story of his witnessing among destitute people in a certain city and of reading them the story of the woman who wiped Jesus' feet with her tears. While he was reading he heard a loud sob and looked up at a young, thin girl whose face was disfigured by smallpox.

After he spoke a few words of encouragement to her, she said: *'Will he ever come again, the one who forgave the woman? I have heard that he will come again. Will it be soon?'* Falconer replied: *'He could come at any time. But why do you ask?'* After sobbing again uncontrollably, she said: *'Sir, can't he wait a little while? My hair ain't long enough yet to wipe his feet.'*

Nothing lovey-dovey

Paul is not speaking here about a sentimental kind of love, or a romantic brand of love, it is not the single red rose and box of Cadbury's chocolates syndrome. It has nothing to do with walking hand in hand on a golden sand under the moonlight, that may be very nice and most enjoyable, but it is not what is in the mind of the apostle Paul as he says: 'I want you to *live a life of love.*'

No, this is earthed to reality, this touches the real world, this influences every corner of our lives, it scratches where people are itching. This goes right to the heart of the matter for, in the final analysis, it really is a matter of the heart—our hearts being synchronised with his.

Boundless love

To walk in love is to give ourselves to others with no strings attached.

It is total commitment. Unconditional. It is when we love for the sake of giving not for what we can get out of it. This is the way the Lord has done it in our lives, he did not just love us when we became his children. Far from it!

We read in Romans 5:8 such tremendous words that they send the shivers down the spine: 'But God demonstrates his own love for us in this: While we were still sinners, Christ died for us.' Real love.

Genuine love. Love with a capital 'L'—*the love that Jesus had for me is more than tongue can tell.* I cannot explain it, let alone adequately describe it, but I know it, and I have experienced it!

Loving the Jesus way

So, says Paul, let us do the same to others. Let us treat them the way that Jesus has handled us. He *gave himself up* (*paradidōmi*) for us in that he held nothing back, he emptied himself on our behalf (*cf.* Philippians 2:8). It was unreserved abandonment and it was all because he passionately cared for us with a heart oozing with compassion.

He demands nothing less from us. Just like him, our love is to extend to every person—believer and unbeliever.

* If God's love can reach out even to his implacable enemies, how can we refuse to love our enemies?
* If he loves his imperfect children with a perfect love, how can we not love our fellow believers whose imperfections we share?

This is the acid test, isn't it! For love just keeps on giving and even when it feels it has nothing more to give, it keeps on loving nonetheless. Why? Because love always finds a way! Love is the sphere in which the believer lives. There is a hefty cost involved when we take on board such a challenging and rewarding lifestyle. It cost Jesus everything. Even a cross.

Love spells ... s-a-c-r-i-f-i-c-e

Inevitably, if we are going to love the way Jesus loved, it will mean a giving up of our so called rights for the sole benefit of others. It may incorporate a degree of pain as sometimes when we show love to others it is not always received in the way we intended it to be. Some people may spurn our love, others may give us the cold shoulder, a few may take advantage of it, and there may even be those who candidly reject it—it does not matter what their response is, positive or negative, all that matters is that we love. Sacrifice.

Learning from Leviticus

Paul describes the Calvary experience of Jesus as *a fragrant offering*—a most interesting turn of phrase that takes us away back to life under the old economy. An old phrase which time has hallowed—it occurs almost fifty times in the Old Testament—goes right to the heart of the message which is found in the early chapters of Leviticus.

In the first five chapters of the third book of Moses we are introduced in a fairly comprehensive way to what are generally called: the five Leviticial offerings. The first three are voluntary and are described as 'sweet savour' offerings—the burnt offering, the meal (grain) offering, and the peace (fellowship) offering. The remaining two are compulsory and are referred to as the sin offering and the trespass (guilt) offering.

* The burnt offering (*cf.* Leviticus 1) depicts Christ's total devotion to God in giving his life to obey and please his Father—the fulness of his devotion.
* The meal offering (*cf.* Leviticus 2) represents Christ's perfection in an unblemished life—the flawlessness of his devotion.
* The peace offering (*cf.* Leviticus 3) typifies his making peace between a holy God and an estranged humanity—the fruitfulness of his devotion.

This trio of offerings spoke of what was pleasing to God for they place the emphasis on the Godward side of Calvary. It is said of each of them that they provided 'an aroma pleasing to the Lord' (Leviticus 1:13; 2:9; 3:5). This simply indicates that the sacrifice was acceptable.

The other two offerings were repulsive to the Lord because they portrayed Christ as bearing the sin of mankind. They symbolised the moment when the Father turned his back on his Son and made him to be sin for us. Their fulfilment was climaxed in those heart rending moments when the Lord Jesus cried out in abject dereliction: 'My God, my God, why have you forsaken me?' (Matthew 27:46).

This was God walking out on God—the hour, when at midday, it was midnight.

While the Lord Jesus was the sin bearer, God could not look on him, he could not rejoice in him, he could not be pleased in him. But when the Father raised him from the dead, the sacrifice that caused him to become sin became the sacrifice that conquered sin. The sin that put him to death was itself put to death and that great act of unsurpassed love was to God as a fragrant aroma.

Valuing a priceless sacrifice

When the burnt offering was made to the Lord, the perfume ascended and was breathed in by the Lord in heaven. This is significant for neither the priest nor the sinful Israelite standing beside him at the altar could fully appreciate or grasp the sheer wonder of it. Only God knew the full value of what had taken place. This shows us what Calvary meant to the Father. Why did it please him? It was:

- a vindication of his throne,
- an exhibition of his wisdom,
- a suitable demonstration of his love, and
- a solid foundation for his grace.

This fragrance spreads its scent to everyone on earth who will place himself under the grace of that sacrifice, and the aroma from this perfume will continue to linger throughout heaven for all eternity—heaven loves to make much of the redeeming work of the Lord Jesus. It is in such a context that Paul says we should pull out all the stops and make it the goal of our lives to please the Lord (*cf.* 2 Corinthians 2:14-16).

5:3

The biscuit tin syndrome

'I can resist everything, except temptation.' (Oscar Wilde)

Down the years the evangelical world has been rocked with many scandals, most of which are either financially related or sexually driven. I have known men (and women) who have fallen and I am sure, without too much effort, you could recite a long list of names as well. Tragic!

Enormous damage is caused to the testimony of the body of Christ, both locally and internationally. Irreparable harm is done to families, friends, and ministries. Innocent people are shell shocked. Some get over it, many do not.

'What tragic irony,' writes R. Kent Hughes, 'for Christianity has by far the most exalted sexual ethics of any religion.' None of the other great world religions—whether Buddhism, Hinduism, Islam, or any other—has such profound sexual ethics. Yet the church of Christ is too often seen making the front page news for all the wrong reasons. Why?

I think part of the answer is the biscuit tin syndrome!

A little boy's mother had just baked a fresh batch of chocolate chip cookies and placed them in the biscuit tin, giving instructions that no one touch them until after dinner. But it was not long until she heard the lid of the tin move, and she called out: *'My son, what are you doing?'* To which a meek voice called back: *'Mum, my hand is in the biscuit tin resisting temptation!'*

No one can resist temptation with his or her hand in the biscuit tin.

Yield not to temptation

Paul brings us down to earth with a bump when he leaves us in no doubt as to what God thinks of sinful behaviour in today's world. He pulls the plug on immorality by reminding us who we are and to whom we belong—*God's holy people.*

We live in a world that has all the pungent stench and filth of a cesspool of iniquity. This world really stinks! And the longer we live in it the more we realise it is not getting any better, if anything, it is getting progressively worse. Third millennium man is racing headlong on a slippery downward slope which can only lead to eternal perdition.

Zero tolerance

The sins which Paul is talking about here powerfully remind us of the vortex of evil which is spiralling out of control all around us. And it is in such an environment that we are called to be shakers and shiners, salt and light! The expression adopted by Paul—*there must not be even a hint* of these things—intimates that such behaviour for the Christian should be unthinkable.

Here we have the zero option in terms of the level of tolerance we should show when such a lifestyle is flaunted openly before us and, so far as the church is concerned, it should never happen there either.

These sins can never in any circumstances be justified and they should never at any time be condoned.

It is a plain fact of life that whatever the Lord does, Satan will always attempt to counterfeit. Where God establishes true love, Satan produces a cheapening counterfeit love. There is all the difference in the world between love and lust. Love is what we were talking about earlier, but lust is what we see portrayed on the soap operas and in the commercial breaks on the television screen. It is the kind of thing we see when we pick up the tabloid newspapers or top shelf glossy magazines; in fact, the more juicy the gossip the more papers are sold.

In a moral tailspin

Man seems to have an insatiable desire for that which is lurid and obscene. That says a lot about how far we have fallen from the standards God has established in Scripture. This kind of so-called love is intrinsically selfish and destructive. It is always conditional and self centred. It is not concerned about long term commitment, only short term satisfaction. It is not concerned about giving, only getting. It has no basis for permanence because its sole purpose is to use and exploit rather than to serve and help. It lasts until the one loved no longer satisfies or until he or she disappears in preference for someone else.

As they say, the grass is always greener on the other side. It does not matter who gets hurt or whose life is made up of shattered dreams and broken pieces, that does not enter into the equation at all—it is what I can get out of it, it is me meeting my immediate need, that is the only proviso. This is the behavioural mindset which Paul roundly condemns—it is *improper*.

And so to bed

Paul addresses the subject of *sexual immorality* first for that is the root of the whole problem and because Ephesus was a mirror for our world. It relates to sexual sin and all sexual sin is against God and against godly love—it can refer to incest (*cf.* 1 Corinthians 5:1), promiscuity (*cf.* 1 Thessalonians 4:3), sexual relations with a prostitute (*cf.* 1 Corinthians 6:13), or illicit sexual relations (*cf.* John 8:41). We get our English word 'pornography' from the word, *porneia*, which the apostle used.

He also speaks about *any kind of impurity* (*akatharsia*)—a more general term—referring to anything which is unclean and filthy. Jesus used the word to describe the rottenness of decaying bodies in a tomb (*cf.* Matthew 23:27). Every other time the word is used in the New Testament it is always associated with some form of sexual sin.

It broadly includes immoral thoughts, passions, ideas, fantasies, and every other form of sexual corruption, including homosexuality. In Athens a great temple to Aphrodite, the goddess of love, was built with the profits from the brothels which were established in the city with this objective.

A famous statement attributed to Plutarch (first century AD) illustrates the laxity in this area: 'Mistresses we keep for the sake of pleasure, concubines for the daily care of our persons, but wives to bear us legitimate children and to be faithful guardians of our households.' Anything goes!

More! Just give me more!

Paul moves on to speak of *greed* (*pleonexia*) which is a most interesting inclusion in this particular context. The plain fact is that greed is inseparable from immorality and impurity (*cf.* 4:19). In matters of sexual impropriety, greed is the driving force.

It is me wanting what does not belong to me, it is me not content with what I already have, it is me driven over the edge with my passion so that I can have what will momentarily satisfy my lust.

I realise that this is all dressed up in more congenial language and presented in more palatable phrases in today's crumbling society. It masquerades as something which is beautiful and thrilling, it looks exciting and good and, if we believe all we read, it is enormously rewarding.

Because it all seems so attractive and promising ...

- spouses are forsaken,
- children are neglected,
- homes are destroyed, and
- friends are disregarded

... as no effort is spared to fulfil one's personal search and quest for pleasure.

Someone asked John D Rockefeller, then one of the richest men alive: *'How much money is enough?'* The multimillionaire replied: *'Just a little bit more!'*

Such is greed—it is never content, it always wants more!

5:4

No laughing matter

Paul continues to highlight some other related areas of major concern as he moves from the twilight zone of immorality to the blue aired world of vulgarity. He sidelines such matters as *obscenity, foolish talk or coarse joking* as being totally *out of place*— and out of character—among God's people. They are like arsenic to the soul.

Obscenity (*aischrotēs*) is a reference to any talk which is degrading, demeaning, and disgraceful. It is risqué—near the knuckle, close to the wind. Obscene language is by its nature destructive language. James M Boice says: 'An obscene person is one who has no regard for standards, nothing commands his respect.'

It is dirty talk emanating from the dirty minds of people who live in a pig's heaven.

When someone engages their minds and mouths in *foolish talk* they are being downright stupid—they are talking the greatest load of drivel. Rubbish. Nonsense of that ilk is the cheapest form of wit. Such ridiculous conversation is only befitting someone who is intellectually deficient—we derive our English word 'moron' from *mōrologia* which Paul uses here.

It is the kind of idiotic language we frequently hear from someone who has had one pint of lager too many, it is the spoken antics of someone who is the worse for wear because he has had too much alcohol to drink. It has no point except to pollute the atmosphere with an air of dirty worldliness.

Coarse joking (*eutrapelia*), on the other hand, refers to chitchat that is more pointed and determined. It carries the idea of a one track mind individual quickly turning something that is said or done, no matter how innocent, into that which is suggestive—a double *entendre*.

It is the flow of vulgar words from a person who uses every word and circumstance to display his immoral wit. It is the stock-in-trade of the clever talkshow host who is never at a loss for sexual innuendo. Sleazy repartee, no less.

Paul is not knocking clean fun. There is nothing wrong with having a real good laugh—humour goes a long way in most people's lives. Good humour is an ice breaker or tension reliever in many situations and, when used properly, can be a source of tremendous cheer to brighten people's otherwise dreary lives. Humour is exhilarating and, according to *American Health* magazine, is like 'inner jogging'.

'The God who made monkeys is not humourless!' (James M Boice)

Try thanksgiving

The true Christian is a person who elevates his conversation to a much higher plane. We should use our tongues to express gratitude to God for all that he is and for all that he has done (*cf.* Philippians 4:6). The contrast is striking and beautiful. In itself, *thanksgiving* (*eucharistia*) is not an obvious substitute for vulgarity since the latter is essentially self centred and the former God centred.

The chances are, this is the point that Paul is making. J H Houlden makes the point that 'whereas sexual impurity and covetousness both express self centred acquisitiveness, thanksgiving is the exact opposite, and so the antidote required; it is the recognition of God's generosity.'

Another way to look at it is that Paul is setting vulgarity and thanksgiving even more plainly in opposition to each other as alternative pagan and Christian attitudes to sex. The reason why Christians should dislike and avoid vulgarity is not because we have a warped or negative view of sex and are either ashamed or afraid of it, but because we have a high and holy view of it as being in its right place God's good gift which we do not want to see cheapened.

All God's gifts—sex included—are deliciously good gifts. Instead of cracking jokes about them, we thank God for them.

To joke about them is to degrade them; to thank God for them is one sure way to preserve their worth as the blessings of a loving Creator.

Enjoying life the way God intended

We can look at it from another angle: the selfish and unloving person does not give thanks because he thinks he deserves whatever good thing he receives. The unselfish and loving person, on the other hand, focuses his life and his concern on the needs of others. Whatever good thing he receives from God or from other people he counts as undeserved and gracious.

He is always thankful because his spirit is one of loving and giving. Instead of using others, he serves them. Instead of trying to turn the innocent into the immoral, he seeks to change the immoral into what is righteous and holy. He is thankful because the holy life is the satisfying life and people see love for God in the thankful person.

Charles Swindoll is quick off the mark to suggest that filthy, foolish, and gutter talk leads us into five danger zones:

- it plays too near the edge of what can degenerate into grossly inappropriate words and actions,
- it breaks down our resistance to things that hinder our intimacy with God,

- it promotes a warped and degrading view of sex and marriage which God created to be beautiful,
- it promotes mental habits of sensuality and disrespect for others, and
- it silences any opportunity to make Christ known.

5:5

Locked out! No admittance!

There is a slight change in emphasis when we leave verse 4 and cross over into verse 5. Even though Paul continues with the topic of sex, he moves on in his treatment of Christian behaviour from models to motivation by adding, in the next few verses, four powerful incentives to righteous living.

It is apparent from what Paul says that we should use our conversational skills to encourage others to think seriously about spiritual matters for the penalty awaiting them is spelled out extremely clearly. Paul categorically affirms (*of this you can be sure*) that such persons—*immoral, impure, or greedy*—have no *inheritance in the kingdom of Christ and of God.*

Paul bundles all three classes of individuals into one when he labels them lock, stock, and barrel: *idolater[s]* (*eidōlolatrēs*). They are guilty of idolatry because they have relegated God to some other place in their lives. They have given him the boot! In his place, they have planted someone or something else on the throne and that has become their central focus of worship.

People who act like that are no better than sitting ducks—easy unmissable targets for God's big guns of judgment.

God's attitude to their sin is unmistakably clear and it attracts his wrath like a fully lit city attracts enemy bombers (*cf.* 1 Corinthians 6:9, 10; Galatians 5:19-21; 1 John 3:7-10).

We are not to be fooled into thinking otherwise lest we lull ourselves into a false sense of security. They may get off Scot free down here but they will not get off with it over there! Sooner or later it will catch up with them. They will not escape detection, conviction, and sentence for ever. 'God does not tolerate sin,' writes John MacArthur, 'and perverted love leads to punishment.' (*cf.* Numbers 25:1-9). God takes sin seriously and, consequently, we need to treat judgment seriously!

Sin has no place in his kingdom and no place in his family.

5:6, 7

Watch out!

Verse 6 gives us a rousing challenge to recognise deception for what it is and then in verse 7 we are exhorted to repudiate deception. *Let no one deceive* (*apataō*) *you* is how the apostle continued. He has himself urged them to acknowledge the truth of divine *wrath* when God decisively acts in judgment—now he warns them of the *empty* (*kenos*) *words* (*logos*) of suave false teachers who would persuade them otherwise. They are totally devoid of any semblance of truth.

Empty words are full of error.

In Paul's day the Gnostics were arguing that bodily sins could be committed without damage to the soul, and with impunity. In our day there are many urbane deceivers peddling their wares in the world and, more often than we care to admit, we even find them strolling around in the church.

They cleverly teach that God is much too kind to condemn everybody in a willy-nilly fashion and that everybody will get to heaven in the end, irrespective of their behaviour on planet earth. But their sugar coated words are empty platitudes and their teaching is deceitful. The plain truth is that universalism is a lie.

Staying clean in a dirty world

No true child of God can compromise when tempted to take part in immoral behaviour. God demands that we make a clean break with the ungodly lifestyle of our unregenerate days. It seems to me that such a break with our past is evidence that we not only profess Christianity but we also possess Christ as our Lord and Saviour. That is why Paul emphatically states: *do not be partners (symmetochos) with them.* If we share in their practices, as Lot was warned in Sodom, we run the serious risk of sharing in their doom.

It would be so easy for us to speed read a paragraph like this, without pausing for reflection, on the assumption that it does not apply to us. We console ourselves by saying it was written primarily for unbelievers.

Home truths

These are immensely challenging words from the apostle and they should cause each of us to sit up and take stock of our own lives. It may be an opportune moment for us to do a personal inventory of our relationship with the Lord.

The only way we can reconcile what Paul is saying here with what he talked about in chapter 1 is by reminding ourselves that salvation is neither a synonym nor an excuse for presumption. And if we should fall into a life of greedy immorality, we would be supplying clear evidence that we are idolaters, not worshippers of God, disobedient people instead of obedient, and so the heirs not of heaven but of hell.

Punching above his weight

I believe Paul gives us a stern and solemn warning in these verses and the man is a fool who does not heed it. In the cold light of day, when we sit down and read these verses through at our leisure, they are not just a stirring summons to the unity and purity of the church, they are much more than that!

'Their theme,' according to John Stott, 'is the integration of Christian experience (what we are), Christian theology (what we believe), and Christian ethics (how we behave).' They emphasise that what I am, what I think, and what I do belong together and must never be separated.

As the people of God there are certain things which we can do, no problem, and there are things which it is wiser and better for us not to do. In a world where it may not be deemed politically correct to say it, the will-not-go-away fact remains that there is a form of behaviour which is acceptable and there is a lifestyle which is totally inappropriate.

5:8

Night and day, darkness and light

In the previous few verses, Paul has encouraged us to *live a life of love*. However, in this section (5:8-14), he exhorts us to *live* (*peripateō*) *as children* (*teknon*) *of light* (*phōs*).

We are to live under the dazzling searchlight of God's truth.

What a lovely picture we have emerging before us. It is something we read of elsewhere in the word of God. The psalmist David testified that 'the Lord is my light and my salvation' (Psalm 27:1)—we have a marvellous promise in Isaiah 60:19 informing us that 'the Lord will be your everlasting light'. The Bible is spoken of as a 'lamp to my feet and a light for my path' (Psalm 119:105). Further down the same Psalm we discover that 'the unfolding of your words gives light' (Psalm 119:130).

Jesus himself is referred to as 'a light for the Gentiles' (Isaiah 49:6). We recall the words penned by the beloved disciple when he sets Jesus forth as 'the true light that gives light to every man' (John 1:9). Our Lord spoke in a similar vein when he introduced himself as 'the light of the world' (John 8:12).

When we put each of these verses together, we say 'amen' to John's perceptively accurate reference that 'God is light' (1 John 1:5). The implication is that if we are to imitate our heavenly Father and copy him as Paul instructs us (*cf.* 5:1), it means we must share in that light and then reflect that light.

Remember the directions Jesus gave us in his Sermon on the Mount, as rendered by Eugene Peterson in *The Message*:

> *You're here to be light, bringing out the God-colours in the world. God is not a secret to be kept. We're going public with this, as public as a city on a hill. If I make you light-bearers, you don't think I'm going to hide you under a bucket, do you? I'm putting you on a light stand. Now that I've put you there on a hilltop, on a light stand—shine!*

Our lives are all about sharing and shining!

Figuratively speaking ...

When we go back to the Bible we note that light is sometimes used in a figurative sense and when it is it always has two facets: intellectual and moral. Intellectually, it represents truth—morally, it represents holiness. To *live in the light*, therefore, is to live in truth and in holiness.

The figure of darkness has the same two aspects. Purely on an intellectual level it represents ignorance and falsehood—on a moral level it represents evil. The intellectual aspect of both figures pertains to what a person knows and believes, the moral aspect pertains to the way he thinks and acts (*cf.* 2 Corinthians 4:4; Romans 1:21; Isaiah 5:20).

When Paul wrote as he did in Romans 13:12, his erudite comments are best seen as an impassioned appeal for God's people to 'put aside the deeds of darkness and put on the armour of light'. John jumped on the bandwagon when he wrote: 'If we claim to have fellowship with him yet walk in the darkness, we lie and do not live by the truth. But if we walk in the light, as he is in the light, we have fellowship with one another, and the blood of Jesus, his Son, purifies us from all sin' (1 John 1:6, 7).

I saw the Light!

A closer look at what Paul has to say about light and darkness is most instructive. It is rich in symbolism and massive in appeal. A question springs to mind when we read Paul's analysis in verses 8-10—what changes are afoot when the bright light of God lights up a person's life? It results always in a change of character!

We have an unbelievable contrast—Paul shows us what we were and he reminds us of what we now are. Before we came to Jesus we were darkness but when we gave our lives to him we were brought into the light. Now, says Paul, you are the *children of light*.

Before and after

The apostle leaves us in no doubt as to the empty lostness of our previous condition. We were not helpless victims of Satan's regime, we were fully subscribed contributors to it. We were not merely in sin, our very nature was characterised and besotted by sin.

It is interesting to note that Scripture gives four basic characteristics of that spiritual darkness:

- It is, unquestionably, the work of Satan (*cf.* John 8:44).
- It is not only the work of Satan, it is also his domain—the unbeliever does Satan's work because he is under Satan's control (*cf.* Colossians 1:13).
- It brings God's penalty (*cf.* 5:6; 2:3; Romans 1:18).
- It leads to the ultimate destiny of eternal darkness—because they choose darkness rather than light, they will forever have darkness rather than light (*cf.* Matthew 8:12).

Eternity simply crystallises the choice they made in a moment of time into one of never ending permanence.

Shades of grey

When we think of the immediate context of this particular truth, we begin to realise that there can be no fellowship between light and darkness. Light drives out the darkness, it dispels the gloom, there is nothing in common between them. It is either one or the other. The Bible says our lives should be lived with no shades of grey.

Max Lucado tells a story about some candles who refused to be taken from a storage closet to provide essential light during an electrical storm. They all have excuses why they should not give off light. When the husband tells his wife that the candles will not work, she explains: 'Oh, they're church candles.' Ouch!

Our principal role in this world is to leave the light switched on! Getting to know the Lord better and walking in the light of his truth means he will change our character. Only God can do that! When we see the light, it makes all the difference.

An author once asked C H Spurgeon for permission to write his life story, to which the great preacher replied: *'You may write my life in the skies, I have nothing to hide.'*

Such is the mindset Paul enthusiastically advocates—the no hidden agenda philosophy.

5:9

Christian glow worms

The effusion of divine light into our lives brings a noticeable change of conduct. It is quite ironic but for some reason this verse is in parenthesis, yet how vitally important a nugget of Scripture it proves to be. Christ's light produces through the prisms of our lives a three-fold cluster of fruit: *goodness (agathōsynē), righteousness (dikaiosynē) and truth (alētheia).*

If we are the children of light, we will display the characteristics of light—if we are the children of God, we will display the intrinsic beauty of the character of God.

Corrie ten Boom tells how during hard times in the watch-making business, when the family was in extreme financial need, she observed her father and a wealthy customer. The wealthy man had decided to purchase a costly timepiece with cash which would have met all their needs. But as her father was handling the cash, the customer related that he was buying the watch because Mr ten Boom's young competitor could not fix the fine old watch.

Corrie's father asked to see it, opened it, made a slight adjustment, and handed it back saying: 'There, that was a very little mistake. It will be fine now. Sir, I trust the young watchmaker. Someday he will be just as good as his father. So if you ever have a problem with one of his watches, come to me. I'll help you out. Now I shall give you back your money and you return my watch.'

Corrie watched horrified as she saw the exchange, and then observed her father open the door for the man and bow deeply in his old fashioned way. She flew at her father in reproof, only to be herself reproved by his patient regard through his steel rimmed glasses and his gentle question: 'Corrie, what do you think that young man would have said when he heard that one of his good customers had gone to Mr ten Boom? Do you think that the name of the Lord would be honoured? As for the money, trust the Lord, Corrie. He owns the cattle on a thousand hills and he will take good care of us.'

Beautiful! Impeccable! Unimpeachable!

Big heart

The basic meaning of *goodness* is a generosity of spirit that overflows from a kind heart. Benevolence. God is described in the Bible as absolutely 'good' (Psalm 34:8). He is so good that he actually litters the world with ample evidence of his generosity.

People should be in no doubt where we live and work as to the big hearted nature of our experience of knowing Jesus. Paul refers here to moral excellence and it is exemplified when we do things for others in a genuine spirit of willingness and sacrifice (*cf.* 1 Thessalonians 5:15).

Right wise, street wise

Righteousness could be defined as behaviour which corresponds to God's ideal. It is a fairly cumbersome word that sounds desperately old fashioned. However, it first appeared in the English language hundreds of years ago as 'right wise' which, when we stop and think about it, does have a third millennium feel to it. It has a contemporary ring. As children of the light we are, therefore, expected to behave right wisely!

Fighting truth decay

The third *fruit of the light* is *truth*. Primarily it has to do with honesty, reliability, trustworthiness, and integrity. This is in stark contrast to the hypocritical, deceptive, and false ways of the old life of darkness.

Integrity is doing what we said we would do.

Other people will see it, they will be very much aware of it, they will recognise it, they will know all about it, for our conduct will reveal it. God always acts according to his character. He never acts out of character. And he is good, righteous, and true, therefore, we should be the same!

- We will not make a habit of being bad,
- we will not make a habit of doing wrong, and
- we will not make a habit of being false.

The living God changes our lifestyle and our style of living.

Spiritual luminaries

The light of God's Spirit has shone into our hearts and the profound effect on us is as visible as *fruit* (*karpos*) on a tree. Therein lies the transforming power of the gospel of the grace of God. We see, therefore, that *goodness* is linked to our interpersonal relationships, *righteousness* zooms in on our relationship with God, and *truth* relates to our personal integrity. This trilogy is reminiscent of the statement in Micah 6:8 that God requires human beings 'to act justly, to love mercy, and to walk humbly' with God.

A man returning from a journey brought his wife a matchbox that would glow in the dark. After giving it to her she turned out the light, but the matchbox could not be seen. Both thought they had been cheated. Then the wife noticed some French words on the box and asked a friend to translate them. The inscription said: 'If you want me to shine in the night, keep me in the light!'

We need to spend quality time alone with Jesus—the Light—in prayer, 'exposing our lives like photographic plates to his presence so that his image, his character, is burnt into ours' (R. Kent Hughes). If we do this, we will be like Moses when he descended from the summit of Sinai after being alone with God—his face shone with the light of God!

5:10

God pleasers

There is a third aspect to this welcome change in our lives—a change of criterion. Here is the bottom line for the child of God. Always, the question of singular importance is: does it *please* (*euarestos*) *the Lord?* It is not whether I like it or not, nor whether other people approve or disapprove!

Does God smile upon it? Or does he frown upon it?

This is all that really matters, this is what really counts more than anything else. Pleasing the Lord! Thankfully, it is not too difficult to ascertain what wins God's approval. We ask three simple questions:

- is it good?
- is it right?
- is it true?

WWJD

All we need to do is to look at the Lord Jesus. He is our standard. We only have to read how he lived, what he did, and what he permitted to be part of his life. From his first breath in the cradle in the cattle shed to his last breath on the cross at Calvary, he spent his entire life as the object of his Father's pleasure and delight. He always brought unsurpassed joy to the heart of God.

That means when we are in any doubt, we ask the question: what would Jesus do? When we are uncertain about a particular course of action, we ask: would it please the Lord or would it embarrass him?

When Jesus is brought into the frame, the choices are clear because the blur evaporates and everything is brought into sharp focus. It seems to me that the light metaphor speaks vividly of Christian openness and transparency, of living joyfully in the presence of Christ with nothing to hide or fear.

5:11

The ostrich mentality

Paul takes, understandably, a hard line approach when he says we must not compromise with anything which smacks of darkness—he emphatically states: *have nothing to do with the fruitless deeds of darkness*. Some things love the dark. Ever walked into a room in the middle of the night and turned on the light, only to catch a glimpse of a cockroach scurrying for cover? Ever turned over a stone on the beach, only to see the creepy crawlies make a speedy exit to another one? They run from the light!

The man is a spiritual nincompoop if he dances in the dark with the devil because his *deeds* (*ergon*) *of darkness* (*skotos*) are all to no avail. They are unfruitful, unproductive, and barren, yielding no beneficial results. Spiritual darkness brings sterility. The siren songs of darkness promise great things but give only desolation and doleful misery—the 'apples of Sodom' as some have called it.

We cannot be tolerant of them, we should be taking a firm stand against them, even though some will label us puritanical bigots. When it comes to issues of light and darkness, the 'live and let live' attitude is a non starter. It should be out of bounds for the Christian. We should not even be guilty by association for we should never identify with any kind of evil.

Sitting on the fence

If we try to run with the foxes and hunt with the hounds, we will only succeed in compromising God's high and holy standards. Any attempt to live with one foot in both camps will significantly weaken and undermine our testimony, personally and congregationally. It will seriously diminish the quality of our Christian character by leaving us badly tarnished.

We should be prepared to tell it for what it is and engage in a necessary ministry of reproof if needs be—it is a willingness to stand up and be counted as we bravely *expose* (*elenchō*) what is wrong.

Evil. To ignore it is to encourage it, to keep quiet about it is to help promote it.

Sin must always be confronted and, when we do oppose it, we do not hold our noses in the air. Nor do we adopt a holier than thou attitude or a self satisfied, smug Pharisaic outlook either. There is no need for us to be prudish or judgmental—we are not moral policemen, nor are we judge, jury, and executioner.

Exposed to the light

In the bazaars of the Middle East, the shops are often little covered enclosures with no windows. A man might wish to buy a piece of silk or an article of beaten brass. Before he buys it, he takes it out to the street and holds it up to the sun so that the light might reveal any flaws or imperfections which happen to be in it. As William Barclay says: 'It is the Christian's duty to expose every action, every decision, every motive to the light of Christ.'

Each situation is different and each will be assessed on its merits but there will be times when such exposure and reproof is direct, on other occasions it will be indirect. Whichever, it should always be immediate in the face of anything that is so blatantly and harmfully sinful. Such appallingly outrageous behaviour must always be taken seriously for sin is no laughing matter.

5:12

Don't play with fire

Paul develops his argument further when he says that which is done in darkness is not something with which we can converse—*it is shameful even to mention what the disobedient do in secret* (*kryphē*). Paul says quite firmly and with more than a hint of brusque bluntness: do not even talk about it! Reason: it pollutes the atmosphere.

It is the late night TV or radio chat show syndrome where everything is up for grabs. Generally speaking, after the 21.00 watershed, there are no bounds to decency on such a program, nothing is sacred in such an atmosphere. For the Christian, living in the light, that kind of scenario is a non starter.

The behaviour Paul is kicking into touch is that which is *shameful* (*aischros*) or 'filthy' (*cf.* Titus 1:11). The word can also mean 'deformed' or 'ugly' in the sense that it is indecent and grossly offensive—it is the gutter press mentality, the tabloid press kind of gossip column.

Talking about it only puts the spotlight on the devil. And the less said about him the better!

5:13, 14

Reveille!

- There is the work of the Spirit (*cf.* 5:13), and
- the work of the Saviour (*cf.* 5:14).

What does Paul have to say, first of all, about the work of the Spirit of God in this wake up call to the church? The word *elenchō* translated *exposed* is a word which conveys the idea of 'convicting'. The whole purpose of this convicting role is to bring in a guilty verdict (*cf.* John 16:8).

That is the unique ministry of the Holy Spirit—to bring the secret works of darkness out into the open light. When the light of the word of God shines on a situation, all is revealed. All is *visible* (*phaneroō*). Nothing, absolutely nothing, can hide from the stunning glare of the bright light.

A Job lot

Remember Job. The book that bears his name is a blow by blow account of how this saint of God faced calamity, criticism, and conviction. To start with we see him in Satan's hands where, even though he was overwhelmed by disaster, he retained his integrity and personal faith in God.

Then we see him in the hands of unreasonable men—so called friends—being roundly accused and scornfully criticised. His response to them was one of angry self defence. In his last recorded speech, he referred to himself by the personal pronoun no less than 195 times (*cf.* Job 29-31).

Finally, we see him in the hands of God and when he is there he totally abhors himself. He did not like what he saw in himself. Here is the man who earlier had loudly protested as he tried to justify himself in the face of hostile criticism. Because of what he did, he exposed all the pent up feelings in his heart—feelings of bitterness, sarcasm, anger, pride, and self righteousness. This same man, believe it or not, is now repenting in dust and ashes.

Open heart surgery

The Holy Spirit can easily and effectively expose our sins to the light. That is his speciality, it is where he excels. He opens up the heart and when he does we see them for what they are—ugly beyond words. In that sacred moment we shrink and shrivel into nothingness in his presence.

Thomas Binney (1798-1874) captured the mood and mystique of that sacred tryst when he wrote:

Eternal Light! Eternal Light!
How pure the soul must be,
When, placed within thy searching sight,
It shrinks not, but, with calm delight,
Can live, and look on thee.

Arise and shine

The great work of the Saviour is capitally highlighted in verse 14 where Paul quotes *ad lib* from Isaiah 60:1, 2. Some commentators believe these words were culled from an Easter hymn sung by the early church and used as an invitation—a first century *Just as I am*— to nonChristians who might have been in the congregation. John MacArthur views it as 'a capsule summary of the gospel.' Other scholars are of the opinion that it was a line taken from an apostolic baptismal hymn sung as the convert emerged from the water.

Be that as it may, the abiding lesson from this paraphrase is that light and life go together. Life craves light. In fact, in its highest forms, life cannot exist without light.

The phrase, *and Christ will shine on you*, is a very special one. Actually, this is the only time we find this phrase used in the unabridged Greek New Testament. It was a word, *epiphauskō*, used to describe the rising of the sun. It means that Christ will shine upon the believer as if it were the dawning of a brand new day.

The Christian has new light and new life.

The story is told of a great fire in the capital city of Edinburgh, Scotland, in which people hurried to exit the building through a narrow passage that led to the cobbled street. They were almost safe when a rush of smoke met them, blowing into the passage from the outside. Instead of running through the smoke, they entered a door into a room that seemed safe. But soon all the oxygen was exhausted and they all suffocated. If only they had seen the light they might have lived.

What a difference the light makes! In our lives, the new light chases away the darkness in which we once grovelled, the new life replaces the darkness that once possessed us. For fairly obvious reasons, it has been called: the Lazarus experience! From death to life! From darkness to light! Nothing short of a miracle of grace!

Horatius Bonar (1808-89) wrote:

I heard the voice of Jesus say,
'I am this dark world's light;
Look unto me, thy morn shall rise,
And all thy day be bright.'
I looked to Jesus, and I found
In him my star, my sun;
And in that light of life I'll walk,
Till travelling days are done.

Some years ago the National Religious Broadcasters held their large annual convention in Washington DC and the President of the United States spoke. Typically, he said what the broadcasters wanted to hear and closed with a quotation of John 3:16. The conventioneers became ecstatic. They leaped to their feet and applauded until long after the President had left the platform. It seemed as though revival had broken out in the capital.

The next speaker was Charles Colson, whose experiences had taught him both the limitations and seductions of political life.

He said that he was glad to have heard the President's speech and believed the Bible quotation. *'But,'* he added, *'we must remember that the kingdom of God is not going to arrive on Air Force One!'*

Profoundly true. In the ultimate sense, the kingdom of God is going to arrive only when Jesus Christ returns to this world and does it himself. He is the one who inaugurates it after he touches down on the Mount of Olives. But until that time it will arrive only to the extent that Christian people—you and me—begin to live like Jesus Christ.

We are lights in this world and, even though we are surrounded by thick impenetrable darkness, the light shines on! The light shines bright!

5:15

Getting our act together

We have just noted the incredible impact that light has on the world in which we live. We looked at the various qualities of light and we saw a rich tapestry of truth begin to emerge from Paul's classic comparison between the children of light and those who are the sons of darkness.

Basically what Paul is talking about in this mini section is the need for us to walk in wisdom. Paul's wonderful insights in these three verses is based on two assumptions:

* Christians are wise people, not idiots.
* Christian wisdom is earthy for it teaches us how to behave.

Paul says in modern tones: be wise!

In the previous half dozen verses we discovered that we were to walk in love and walk in the light—now, Paul says, walk wise.

Wise up!

The mega challenge facing us is not to be foolish! We are not intended to be spiritual cranks or some kind of hyped up spiritual eccentric cum oddball. Neither is Paul casting aspersion or making any stage whispered comment about us being clever or having a certain level of IQ!

It has nothing to do with intelligence, everything to do with wisdom.

According to John MacArthur, the wise Christian is someone who knows:

- his life principles (*cf.* 5:15),
- his limited privileges (*cf.* 5:16), and
- his Lord's purposes (*cf.* 5:17).

Eyes open

The first word in the verse is *be* meaning 'look' or 'observe'. Paul's command that we should walk wisely or circumspectly is based on what he has just been teaching in the previous verses—we have come out of darkness into the light of the Lord, we have been raised from the place of death to receive a brand new life, we are to imitate and copy our heavenly Father, we have been born and brought into the global family of God—therefore, be ultra careful how you live and walk. In other words, we may not come from the East, but we are still to walk as *wise* men.

We are to walk as sensible men, not as simpletons!

We are to live like the people we are. In Christ we are *wise* (*sophos*) and what we do should correspond to what we are. There is no room for an apparent contradiction in what I am and what I do.

The two are to harmonise beautifully in a note of sweet snychronisation. What do I mean?

At the moment of salvation, every believer in Christ has been made wise (*cf.* 2 Timothy 3:15; 1 Corinthians 1:30; Colossians 2:3). This is absolutely thrilling for here is the miracle of our conversion experience. When in grace God reached down and saved us, he made us immediately righteous, holy, and redeemed—at the same time, he also made us wise!

Paul's reasoning here would lead us to conclude that we cannot have salvation without God's wisdom any more than we can have salvation without his righteousness, his holiness, and his redemption. Simply, we cannot have one without the other, it is either all or nothing! We have been given wisdom and we thank God for that.

Growing pains

There is more to it than meets the eye for we also grow in wisdom as we mature in the Christian life. Peter challenges us to 'grow in the grace and knowledge of our Lord and Saviour Jesus Christ' (2 Peter 3:18). As we become more like Jesus, we will grow more and more in his love, in his joy, in his peace, and in every other fruit of the Spirit. It is a paradox and something we cannot easily explain.

When we place each of these references side by side, they remind us that when we give our hearts and lives to Jesus Christ, we get the wisdom that we need to daily live for the Lord, then we continue to grow in wisdom, so that we can be more mature, more faithful, and more fruitful in his service.

- Be wise!
- Be what you are!

Watch your step

Paul invites us to *be very careful* (*akribōs*) and to live our lives on the highest level of vigilance—on red alert.

'Be a lert! The world needs all the lerts it can get!'

The vivid picture painted here on the canvas of Scripture is of a cat walking on top of a wall into which pieces of sharp glass have been embedded. The wise old cat will be circumspect, to say the least. He will watch where he puts his feet, treading cautiously and carefully. He will take his time to pick his spot. He is precise. Exact.

That is the way we should be in our walk in this world. Pardon the pun, we should be copycats! Every step we take should be wisely considered. We are to walk assiduously. We need to keep our eyes wide open, watch where we are walking, and look where we are going. If we fail to watch how and where we walk, we end up acting rather foolishly (*cf.* 1 Samuel 26:21; 2 Samuel 24:10). It happens. It happens to all of us. And it can happen a lot easier than we think sometimes. We are not immune.

- We play the fool by not believing God completely (*cf.* Luke 24:25).
- We play the fool when we are openly disobedient to the Lord and his word (*cf.* Galatians 3:1, 3).
- We play the fool when we set our heart on wrong things (*cf.* 1 Timothy 6:9).

Paul says: do not be a fool! Be wise. Be careful. That is the best principle to live by this side of heaven and the man is a wise man who knows how to do it, and goes ahead and does it.

5:16

Getting beyond the halfway stage

The chances are that most of us are fairly good starters, probably very few of us are good finishers. We start well, we do not always end well! It has been said that too many fall out on the last lap.

Sometimes—a symphony is unfinished, a painting is not completed, a project is left half done because the musician, the artist, or the craftsman dies. Nine times out of ten, however, the main reason why jobs are left unfinished is because the person's commitment has died.

Dreams fail to turn into reality, hopes never materialise because the participants never get beyond the first few tentative steps. They lose heart, their enthusiasm wanes, their zeal and keenness evaporates and, for them, life is a series of unfinished symphonies.

We have a lot of people walking about in today's world whose lives are a sad and sorry tale of untapped potential. It is pathetic for not only have they short changed themselves, in the process they have deprived the church worldwide of their valuable contribution.

Time management skills

The man who makes an impact on other people, the person who makes an impact for the Lord Jesus, is the individual who has learned to master the time at his disposal. In the words of Paul, he *makes the most of every opportunity*. If we are to achieve our potential for God we need to maximise the time he has given to us.

It is interesting to note that the word which Paul employs for *opportunity* is not the word *chronos*—clock time that we measure in hours, minutes, and seconds. The word specially chosen for this situation is *kairos* which refers to a fixed season, an epoch, an allocated period (*cf.* Exodus 9:5; 1 Peter 1:17). The thought is:

God has set boundaries to our lives and our opportunities for service exist only within these limits.

Time is ring fenced

It is so vitally important for us to realise that the Bible speaks of these times being shortened but never of them being lengthened. God clearly defines the parameters. He has bounded our lives with eternity (*cf.* Ecclesiastes 3:11). God knows both the beginning and the end of our time on this world. That means we can be all that God wants us to be only as we make the *most of every opportunity* given to us.

The phrase *make the most of* (*exagorazō*) or 'redeem' (KJV) is fascinating. It refers to 'buying back' or 'buying out'. It was used of buying a slave in order to set him free. Hence the idea of redemption. We are to buy up—redeem—all the time that we have and devote it entirely to the Lord Jesus.

'Opportunity has a forelock so we can seize it when we meet it. Once it is past, we cannot seize it again.' (Chinese proverb)

Buy now, play later

Again the emphasis is on grasping the moment, seizing the chance, for life is short. So many people fritter their lives away as if they were involved in a game of trivial pursuits and, before they know it, they come to the end of the journey and it is too late to do anything about it.

The epitaph on the tombstone of their lives pays silent testimony but not eloquent tribute to wasted years. They leave this world with regret written in bold capital letters all over their hearts. Many echo the sentiments of the gospel song when, with tears streaming down their faces, they *wish they had given him more.* There is a crucial need for us to be proactive and make hay when the sun is shining.

The Shakespearian classic *Julius Caesar* reveals a similar mindset:

> *There is a tide in the affairs of men,*
> *Which, taken at the flood, leads on to fortune;*
> *Omitted, all the voyage of their life*
> *Is bound in shallows and in miseries.*

Napoleon was thinking along these lines when he wrote: *'There is in the midst of every great battle a ten to fifteen minute period that is the crucial point ... take that period and you win the battle, lose it and you will be defeated.'*

One day at a time

Tomorrow is not guaranteed. It may never come. We may never see it! It does not matter who we are or where we have come from, we all have at least one thing in common—the gift of time. All of us have twenty four hours each day to spend as we please but we cannot credit any of today's hours on tomorrow's account.

No matter how hard we may wish for it to be so, we know there will never be more than twenty four hours in a day. None of us can stretch time. We get only one opportunity to use each minute we have—once passed, it is gone forever.

An advertisement appeared in a local freebie newspaper which read: *'Lost, yesterday, somewhere between sunrise and sunset, two golden hours, each set with sixty diamond minutes. No reward offered for they are gone for ever.'*

Stewardship is not only about how we manage our personal finances, or how we exercise the gift which we feel the Lord has given to us, it is about personal time management as well.

Jonathan Edwards (1703-58), who became God's instrument in the Great Awakening in America in 1734-5 wrote in the seventieth of his famous *Resolutions* just before his twentieth birthday: 'I resolve never to lose one moment of time, but to improve it in the most profitable way I possibly can.'

The Melanchthon mindset

Philip Melanchthon (1497-1560) was one of the great reformers of the sixteenth century. He was the gentle genius who honed Martin Luther's theology and spread it throughout Germany. It was said of him that he kept a record of every wasted moment and took his list to God in confession at the end of each day.

The lessons are clear: it pays handsome dividends to keep in touch with God, and here was a man who was so in tune with the Lord that he was sensitive to those lost and missed opportunities.

Small wonder that God used him in such great and momentous ways.

Time ... an ever flowing stream

Many Bible texts stand as warning beacons to those who think they will always have time to do what they should. It is all about getting a firm grip on a rather slippery subject. Procrastination is the thief of time—it is the person who puts off until tomorrow what he can do the day after tomorrow!

When Noah and his family entered the ark and shut the door, the opportunity for any other person to be saved from the flood was gone. That was it! Everyone else missed the boat, they were left standing on the dockside (*cf.* Genesis 7:1-16). The five foolish virgins had a profoundly unhappy experience when they blew it, big time. They let their oil run out before the bridegroom came. Needless to say it all ended in tears when they were shut out from the wedding feast (*cf.* Matthew 25:1-13).

Jesus himself said: 'As long as it is day, we must do the work of him who sent me. Night is coming when no one can work' (John 9:4). I suppose one of the most tragic examples of wasted opportunity is seen in the life of Judas—he spent three years in the immediate presence of the Son of God as one of the inner circle of trusted disciples, yet he betrayed the Lord and forfeited his own soul for thirty pieces of silver.

When we take each of those illustrations and think them through, the message is loud and clear:

- none of us can rewrite history,
- none of us can put time on playback.

Once the moment has slipped through our buttery fingers, it can never be retrieved. We cannot press a key and go into recovery mode. It is past, it is yesterday, it has gone—it is the memory lane syndrome. A few months back, I was in the quintessentially English city of Chester and, with a few minutes to spare, I happened to pop in to the cathedral for a quick visit. I stood by the old clock and read these words:

When as a child I laughed and wept,
Time crept.
When as a youth I grew more bold,
Time strolled.
When I became a full grown man,
Time ran.
Soon I shall find as I journey on,
Time gone.

Tomorrow

I was moved recently when I read in the book *A Distant Grief* the touching story of Kefa Sempangi. He was a national pastor in Africa and barely escaped with his young family from the brutal oppression and terror in his home country of Uganda. They made their way to Philadelphia where a group of Christians began caring for them. One day his wife said to him: 'Tomorrow, I'm going to go and buy some clothes for the children.'

No sooner had she said it, but she and her husband broke down into floods of tears. Because of the constant threat of death under which they had lived for so long, that was the first time in many years they had dared even speak the word *tomorrow*. Their terrifying experiences as a family forced them to realise what is true for every single one of us—we have no assurance of tomorrow.

The only time we can be sure of having is what we have at this precise moment. Now! Remember the phenomenally rich farmer in the story Jesus told in Luke 12:20—he had already lived his last tomorrow.

The hourglass is almost full

Why should we pull out all the stops and maximise the potential of every opportunity? *Because the days (hēmera) are evil (ponēros).* That says it all, doesn't it.

Times were bad then. Two thousand years have come and gone and they certainly have not improved. Sin abounds in every strata of society, standards are plummeting all around the world, it is a downward spiral as we progress from bad to worse. It is an age when anything goes and everything is deemed to be ok and the Bible makes it clear that it is going to get even worse the nearer we get to the second advent of Jesus Christ.

Turn on the television in the evening, switch on the car radio, pick up a magazine from a newsstand and before we know it, we are bombarded with an unthinkable volume of evil. It is unimaginable! Horrific. Real.

We live in a godless era. We are back to the days of Noah and Lot having gone full circle in terms of personal morality and the incredible decline in public standards and decency. This simply underlines the relevance of what the apostle is saying.

5:17

First things first

Paul starts the ball rolling in this verse with a terse *do not be foolish*. He has said it before, he says it again: be wise! He goes for the jugular, he pulls no punches. We need to prioritise our lives. This is fundamental if our relationship with Jesus Christ is to mean anything. We need to set our personal agenda so that it tallies with God's personalised plan for our lives.

There is a real sense of urgency about Paul's comment for 'wisdom consists in perceiving where God is going and then jumping on his bandwagon' (James Montgomery Boice).

Not being *foolish* (*aphrōn*) also means 'do not become anxious or panicked'. When we look around us and see the appalling rise of evil on every hand, combined with the forward advance of the enemy, we see the enormous need to evangelise—in moments like that, it is easy to be overwhelmed with it all, we could be tempted to give up and give in, or we could become hyperactive and lose precision. We could waver on our purpose statement and become ineffective in a frenzy of activity which only leads to burnout and discouragement.

Trying to run ahead of the Lord only puts us further behind in his work.

Discovering God's will

When we see the need, it should drive us to *understand (syniēmi) what the Lord's will (thelēma) is.* We need to prayerfully discern his will and, when we have done that, we need to get out there and do it. Nothing is more important in our lives than for us to discover and do the will of God. We need to be on the same wavelength as Jesus. Only then will he be able to accomplish and achieve great things through us.

What is God's will for our lives? Well, we find it clearly elucidated in the word of God. Because of its huge significance, he will not leave us guessing or grasping at straws. Sussing out God's will is not some airy fairy experience. There is nothing mystical or esoteric about it.

God has given us a mind and he expects us to use it, he wants us to think clearly as we seek to ascertain his will for our lives. Of this we can be sure, the Lord will guide us according to the timeless principles established in Scripture.

The will of God for the people of God is revealed in the word of God.

- He wants us to be saved (*cf.* 1 Timothy 2:3, 4).
- He wants us to be Spirit filled (*cf.* Ephesians 5:18).
- He wants us to be sanctified (*cf.* 1 Thessalonians 4:3).
- He wants us to be submissive to others (*cf.* 1 Peter 2:13-15).
- He wants us to experience a degree of suffering (*cf.* 1 Peter 2:20).
- He wants us to always be thankful (*cf.* 1 Thessalonians 5:18).

At the end of the day, it is all about you and me actively engaging ourselves in the full blown will of God (*cf.* Romans 12:2). It may not always be the easiest option, but it is the best!

5:18

God's chief executive

Paul is focusing in this verse on one of the greatest and finest ministries of the Holy Spirit in the life of the Christian—the fulness of the Spirit. This should not catch us on the back foot for throughout his epistle Paul has drawn attention to various aspects of the Spirit's influence in our lives.

He is the third person of the trinity and as such is the executive of the Godhead, fulfilling the express wishes of the Father and the Son. This was so on the morn of creation and it continues up to this day.

The ministry of the Holy Spirit in a person's life begins long before they are consciously aware of it. It is the Holy Spirit who draws us into that place where God can begin to work a work of grace in our hearts. From the new birth right through to the painful growth in holiness, it is the Holy Spirit who is constantly at the believer's side. Which means, when Paul wrote in this section about the Christian life, it would have been most surprising if he had not urged us to *be filled with the Spirit*.

Never a dull moment

We need to be clear in our own minds that the experience of the Holy Spirit is not the preserve of an exclusive band of blue-blooded believers. He is at the very heart of the Christian life and, if we lift him out of the picture, we immediately cease to be talking about biblical Christianity.

The believer is marked with the seal of the Spirit (*cf.* 1:13), we have access to the Father by the Spirit and at the same time he is indwelling us by the Spirit (*cf.* 2:22), he has strengthened us in our inner man (*cf.* 3:16), we are to make every effort to keep the unity of the Spirit through the bond of peace (*cf.* 4:3).

When we put each of these together, it means the Holy Spirit is not assuming a kind of laidback or passive role—on the contrary, he is always doing something in our hearts and lives. Supremely, his goal is to make us more and more like the Lord Jesus. It is all about striking a balance, isn't it. We can look at it like this:

- if we are all word and no Spirit—we dry up,
- if we are all Spirit and no word—we flare up,
- if we are all word and all Spirit—we grow up.

That is what God desires from each of us today and every day. He wants us to pursue a life of holiness and godliness. He wants us to become increasingly more conformed to the image of his Son, the Lord Jesus Christ. He wants us to have an eternal dimension to our lives on planet earth. He wants us to feel the beat of his heart and reach out to those for whom his Son has died.

Par for the course

I would suggest that life lived in the fulness of the Holy Spirit is the normal Christian experience. It is when we come to a place where our all is yielded to the Lord and, in return, we are brought into the blessing of a surrendered life.

When we are abandoned to him, then we allow him to monopolise and master us. He is number one on the agenda of our lives. He is top of our priority list. Without Christ, our lives were like a vast empty reservoir awaiting the coming of a downpour.

However, when the experience of God's salvation became a glorious reality, this emptiness became full to the point of running over. The Spirit of God has filled our internal capacity with power and dynamic.

A couple of metaphors help us understand it: like the wind that fills the sails, we allow his power to propel our lives; what fuel is to a car, the Holy Spirit is to the believer—he energises us to stay the course, he motivates us in spite of the obstacles, he keeps us going when the road gets rough.

Up close and personal

There is nothing la-di-da about the Holy Spirit—he comforts us in our hour of distress, he calms us in times of calamity, he becomes our constant companion in loneliness and grief, he spurs our intuition into action, he fills our minds with discernment when we are uneasy about a certain decision.

In short, the Holy Spirit is our high octane spiritual fuel. When we attempt to operate without him or perhaps try a substitute fuel, we know what happens, all systems grind to a halt. We sometimes sing the words of M E Maxwell's song which is really a prayer:

Jesus, fill now with thy Spirit
Hearts that full surrender know,
That the streams of living water
From our inner man may flow.

It is one thing to sing it and pray it, but what does it mean to be filled with the Holy Spirit? Again we go back to the Bible for the answer to that question of mega importance. John Phillips has a most intriguing outline of these four verses:

- be filled with the Holy Spirit (*cf.* 5:18),
- be thrilled in the Holy Spirit (*cf.* 5:19, 20), and
- be drilled in the Holy Spirit (*cf.* 5:21).

Where the rubber hits the road

When we turn back to Ephesians 5 we are confronted with a most interesting situation. This great experience of the fulness of the Holy Spirit is set in quite a remarkable context. It is not just something for preaching from the pulpit or something we experience in a Bible convention. It is essential for everyday living among men.

It is found in a paragraph which has an awful lot to say about husbands and wives, parents and children, management and employees.

Optional or obligatory

There is a command to be obeyed. It is important to note that in the Bible there are some things we are never commanded to be:

- we are never told to be baptised in the Spirit,
- we are never told to be indwelt by the Spirit,
- we are never told to be gifted with the Spirit,
- we are never told to be sealed with the Spirit.

But here we strike a different chord because two commands are issued—one negative, the other positive. *Do not get drunk on wine* (negative) ... *instead, be filled with the Spirit* (positive). In other words, do not get drunk with the devil's booze but be intoxicated with the new wine of the Spirit of God.

A person who is drunk is under the influence of alcohol—a Spirit filled Christian is under the influence and power of the Holy Spirit. Of course, in the heathen cult of Dionysus, which was rampant in Paul's day, intoxication was regarded as a means of inspiration. The man is a fool who goes down that road!

We need to realise this is not some kind of tentative proposal which Paul is floating for them to think about, it is not another hat which he is throwing into the ring of pneumatology—it is an authoritative command. We have no more liberty to avoid this huge responsibility than the many others which surround it in the book of Ephesians. To *be filled with the Spirit* is obligatory, it is not optional.

Something for everyone

The verb, *plēroō*, which Paul employs in the text is in the plural form and that means these words are addressed to the whole Christian community. *Be filled* excludes no one for every member of God's global family is included here. None are eliminated. None are left out in the cold. It is for everyone who has a personal relationship with Jesus Christ.

None of us is to get drunk, all of us are to be Spirit filled.

Because life is complicated enough

I was intrigued to discover that the verb is also in the passive voice. In other words, there is no technique for us to learn—there is no, one, two, three, and whoosh, got it—there is no formula to recite. None of these is required! He has kept it simple. What is essential is such a penitent turning from what grieves the Holy Spirit and such a believing openness to him, that nothing hinders him from filling us.

The right tense

The tense of the verb is most instructive for it is in the present tense. When Paul says *be filled with the Spirit* he could just as easily have said 'go on being filled with the Spirit' because he used a present imperative.

In other words, it is not an initial and final happening, it is a daily moment by moment infilling. It is not a once for all experience which we can never lose, but a privilege to be renewed on an uninterrupted basis by continuous believing and obedient appropriation. It is not some great high and mighty, once in a life-time moment where we experience the fulness of the Spirit and from then on we are on a super high that never wanes.

It is an ongoing experience as we say to him: *'Lord, I want to be filled. Lord, I want to be used. Lord, I want to be available. Lord, I consciously make myself dependent upon you.'*

A triple allusion

The word which Paul uses to describe this experience means more than filling something up as when someone pours water in a glass up to the rim. The term was used in three additional senses that have great significance for Paul's use of it here.

One, it was often used of the wind filling a sail and thereby carrying the ship along. To be filled with the Holy Spirit, therefore, is to be moved along in our Christian life by God himself—it is to be borne along by the same dynamic with which the writers of Scripture were moved (*cf.* 2 Peter 1:21).

Two, it also carries the idea of permeation for it was used of salt permeating meat in order to flavour and preserve it. In other words, God wants his Holy Spirit to so percolate through our lives so that everything we think, say, and do, will reflect his divine presence.

Three, it gives the impression of total control. The person who is filled with sorrow is no longer under his own control, but is totally under the control of that emotion (*cf.* John 16:6). To be filled in this sense is to be totally dominated and controlled by the Holy Spirit.

- Baptism in the Spirit—an immersion—focus on relationship.
- Anointing of the Spirit—an investment—focus on responsibility.
- Fulness of the Spirit—an infilling—focus on realisation.

It was only as the members of the early church were filled with the Holy Spirit that all that the Lord was—in the value of his cross, in the victory of his resurrection, in the virtue of his ascension—became real in them.

If the greatest sin of the unbeliever is his refusal of new life in Christ, perhaps the greatest sin of the Christian is when he declines life more abundant in the Spirit's fulness.

Angles on the analogy

When a man is drunk with the wine of the world, there are at least three traits reflected in his character. By inference, there is a bare minimum of three enhancing qualities found in the life of a person who drinks deeply from the well of God's salvation.

* A drunken man loses self consciousness whilst the Christian is someone who is lost and absorbed in Christ. The Lord Jesus is everything to him.
* A man who is the worse for drink loses a degree of self control but the Christian is an individual who will be led by the Holy Spirit because God is sitting in the driving seat of his life.
* The person who is inebriated loses self conceit and, so far as the Christian is concerned, there is no place for pride in our hearts as we owe all that we are to the amazing grace of God.

Life in the Spirit means we are captivated by Christ, motivated for Christ, and activated by Christ.

The Spirit filled life is not one of dejection, despair, and defeat. It does not lead to *debauchery* (*asōtia*) like drunkenness does (*cf.* Proverbs 23:29-35). There are no dreadful hangovers when our lives are fully governed by him. There are no 'morning after the night before' headaches to cope with when our lives are given over entirely to him. An individual filled with the Holy Spirit is said to be under new management. In addition to this, we must understand that 'alcohol is a depressant, while the Spirit is a stimulant' (D. Martyn Lloyd-Jones).

Playing by the rules

Because this is an experience destined to lead us into a place of real blessing it means there are certain conditions to be observed.

* To be filled with the Holy Spirit means an emptying—we must be empty before he fills us—empty of me!
* It also suggests a cleansing because the people that God is pleased to use are those who have been purged and purified—such

men and women are 'useful to the Master' (*cf.* 2 Timothy 2:20, 21).

Experiencing a personal Pentecost

When an individual believer is filled with the Holy Spirit of God the change is glaringly obvious. Look at the incredible difference before and after Pentecost (*cf.* Acts 2:2-4) with the band of disciples.

- They were all filled for the glory of God,
- they were all filled so that Christ would be exalted,
- they were all filled so that his word would be magnified,
- they were all filled so that his name would be honoured.

A quick look through the Acts of the Apostles unearths some wonderful stories of God's grace and ability as he worked in and through the lives of very ordinary people who had one thing in common—they were filled with the Holy Spirit.

True, it is only a vignette of life in the first century church but it serves to highlight the truth that the Spirit filled life is the victorious Christian life—a life of conquering sin, Satan, and self—a life where we have an overwhelming sense of personal unworthiness allied to a deep consciousness of the reality of Christ and his preciousness to us.

- Peter was filled to preach for the Lord (*cf.* Acts 4:8).
- The first deacons were filled to serve the Lord (*cf.* Acts 6:3).
- Stephen was filled to suffer for the Lord and ultimately lay down his life for the sake of the gospel (*cf.* Acts 7:55).
- Barnabas was filled to encourage others to go on with the Lord (*cf.* Acts 11:24).
- Paul was filled to enable him to promote the truth about God (*cf.* Acts 13:9).
- The early Christians were filled to live for the Lord (*cf.* Acts 13:52).

5:19

Songs of praise

There is a significant number of beneficial and salubrious results to being filled with the Holy Spirit. The first—the Spirit filled life produces music—is mentioned in this verse where Paul says: *Speak to one another with psalms, hymns and spiritual songs. Sing and make music in your heart to the Lord.*

- *Psalms (psalmos)*—the Old Testament Psalms put to music, usually accompanied by a harp—such as: Psalms 23 and 84.
- *Hymns (hymnos)*—songs of praise which exalt God and specifically praise the Lord Jesus—such as: *A Mighty Fortress is Our God* and *The Old Rugged Cross.*
- *Spiritual songs (pneumatikos ōdē)*—songs of testimony that include any music expressing spiritual truth—such as: *O How He Loves You and Me* and *I'd Rather Have Jesus.*

There is a joy that we experience within, which extends to others for there is something contagious about it, and then reaches heavenward in glad worship to the Lord.

When we are filled with the Holy Spirit we begin to relate to each other in the family of God.

We want to hear what others have to say, we want to learn from our brothers and our sisters, we want to contribute to each other's welfare by adding to one another's lives. Harmony enters all the interpersonal relationships we share. We enjoy being with one another and we have a wonderful time without resorting to the false stimulants of this world. Life takes on a special lilt for joy is much in evidence.

Worship 24/7

One of the characteristics of Spirit filled believers is that they do not have to wait until Sunday morning to worship the Lord—they have a daily worship service in their hearts.

You may be a gifted singer, marvellous. On the other hand, if you are anything like me and cannot carry a tune, you will be as flat as a Scotch pancake or a Yorkshire pudding gone wrong. But that does not matter for all of us have an inner melody that bubbles up spontaneously in our lives. When we are walking in the Spirit, there is usually a song on the tip of our tongues because there is a melody flowing through our hearts—the Spirit filled Christian is a singing Christian.

Best of times, worst of times

It is good to remind ourselves that we can know this joy even when circumstances are less than conducive. Even when the dominoes are falling and our backs are to the wall, we can still know this joy deep within for our lives are filled with the Spirit of God.

Joy is not a thermometer, rising and falling with the circumstances in which we find ourselves—it is a thermostat that determines the spiritual temperature of the situation.

Much ado about something

It is also worth noting the emphasis which Paul places in this verse on praise and worship. It is not restricted to our personal times with the Lord, it also incorporates the various occasions when we gather together for acts of public worship. Whenever the people of God assemble, they love to *sing* (*adō*) and *speak* (*laleō*)—both to God and to one another.

For over a thousand years of its history (c.500-1500), the church in general did not sing. From shortly after New Testament times until the Reformation, what little music the church had was usually performed by polished professional musicians. The music they presented could not be understood or appreciated by the average church member. In any case, they could only sit and listen, unable to participate.

However, when the Bible came back into the church during the Reformation, singing came with it. Martin Luther and some of the other Reformation leaders are among the greatest hymn writers of church history. As John MacArthur points out: 'Where the true gospel is known and believed, music is loved and sung. God's Spirit in the heart puts music in the heart.'

Sometimes we sing responsively as the Jews did in the temple and synagogue, and as the early Christians did also, meeting after daybreak 'to recite a hymn antiphonally to Christ as God'. That much info we glean from a letter addressed to the Emperor Trajan around 112 AD by Pliny the Younger, procurator of Bithynia.

Tertullian (c.160/70-c.215/20), writing from North Africa toward the end of the same century, describes a Christian feast at which 'each is invited to sing to God in the presence of others from what he knows of the Scriptures or from his own heart.'

John Stott reckons that 'some of the Psalms we sing are in reality not worship of God, but mutual exhortation.' A good example is Psalm 95, the *Venite*, in the singing of which we should turn to one another: 'O come, let us sing to the Lord; let us make a joyful noise to the rock of our salvation!' Here is rich fellowship in worship, a reciprocal invitation to praise.

J B Phillips has a lovely translation of the phrase when he writes: 'Making music in your hearts for the ears of the Lord.' Spirit filled Christians have a song of joy in their hearts and Spirit filled public worship is a joyful celebration of God's mighty acts.

Johann Sebastian Bach, probably the greatest musician of all time, said: *'The aim of all music is the glory of God.'*

The anonymous poet expressed it thus:

My life flows on in endless song
Above earth's lamentation.
I hear the real, though far-off hymn
That hails a new creation.
No storm can shake my inmost calm
While to that rock I'm clinging.
It sounds an echo in my soul,
How can I keep from singing?

5:20

Thanks a million, Father

Paul introduces us to the delightful theme of thankfulness with an exhortation to be thankful for all things at all times—*always* (*pantote*) *giving thanks* (*eucharisteō*) *to God the Father for everything* (*pas*).

Not easy! And it does not come naturally. It goes against the rough textured grain of human nature. But when we are happy to leave everything with the Lord, he gives us a spirit of gratitude and also an attitude of heartfelt appreciation no matter what falls into our lap.

Show me a grumbler, take me to a complainer—it is a sad fact but I know before I meet them that I will be introduced to a couple of negative, dour, miserable individuals who have effectively distanced themselves from the Spirit of God. In *King Lear*, Shakespeare wrote: 'Ingratitude, thou marble-hearted fiend! … How sharper than a serpent's tooth it is to have a thankless child!' However, when we are filled to overflowing with the Holy Spirit, there is an overwhelmingly profound sense of thankfulness in our lives.

One day Tauler, the fourteenth century mystic and preacher, met a beggar. 'God give you a good day, my friend,' he said. The beggar answered: 'I thank God I never had a bad one!' Tauler said: 'God give you a happy life, my friend.' 'I thank God,' said the beggar, 'I am never unhappy!' Tauler, in amazement, responded: 'What do you mean?' 'Well,' said the beggar, 'when it is fine, I thank God; when it rains, I thank God; when I have plenty, I thank God; when I am hungry, I thank God … why should I say I am unhappy when I am not?'

We are not too hard to please, we are happy to have whatever God provides for us, we are not spoiled or pampered, we are not picky and choosy.

Hammered out on the anvil of experience

This may be the right moment to remind ourselves that Paul was not writing these words from a plush five star hotel in some idyllic coastal resort! He just happened to be a prisoner chained to a disgruntled soldier for days and weeks on end. It was tough, and torrid. It was not the nicest experience to encounter—yet he was immensely appreciative in his attitude to the Lord.

I think it is interesting to note that *gratitude* comes from the same root word as *grace*. In other words, if we have experienced the grace of God in our hearts, then we ought to be extremely grateful for whatever the Lord brings into our lives.

Thank and *think* come from the same root word. Maybe if we would think more, we would thank more!

A medieval legend tells of two angels sent to earth by the Lord to gather the prayers of the saints. One was to gather the petitions and the other the thanksgivings. The angel responsible for petitions was not able to carry them back to heaven in one load, while the angel responsible for thanksgivings carried his back in one hand (*cf.* Luke 17:11-19).

Joni Eareckson Tada, a quadriplegic author, observed: 'Giving thanks is not a matter of feeling thankful, it is a matter of obedience.'

A city missionary in London was called to an old tenement building where a woman lay dying in the last stages of a terrible disease. The room was cold and she had nowhere to lie but on the floor. When the missionary asked if there was anything he could do, she replied: 'I have all I really need, I have Jesus Christ as my Lord and Saviour.' Deeply moved, the missionary went home and penned these words:

In the heart of London city,
Mid the dwellings of the poor,
These bright and golden words were uttered,
'I have Christ. What want I more?'
Spoken by a lonely woman
Dying on a garret floor,
Having not one earthly comfort,
'I have Christ. What want I more?'

OTT in PTL

It is helpful if we keep all of this in perspective for a strange notion is gaining popularity in some Christian circles that the major secret of Christian freedom and victory is unconditional praise—that a husband should praise God for his wife's adultery and a wife should praise God for her husband's drunkenness—and that even the most appalling calamities of life should become subjects for thanksgiving and praise.

To me such a suggestion is at best a dangerous half truth and at worst ludicrous, even blasphemous. Sure, God's children learn not to argue with him in their suffering, but to trust him, and indeed to thank him for his loving providence by which he can turn the worst of times into the best of times (*cf.* Romans 8:28)—that, however, is praising God for being God, it is not praising him for evil.

5:21

Submission with a smile

Paul brings another factor into the equation when he speaks of submission—*submit (hypotassō) to one another out of reverence (phobos) for Christ.* Such an attitude will be:

- seen in the home,
- evident in the local church, and
- reflected in our hearts before the Lord.

That means if we are in any kind of leadership role, a servant hearted style will replace a demanding dogmatic style—a God directed humility combined with a healthy fear of the Lord will emerge in our lives. And if we are married, then our Spirit filled heart prompts us to want to serve our partner, not control them. It is not a matter of us throwing our weight around or seeking to become top dog at someone else's expense (*cf.* Mark 10:42-45; Philippians 2:3-8).

In this context, if our marriages are to be healthy and God honouring then there is to be a mutual submission to one another, a teachability of heart, an openness in communication. Needless to say, it works both ways—from the wife toward her husband and the husband toward his wife.

Submission is not a one way street.

A bridge

It is worth noting that there is no verb at all in verse 22 because the call for submission in verse 21 is intended to be carried over into it. This fascinating insight means that verse 21 is best seen as a transition verse—a connecting link—forming a bridge between two sections. We know what has gone before, what follows is most illuminating for Paul gives us three excellent examples of what true submission is all about:

- wives are addressed before their husbands and told to *submit* to them (5:22),
- children are mentioned before their parents and told to *obey* them (6:1), and
- slaves are addressed before their masters and told to *obey* them (6:5).

'The key to submission is profound, reverent submission to Christ. What a beautiful grace this is in today's assertive, rung-dropping world! What a magnet to Christ!' (R. Kent Hughes)

5:22-24

Happy hearts, happy home

In the remaining verses, Paul touches on an area which affects all of us to one degree or another, directly or indirectly—the issue of interpersonal relationships. Here he specifically zooms in on the tie-in between a husband and wife where the emphasis is on harmony in the Christian home.

Life is enriched by relationships, the most meaningful being the marriage relationship.

Paul's comments make a lot of sense especially in today's secular environment and when carried out are guaranteed to bring stability and blessing to the family. He reminds us that if our homes are to reflect the love of Christ then each partner has a distinctive role to fulfil—something special for wives to do and something unique for husbands to do. Consequently, when we both do our part, God opens the windows of heaven and showers his mercies upon us as a couple.

At close quarters

Ever wondered, why does Paul spend so much time talking about the home? It seems to me this cannot be over emphasised enough. The home is where we spend so much of our time and it is often the place where we are not always seen in our best colours. Sadly, it can be said of many professing Christians that they are saints outside but devils at home!

With other believers, they are often very good company and are most plausible, with a winsome word and a bright cheery smile. In their place of employment and in the world at large, they resolutely stand against wrong and they appear to be fairly genuine and real in their experience of grace. However, at home, in their own wee corner, it is a different ball game—they are impossible to live with! They relax and lower their defences. As they put on their slippers, they take off their masks!

Double standards

Home is where we are seen as we really are for we cannot fool our partners. For such rascals, their life at home is best labelled a shocking disgrace. The apostle sets his face against such blatant inconsistency. Home is where we are all known the best and misunderstood the most, where we are constantly open to scrutiny and criticism. But this is where the Christian life has to be lived and this is where the gospel is put to its severest test.

'He whose light shines furthest, shines brightest nearest home.' (Anonymous)

The true spirituality of a church leader is not measured best by how well he leads a deacons meeting or an elders meeting, it is not gauged by the way he participates in all age Sunday school, or by the way he speaks from the pulpit—but by the way he treats his wife and kids at home when no one else is around.

A wee word to wives

How can we be the kind of people God wants us to be within the privacy of our own four walls? I want us to look first of all at the role carved out for the wife in the marriage relationship (*cf.* 5:22-24). It can be summed up in one word—submission. There are two main reasons for this:

- the Lordship of Christ, and
- the headship of the man in Christ.

When the Christian wife submits herself to Christ and lets him be Lord of her life, she will have no difficulty submitting to her husband. That perspective lifts this whole concept to a higher, holier, and more heavenly plane.

What woman in all the world who has met and fallen head over heels in love with the Lord Jesus would not willingly do anything for him?

- Never in the gospel narrative do we find a woman treating Jesus badly,
- never do we read of a woman speaking against him,
- never do we meet a woman doing anything to harm him.

In actual fact, the women of the New Testament loved and honoured Jesus—he was so manly, so honourable, so attractive, so kind, and so thoughtful. When we put two and two together, it was a logical step for them to submit themselves to the Lordship of Jesus Christ.

Is he better than me?

In relation to the home, this certainly does not mean that the wife becomes a veritable slave. Far from it. When she does what God wants her to do, when she is what God wants her to be, she actually enters into a whole new experience of freedom as her heart is bonded to her husband's in a genuine feeling of mutual love and respect.

Headship is not dictatorship! It has nothing to do with her husband ruling with a rod of iron. It can never command what God forbids or forbid what God commands. There should be no sense of threat or feeling of fear associated with this unique role she is called upon to fulfil.

As Jill Briscoe observes: 'A man of quality is never threatened by a woman of equality.' A country song says: 'A woman wants a man she can look up to who won't look down on her.' The *head* (*kephalē*) has authority but he is not to be authoritarian! There is no room for tyranny or bullying—'Me Tarzan! You Jane!'

The husband is not to treat his wife as a servant or a child, he is to treat her as an equal because she is one whom God has given him special responsibility for. She is not his to order about, she is not there to respond like a lapdog to his every whim and fancy, his every wish and command.

No matter what the husband says and thinks, he is not the boss!

A Christian wife who willingly and lovingly responds to her husband's leadership as to the Lord is an honour to the Lord and, in so doing, she pays an impressive testimony to the grace of God in her heart. It may be a silent tribute but it speaks volumes.

There is nothing demeaning about this for her submission is not to be an unthinking obedience to his rule but rather a grateful acceptance of his care. Whenever the husband's headship mirrors the headship of Christ—our Provider, Protector, Head, and Saviour—then the wife's submission to the protection and provision of his love, far from detracting from her womanhood, will positively enrich and enhance it.

Back to Eden

God's order in human relationships goes away back to the beginning of time—to the Garden of Eden—and we cannot go much further back than that! We read in Genesis 2:7 that God created the man first, investing in Adam the position of headship. God created the woman second, giving to Eve a subordinate but not subservient position in relation to the man (*cf.* Genesis 2:21, 22).

Adam was made to be ruled from his head and Eve was made to be ruled from her heart.

Paul develops his understanding of such a position when he points out that:

- woman was made *after* man,
- woman was made *out of* man, and
- woman was made *for* man.

He adds that man is also born from woman so that man and woman are dependent on one another (*cf.* 1 Corinthians 11:3-12; 1 Timothy 2:1-13). It was to this 'beginning' that Jesus himself went back when he confirmed his understanding of what happened in the Garden of Eden (*cf.* Matthew 19:4-6). And so must we! What creation has established, no culture is able to destroy!

Nevertheless, in this section, Paul's emphasis is on the order, mode, and purpose of the creation of Eve. There is nothing chauvinistic here, it is just God's way of doing things. As John Howard Yoder has said: 'Equality of *worth* is not equality of *role*.'

A rare jewel

When a wife exercises such an attitude of heart and mind, she will find total fulfilment in her ministry in the home and she will be seen, in every sense, as a complete woman.

Gone is the feminist syndrome, the chic emancipated woman mindset of the third millennium, and the modern woman of the twenty first century as promoted in many upmarket glossy magazines. In will be the wonderful wife so glamorously portrayed in Proverbs 31:10-31, someone whose worth is 'far more than rubies'.

If only he knew it, such a gem of a woman is a priceless asset to the man in her life.

5:25

Men and marriage

Having addressed one side of the coin of marriage, Paul looks at the other—the role of the husband. Actually, he has a lot more to say to him and about him than he did to the wives. The apostle sets for the

husband an exceptionally high standard for they are to *love [their]
wives just as Christ loved the church.*

With one stroke of the pen on the papyrus, the inspired Paul
elevates married love to the highest level possible for he sees in the
Christian home a beautifully profound illustration of the hugely
intimate and personable relationship between Christ and the
church.

A flick through the pages of Scripture reveals that God
established marriage for all the right reasons:

- Emotional—for love, companionship, and support (*cf.* Genesis
  2:18).
- Social—for procreation, when children are born into the home
  (*cf.* Genesis 1:28).
- Physical—for the pleasurable fulfilment of normal sexual
  desires (*cf.* 1 Corinthians 7:1-3).
- Spiritual—as they experience and share Christ with each other
  (*cf.* Ephesians 5:25-33).

Vital verbs

What stands out in Paul's development of this noble theme is the
sacrificial steadfastness of the heavenly bridegroom's covenant love
for his bride. Paul uses five verbs to indicate the unfolding stages of
Christ's long term commitment to his bride, the church—he *loved*
her, he *gave himself up* for her, to *make her holy,* having *cleansed*
her, that he might *present* her to himself.

This statement is so concise, complete, and comprehensive that
some biblical scholars think it may be a quotation lifted from an
early Christian confession, liturgy, or hymn.

Five verbs that trace Christ's unbreakable and unstoppable care
for his church from eternity past to eternity future.

Certainly the words *Christ loved (agapaō) the church,* preceding as they do his self sacrifice on her behalf, seem to look back to

his eternal pre-existence in which he set his love on his people and determined to come to save them.

Having loved the church, he *gave himself up* (*paradidōmi*) *for her.* That reference is, of course, primarily to the cross at Calvary. If the husband makes Christ's love for the church the pattern he adopts for loving his wife, then he will love her sacrificially.

We read that *Christ gave himself up* for the church, likewise, the husband, in love, gives himself unreservedly for his wife and to his wife—Jacob so loved Rachel that he happily worked and immolated fourteen long years to win her (*cf.* Genesis 29:14-30).

In my place

We are told in one of the Greek histories that the wife of one of the generals of Cyrus, the ruler of Persia, was accused of treachery and was condemned to die. At first her husband did not know what was taking place. But as soon as he heard about it he rushed to the palace and burst into the throne room. He threw himself on the floor before the king and cried out: 'Oh, my Lord Cyrus, take my life instead of hers. Let me die in her place.'

Cyrus, who by all historical accounts was a noble and extremely sensitive man, was touched by this offer. He said: 'Love like that must not be spoiled by death.' Then he gave the husband and wife back to each other and let the wife go free.

As they walked away happily the husband said to his wife: 'Did you notice how kindly the king looked at us when he gave you the pardon?'

The wife replied: 'I had no eyes for the king. I saw only the man who was willing to die in my place.'

Undying love

The brand of love Paul refers to is a boundless love—a love which keeps on loving even though the circumstances may be constantly changing all around us. There is nothing fickle or erratic, wishy washy or capricious, unpredictable or moody about it. This love is constant, unflagging, loyal, and unwavering!

This love has absolutely nothing to do with the other person's character, temperament, or personality—no matter what she is, or is not—she deserves to be loved, she needs to be loved.

This is love with no strings attached and no ulterior motives. It is a love which gives even when there may be a serious risk of not receiving something in return.

Macho man. God's man.

The world continually tells modern man to be macho and defend himself, to assert and bring attention to himself, to live totally for himself. But God breaks the mould when he challenges the Christian man to give himself up for others, especially his wife.

Headship implies a degree of leadership and initiative as when Christ came to woo and ultimately win his bride. But, more specifically, it implies sacrifice in a generous act of self giving for the sake of the one loved as when Christ gave himself for his bride. If headship means power in any sense, then it is:

- power to care, not to crush,
- power to serve, not to dominate,
- power to facilitate self fulfilment, not to frustrate or destroy it.

In all this, the standard of the husband's love is the cross of Christ on which he voluntarily surrendered himself, even to death, in his selfless and reckless love for his bride.

Love, love, love

If the husband's obligation to *love* is repeated three times (*cf.* 5:25, 28, 33), so is the requirement for him to model his attitude and behaviour on Christ as his role model.

- He is the *head* of his wife as *Christ is the head of the church* (5:23),

- he is to *love* his wife as *Christ loved the church* (5:25), and
- he is to *feed and care* for her as *Christ does the church* (5:29).

The highest pinnacle of demand is reached when the husband is exhorted to love his wife *as Christ loved the church and gave himself up for her*. Total self sacrifice. Calvary love. A Christian husband who even partially fulfils this ideal preaches the gospel without ever opening his lips—people can see in him that quality of love which took Jesus to his cross. It costs! Everything!

Samuel John Stone (1839-1900) echoed this truth when he penned:

> *The church's one foundation*
> *Is Jesus Christ her Lord;*
> *She is his new creation*
> *By water and the word;*
> *From heaven he came and sought her*
> *To be his holy bride;*
> *With his own blood he bought her,*
> *And for her life he died.*

5:26, 27

Till death us do part

Sacrificial love. Sanctifying love. The phrase *to make her holy* (*hagiazō*) is based on the word 'sanctify' or 'set apart'. In the marriage ceremony the husband is set apart to belong to his wife and the wife is set apart to belong to her husband. It is each to the other for as long as both are alive.

It has to be said that any interference from any quarter with this God given arrangement is sin.

Today, Jesus Christ is *cleansing* (*katharizō*) his church through the ministry of the word of God. The love of the husband for his wife should have a purifying influence on her so that both are becoming more and more like Christ. William Barclay comments that 'real love is the great purifier of life.' Even their physical relationship should be so controlled by God that it becomes a means of spiritual enrichment as well as personal enjoyment (*cf.* 1 Corinthians 7:3-5).

What every husband should know

The husband is not to use his wife purely for his own pleasure and satisfaction, rather he is to show the kind of love to her that is mutually rewarding and sanctifying. As her loving and devoted head, he serves her and prays for her and adores her with an unconditional love. The whole marriage experience is one of constant round the clock growth—intellectually, emotionally, and spiritually—when Christ is Lord of the home. Love always enlarges and enriches, it never stifles!

He will seek to protect his wife from the contamination of the world. He will never induce her to do that which is wrong or unwise, he will never expose her to that which is less than good. His love is such that he will only want the finest and best for her. Anything less is not good enough. As men, we have a huge responsibility! It is something each of us needs to ask ourselves personally:

- Is my wife more like Christ because she is married to me?
- Or, is she like Christ, in spite of me?

The imperfect church

The church today is not perfect, we all know that! It has many *stains* (*spilos*) and loads of *wrinkles* (*rhytis*).

'*Spots are caused by defilement on the outside, while wrinkles are caused by decay on the inside.*' (Warren Wiersbe)

Because the church becomes polluted and soiled by the world, it needs perennial cleansing, and the word of God is the cleansing agent. Strictly speaking, there should be no wrinkles in the church, because wrinkles are an evidence of old age and internal decay. As the church is nourished by the word, these wrinkles should disappear. Like a bonny and beautiful bride, the church should be clean and youthful, which is only possible through the Spirit of God using the word of God.

The perfect church

One day the church will be presented to the Lord Jesus in heaven as a *radiant* (*endoxos*)—glorious and gorgeous—church. On that special day, his transforming work will be finished and the romance of the ages will be sealed for time and eternity.

- The church *without stain*—she is beyond the reach of temptation.
- The church *without wrinkle*—she is beyond the reach of time.

What a day that promises to be. Exciting!

A bridal bath

I want us to backtrack for a moment and view these happenings from a slightly different perspective. Paul reminds us in verse 26 that it is the aim of Christ *to make [the church] holy, cleansing her by the washing with water through the word.*

Is this a deliberate allusion to the ritual, nuptial bath which took place before both Jewish and Greek weddings? In Athens, for instance, the bride was bathed in the waters of the Callirhoe, which was sacred to the goddess Athene. The tenses of the verbs suggest that the cleansing of the church precedes her consecration or sanctification. Indeed, the cleansing seems to refer to the initial purification or cleansing from sin and guilt which we receive when we first repent and believe in Jesus as Lord and Saviour. It is accomplished *by the washing of water with the word.*

I have a strong hunch that the *washing of water* is a clear and unambiguous reference to baptism, while the additional reference to *the word* indicates that baptism is no magical or mechanical ceremony. When it happens, it needs an explanatory word to define its significance—the same word will also express the promises of cleansing and new life in the Spirit which it symbolises, and it will also arouse our faith.

Presented to ...

The next logical step, having cleansed his bride by water and word, the heavenly bridegroom's plan is to sanctify her and finally *to present her to himself.* The sanctification appears to refer to the present process of making her holy in character and conduct by the power of the indwelling Holy Spirit, while the presentation has a distinct eschatological flavour associated with it, for it will take place when Christ returns to the air for his people (*cf.* 1 Thessalonians 4:16, 17).

We read that he will *present her to himself as a radiant church.* It is interesting to note that the word *endoxos* suggests that he will present her to himself in effulgent 'splendour'. The word may hint at the bride's intricately designed wedding dress since it is used of clothing in Luke 7:25 (*cf.* Revelation 19:7, 8). But it means more than this!

Glory!

Glory is the radiance of God! It is the shining forth and manifest-ation of his otherwise hidden being. So too, in that final day, the church's true nature will become apparent. In this world she is often seen in rags and tatters, she is frequently portrayed as stained and ugly, she is more often than not despised and persecuted.

On that day, her finest hour, she will be seen for what she is, nothing less than the exquisitely beautiful and glorious bride of Christ.

John Stott writes: 'It is to this constructive end that Christ has been working and is continuing to work.' The bride does not make herself presentable—it is the bridegroom who works hard behind the scenes to beautify her in order to present her to himself. His love and self sacrifice for her, his cleansing and sanctifying of her, are all designed for her liberation and her perfection, when at last he presents her to himself in her full glory. What a wonderful moment that will be!

5:28-30

Good for the goose, good for the gander

The love of the husband for his wife should also be a satisfying love. Having said that, after climbing with Paul to these sublime heights of romantic love, many of us sense an anticlimax in verse 28 where Paul says: *in this same way, husbands ought to love their wives as their own bodies.*

In his instruction to husbands to love their wives, he seems to come down from the lofty standard of Christ's love to the rather low standard of self love. Many commentators have been inventive in trying to wriggle their way out of this one! They have not succeeded for in the next sentence Paul pulls the rug from under their feet when he says: *he who loves his wife loves himself.*

The probable explanation for Paul's descent to the more mundane and legitimate level of self love is that he is always a realist. We cannot fully grasp the greatness of Christ's love for it surpasses knowledge (*cf.* 3:19). Nor do husbands find it easy to apply this standard to the realities of family life.

The payback principle

Greek mythology tells of a beautiful youth who loved no one until one day he saw his own reflection in the water and fell in love with that reflection. He was so lovesick that he finally wasted away and died and was turned into the flower that bears his name—*Narcissus.*

We cannot stand the sight of narcissism. Rightly so! But we all know from every day experience how to love ourselves—we know how to look after Number One. No coaching needed on that score! Hence the practical usefulness of the Golden Rule that Jesus enunciated—we should treat others as we would like them to treat us (*cf.* Leviticus 19:18; Matthew 7:12).

In the marriage relationship, the husband and wife are said to become *one flesh* (5:31). Apart from anything else, this means, whatever each does to the other, he does to himself or herself. It is a mutually satisfying experience with two huge pluses—it is a union of bodies and a union of personalities.

The man who loves his wife is actually loving his own body, since he and his wife are one flesh. As he loves her, he is 'nourishing' (KJV) and 'cherishing' (KJV) her—*he feeds* (*ektrephō*) *and cares* (*thalpō*) *for it*. When she needs strength, he gives her strength. When she needs encouragement, he gives her that. And so with every other thing she needs.

The marriage which is well blessed is the one where the husband loves his wife with unlimited caring.

Something is seriously wrong if a wife is looked at only as a cook to dish up the latest recipes, a housekeeper to keep the place neat and tidy, a laundry maid to wash and iron shirts, an occasional companion for the odd night out, or whatever. She is a God given treasure to be loved and cared for.

- To nourish a wife is to provide for her needs, to give her that which helps her grow and mature in favour with God and man.
- To cherish her is to use tender love and physical affection to give her warmth, comfort, protection, and security.

Winston Churchill once attended a formal banquet in London at which the attending dignitaries were asked the question: 'If you could not be who you are, who would you like to be?' Naturally everyone was curious as to what Churchill, seated next to his beloved Clemmie, would say.

When it finally came Churchill's turn, the old man, who was the dinner's last respondent to the question, rose and gave his answer. 'If I could not be who I am, I would most like to be'—here he paused to take his wife's hand—'Lady Churchill's second husband!'

Well done, Sir Winston! The old boy made some superbly good points that night but his apt comments also apply to everyone who already has a good marriage and aims to make it better.

Just as love is the circulatory system of the body of Christ, so love should be flowing through the veins in the Christian home. As Charles Swindoll writes: 'The Lord wants a husband's arms to be a safe place for his wife, as the church is in his arms.'

5:31-33

Eden revisited

Paul refers back in verse 31 to the creation of Eve and the forming of the first home in the garden of Eden. The full story is detailed in Genesis 2:18-24. Adam had to give part of himself in order to get a bride, but Christ gave all of himself to purchase his bride at Calvary. God opened Adam's side, but sinful men pierced Christ's side.

So united are a husband and wife that they are *one* (*heis*) *flesh* (*sarx*). Their union is closer than that of parents and children. The believer's union with Christ is even closer and, unlike human marriage, it will last for eternity. For a husband to love his wife as Christ loves his church, he must love her with an unbreakable love.

R. Kent Hughes makes the point that 'marriage ideally produces two people who are as much the same person as two people can be.' Christians in marriage have the same Lord, the same family, the same children, the same future, and the same destiny.

Paul's direct quote from Genesis 2:24 emphasises the permanence as well as the unity of marriage.

God's standard for marriage did not change from the time of Adam until the time of Paul, and it has not changed to this day.

Leaving and cleaving

One of the greatest barriers to a successful marriage is the failure of one or both partners to *leave (kataleipō) father and mother*. In marriage, a totally new family is begun and the previous relationships are to be severed as far as authority and responsibilities are concerned. Parents are always to be loved and cared for, but they are no longer to control the lives of their children once they are married.

The word 'cleave' (KJV)—*be united (proskollaō)*—literally means 'to be glued or cemented together'. A newly married couple break one set of ties as they establish the other. As they leave their parents, so they cleave to one another. They are interlocked.

Love and respect

Paul was a realist right to the very end and so he closes the chapter with a double parting shot when he says that *the husband must love his wife as he loves himself, and the wife must respect her husband.* In some ways, this is a succinct summary of the fuller teaching which Paul has been giving to husbands and wives.

For both—husband and wife—to do what is expected of them, they require the power of the Holy Spirit to enable them and the example of Christ to encourage them. When this is our daily experience, then we will really know heaven in our homes and our marriage will be a mirror of his awesome grace.

Paul began with one couplet—love and submission. He ends with another—love and respect.

We have seen that the love he has in mind for the husband is one that sacrifices and serves with a view to enabling his wife to become what God intends her to be. So the submission and *respect (phobeomai)* he asks of the wife expresses her response to his love and her desire that he too will become what God intends him to be in his leadership. Potential is, therefore, realised on both sides!

Divinely designed

It reverts back to verse 32 for the marriage of every believer is a fantastically brilliant illustration of the unique relationship—*a profound mystery*—between *Christ and the church.* Something sacred and special. A hint, perhaps, that in Christian marriage there are not two partners, but three—husband, wife, and Jesus Christ.

When it comes to marriage there is something we should never forget: it was God's bright idea in the first place! Marriage was a divine brain wave. John Phillips writes that 'the golden purpose of a Christian marriage was to make paradise complete—to bring heaven down to earth.'

Take 2

I find it ironic that the first and second references to love in the Bible actually occur when and where they do. The first is the love of the father for the son (*cf.* Genesis 22:2). Abraham loved Isaac, yet God demanded that he take his only son to mount Moriah and enact the scenes of Calvary. I believe the spiritual significance of this illumines all of a past eternity.

The second is the love of the son for his bride (*cf.* Genesis 24:67). On a similar note, I believe the spiritual significance of the marriage of Isaac and Rebekah illumines all of the endless ages yet unborn.

There are hidden depths in Christian marriage that are inextricably linked with God's eternal purposes. Paul gave us some fleeting glimpses of this in Ephesians 5 and a comprehensive study of Old Testament brides reveals so much more—for example, Adam and Eve, Isaac and Rebekah, Joseph and Asenath. If we take them together, these three marriages are pictures which typify the church's past, present, and future.

Spare rib

The story of Adam and Eve vividly illustrates the past and it shows us how the church was formed. Adam was put to sleep in the will of God. Then God opened his side and took from him what was needed to form his bride. This scene is reminiscent of Calvary where the Lord Jesus entered into the sleep of death in the will of God. Jesus' side was opened and out gushed water and blood, the elements that made possible the creation of the church, his bride.

A spiritual Cupid

The story of Isaac and Rebekah beautifully illustrates the present. Their love story typifies the work of the Father and the Spirit in finding a bride for the Son. In Genesis 22, Isaac went to the mountain as a willing sacrifice, obedient unto death. In Genesis 24, however, he was a passive observer waiting with his father for the coming of the bride. All the action was in the hands of the unnamed servant whom Abraham sent to seek, invite, persuade, and eventually bring the responsive bride to his son.

In this present age, the Son's work of redemption is finished and he sits on his Father's throne. The Holy Spirit is the active one. He is here to seek out a bride, the church, for the Father's beloved Son who is waiting at his right hand in glory.

Tomorrow's world

The story of Joseph and Asenath powerfully illustrates the exciting prospects of the church as told in Genesis 41:45. Asenath was taken from relative obscurity and elevated to share the lofty position occupied by Joseph at the right hand of Pharaoh. In the same way, our past is blotted out and our ultimate destiny is to sit with Christ on his throne and share his glory for all eternity.

Selah

Since the brides of the Bible are obviously intended to typify the unique relationship between Christ and his church, so the marriage of every believer on earth should do the same.

Anne Ross Cousin (1824-1906) was thinking along similar lines when she wrote:

The bride eyes not her garment,
But her dear bridegroom's face;
I will not gaze at glory,
But on my King of grace;
Not at the crown he giveth,
But on his piercèd hand:
The Lamb is all the glory
Of Immanuel's land.

6

Big on Conflict

6:1-3

Battle stations

This chapter is a familiar one, renowned as it is for the practical teaching it gives in relation to the ongoing conflict we face in the Christian life. With military precision, Paul shows us what we are to wear in the hour of battle—the armour of the soldier of the Lord (*cf.* 6:10-17).

Initially, Paul zooms in on two of the most fundamental relationships in our daily lives—*children* and *parents* (*cf.* 6:1-4) together with management *[masters]* and employees *[slaves]* (*cf.* 6:5-9). In a chapter that deals with conflict, it is ironic that both these areas have awesome potential for turning into a battle field!

All age worship

Paul pictures the local congregation in Ephesus and elsewhere as a church family, consisting of both sexes and people of all ages. Since he addresses the children in this paragraph as well as their parents, he evidently expects whole families to come together for public worship, to praise God and listen to the exposition of his word.

As a family unit—mum, dad, and 2.4 kids—they would hear the Old Testament Scriptures and the apostle's letters read aloud in their midst and explained. When the apostle's inspired comments were read out they would, most importantly, learn their own Christian duties. No doubt, human nature being what it is, they would also have more than a passing interest in the various duties assigned to other family members.

It's for you

I can just imagine the wives sitting up, all eyes and ears, listening with rapt attention to what was directed towards them. I can see the husbands sitting on the edge of their seats apprehensively wondering what was going to apply to their situation.

So far as the boys and girls were concerned, they would have heard in distinctive tones the responsibilities resting on their young shoulders, but they would also have heard of the unique role of their parents in their ongoing development.

It must have been quite an historic occasion when this epistle had its premiere reading—a moment to savour when it was first read out loud in public!

When life goes pear shaped

After watching a current affairs programme on television about young people, a disillusioned husband turned and said to his wife: *'Darling, what a mess! Where did our generation go wrong?'* The wife calmly answered: *'Honey, we had children!'*

We smile! However, I suppose many of us can readily identify with that tongue in both cheeks comment!

A kids charter

Let us look at what the Bible says about the attitude of children. The word that Paul uses for *children* (*teknon*) does not refer particularly to young children. He is not just talking about little people—boys and girls. He is speaking to all those who are still dependent on their parents. And he says they are to *obey* (*hypakouō*) them and *honour* (*timaō*) them.

- *Obey* has to do with action.
- *Honour* has to do with attitude.

These verses summarise the whole duty of a child manward and Godward. When there is a heart love for the Lord Jesus, there will be a real desire to do what is right in the home.

The child who is brought up to obey and honour his parents will always be sensitive to their wisdom, counsel, and welfare. The word *obey* literally means 'to hear under'. It means to listen with attentiveness and to respond positively to what is heard. In other words, children are to put themselves under the words and authority of their parents.

The little phrase *in the Lord* refers to the sphere of pleasing the Lord. It means when a child obeys his parents he is doing it for the sake of the Lord Jesus. When children obey their mothers and fathers it is a reflection of their obedience to the Lord Jesus Christ. The context makes it crystal clear that *in the Lord* applies right across the board—to honouring and obeying.

Parenting skills

Paul speaks here about *parents*—our mothers and fathers—and he implies that they are God's stewards. We must never forget that our children are loaned to us in trust by our heavenly Father.

Mothers and fathers are his proxy authority in relation to their children.

That is why children are commanded in another of Paul's epistles: 'Obey your parents in everything, for this pleases the Lord' (Colossians 3:20). The only exception to such obedience is in the matter of doing what is inherently wrong. If and when that happens and, hopefully, it will be very rare, then the abiding principle to steer by is found in the experience of Peter and John as recounted in Acts 4:19, 20.

A major message for minors

Why are children to treat their parents in such a manner? The basic reason we glean from verse 1 is that *this is right* (*dikaios*). This is God's standard! Who are we to mess around with it? If it is right, it cannot be wrong! It is the proper thing to do, it is the correct line of approach. It has nothing to do with psychological case studies and even less to do with the writings of learned individuals.

Having said that, it is not confined purely to Christian ethics—it is standard behaviour in every society. Pagan moralists, Greek and Roman, taught it. Stoic philosophers saw a son's obedience as self evident, it was the done thing, as it were! Much earlier, and in oriental culture, one of the greatest emphases of Confucius was on filial respect, so that still today, though centuries later, Chinese, Korean, and Japanese customs continue to reflect his influence. 'Indeed, virtually all civilisations have regarded the recognition of parental authority as indispensable to a stable society,' writes John Stott.

It is no wonder then that Paul included 'disobedience to parents' as a mark both of a decadent, degenerate society which God has given up to its own godlessness and as a clear indicator that we are living in the last days (*cf.* Romans 1:28-30; 2 Timothy 3:1, 2).

Swallow the tablet

Why then is it right for children to obey their parents? Because everything God commands is right. Simple! The right attitude behind the right act of obedience is *honour* and that is taken for granted in verse 2. It means 'to value highly and to hold in the highest regard and respect'. It is frequently used as a term of reverence, preciousness, and honour regarding God the Father and the Lord Jesus. It is also used by the Father in reference to the Son (*cf.* Hebrews 2:9; 2 Peter 1:17).

Children are to honour both their father and their mother. This is based on the Law that God gave to Moses on Mount Sinai (*cf.* Exodus 20:12). It is interesting to note that this is the only diktat of the ten that relates specifically to the family unit.

Since this is the fifth of the ten commandments and appears at first sight to concern our duty to our neighbour, many Christians have come along and unwittingly divided the Decalogue into two uneven halves of four and six—the first four commandments specifying our duties to God and the remaining six our duties to our neighbour.

The Jews did not fall into that trap! They regularly taught that each of the Law's two stone tablets contained five commandments. The significance of this arrangement is that it brings the honouring of our parents into line with our duty to God.

At least during our childhood, our parents represent God to us and they mediate to us both his authority and his love. We are to honour them by acknowledging their God given authority, and so give them not only our obedience, but our love and respect as well.

Off to a good start

When a young person grows up respecting his parents, it lays a good solid foundation for the rest of his life. Respect for other people will then flow naturally, it will be the norm. Generally speaking, it will not be a huge problem to him. The children have seen a lot of healthy mutual respect displayed in the home between mother and father and, for them, it will be a matter of course to follow their parents fine example in how they handle others throughout life.

'One generation plants the trees and the next gets the shade.'
(Chinese proverb)

What a tremendous blessing it is to see children who really love their parents. I find it a great thrill to walk into a home where there is a genuine respect for mum and dad, where there is loving discipline, and where boys and girls bring much joy rather than the pain of sadness to their parents.

Obviously, the finest recorded example we have is Jesus. As a child, he was subject to his parents and as he grew to manhood we read that 'he kept increasing in wisdom and stature, and in favour with God and men' (Luke 2:52). The Lord Jesus grew intellectually, physically, spiritually, and socially. His was a well-rounded experience, one of balanced development.

Get a life!

When this all happens in the context of a Christian home, the two-fold promise of verse 3 can then be claimed:

- *that it may go well with you*—the quality of life, and
- *that you may enjoy long life on the earth*—the quantity of life.

What a rich double blessing!

Live life to the full and have a full life.

That is the reward guaranteed to all those who honour their parents! Yes, children can do it. We should not underestimate them. On the other hand, we have to be realistic and not expect too much from them either. It is a matter of striking a balance in all our expectations.

Never too young

There are many excellent examples documented in Scripture:

- Samuel's close relationship to the Lord started when he was fairly young,

- King Josiah was the instigator of a spiritual revival in Judah when he was still a teenager,
- David was only a boy when the Lord first started using him,
- Queen Esther was a young woman when the Lord used her to save her people from ethnic cleansing,
- John the Baptist was filled with the Holy Spirit from his mother Elizabeth's womb.

6:4

First century fathers

This time fathers are singled out for special mention—much to any mother's relief, they do not get off the hook! Having said that, in the average home in today's western world, both parents should find this recommendation relevant and appropriate.

In Paul's day this was a totally new concept, especially for such nullifidian strongholds as Ephesus. The overwhelming majority of families were in a state of shambles, almost to the point of being dysfunctional. Mutual love among family members was almost unheard of. When it came to children, it was the survival of the fittest—the dog eat dog and the puppies do not survive syndrome!

In a male dominated society, a father's love for his children would have been extremely hard even to imagine. For example, a father would never take a child by the hand, he would never give it a cuddle! Roman law dictated that the father had virtual life and death powers over his entire household.

- He could throw his children out at any time,
- he could sell them off as slaves,
- he could make them work in his fields even in chains,
- he could take the law into his own hands for the law was in his own hands,
- he could even kill them, and
- he would be accountable to no one.

A new born child was placed at its father's feet to determine its fate. If the father picked the baby up, the child was allowed to stay in the home—if the father walked away, the child was simply disposed of. It was as clinical and as cruel as that! Discarded infants who were healthy and vigorous were collected each night and taken to the town forum from where they would be picked up and raised to be slaves or prostitutes.

Seneca, a renowned statesman in Rome at the time Paul was writing his letter to the church in Ephesus, said: *'We slaughter a fierce ox, we strangle a mad dog, we plunge a knife into a sick cow. Children born weak or deformed we drown.'*

Such hard bitten callousness makes me sick! Chilling. It sends a shiver down the spine, but that was life in the raw in the first century.

Fathering God's way

Completely different was the Christian father, especially if he remembered what Paul had written earlier, namely that his fatherhood was derived from the *one God and Father of all* (3:14, 15; 4:6). The overarching theme of Ephesians is that through the reconciling work of the Lord Jesus, there is now one multinational, multicultural family of God—we are an integral part of the international community of God's people.

Because of this linkup, it means that human fathers are to care for their families as God the Father cares for his. What on earth did Paul mean? How can this kind of thing happen? How can we avoid bringing out the worst in our children? Can we prevent it? Legitimate questions.

What kids think of their dads

'When I was sixteen my father didn't know anything. When I was

twenty two, I was amazed at how much he had discovered in six years.' (Mark Twain)

When we are young, we think we know it all—the older we get, the more we realise how little we really do know! That is the kind of mindset Paul is referring to when he says: *Fathers, do not exasperate (parorgizō) your children; instead, bring them up (ektrephō) in the training (paideia) and instruction (nouthesia) of the Lord.*

All credit to Paul, he obviously recognises how delicate a child's personality is. Some commentators have speculated that in his own childhood he was comparatively deprived of love and that, in this instruction to parents, there is a flashback to some early childhood reminiscence. Maybe. Maybe not. It may even have been the last thing on his mind.

How not to do it

How many angry young men, hostile to society at large, have learned their hostility as children in an unsympathetic home? How many youngsters have gone off the rails and made a mess of their lives because they have been brought up in an overly strict environment where love was rarely experienced?

Such treatment is not intended to have this effect, parents do it with the best will in the world, often they feel it is for the good of the child in the long term. None of us can rewrite history and, I imagine, if we had it all to do over again, there would probably be some changes that we would want to make if we had a second chance!

If we cannot turn the clock back, what can we do to turn the hearts of our young people back to home?

Well, it is a matter of realising there is a way to handle them, and there are certain things which we need to understand if we are going to pay more than lip service to Paul's serious injunction. How do parents succeed in bringing out the worst in their children?

- One, we wrap them in cotton wool.

Parents who smother their children, who overly restrict where they can go and what they can do, who never trust them to do things on their own, who continually question their judgment—such may be done under the umbrella of love, but it is fraught with serious danger. If we choose to go down this road we only end up building a barrier between parents and children, when the preferred option should be to build a bridge.

- Two, we play one child off against another child.

Favouritism is a big, big problem. Isaac favoured Esau over Jacob, Rebekah preferred Jacob over Esau. It caused huge problems then and it does the same today with their descendants. That is why we have one crisis after another in the cauldron of the Middle East, the repercussions of such an attitude are scarily frightening and they are felt for generations down the line.

For parents to compare their children with each other, especially in their presence, can be a devastating and demeaning experience for the child who is less favoured or talented. It is an awful putdown for a young child and they never forget it. Nine times out of ten, that child will become withdrawn or discouraged, they may even become resentful and bitter.

Nothing is achieved by talking one child down and talking the other child up!

- Three, we expect too much from them.

A child can be so pressured to achieve that he is virtually destroyed. The child quickly learns that nothing he does is sufficient to please his parents. No sooner does he accomplish one thing than he is challenged to accomplish something bigger and better. Parents have an unfortunate and uncanny knack of moving the goal posts.

It seems to me that some parents live in a world of fantasy and make believe—they want their kids to be high achievers, always performing at their peak. To them, anything less than an A grade is a failure!

- Four, we constantly nag at them.

A child who is never complimented and encouraged by his parents is usually destined for trouble. If the child is always told what is wrong with him and never told what is right, that child will soon lose hope and become convinced that he is incapable of doing anything right.

Today's innocence can quickly become tomorrow's delinquency.

At such a point the child has no reason to even try for he just cannot win anyway. He is on a hiding to nothing. Parents should always commend a child for what is good and they should seek to be positive in their praise. It does not take much to show how much we appreciate them and it always pays handsome dividends.

Nothing causes a child's personality to blossom and gifts to develop like the positive encouragement of loving and understanding parents. Children have a life and personality of their own—they are little people in their own right!

- Five, we see them as a pain in the neck.

Children who are made to feel that they are an intrusion or a nuisance in their parents lives, that they are always in the way and interfere with the plans and happiness of the parents, cannot help becoming resentful and riled. And it is perfectly understandable if they do. It does not matter who we are, we all need to feel as if we belong, we all need to feel loved and wanted.

- Six, we put an old head on young shoulders.

Chiding our children for always acting in a childish manner, even when what they do is perfectly normal and harmless for their age, does not contribute to their maturity. When parents get on their children's backs like this, it only helps confirm them in their childishness.

Every child must be allowed to be himself. Wise parents recognise that not all the non-conforming responses of childhood deserve to be styled as rebellion. On the contrary, it is by experiment that children discover both the limits of their liberty and the quality of their parents love. To help them grow up, they have to develop their independence, not because they are resistant to their parents authority, but because they need to exercise their own.

- Seven, we use love as a juicy carrot or a big stick.

We give a child our love when they are good and we withdraw it when they are bad. Oftentimes the practice may be unconscious, but a child, especially a sensitive child, can easily tell if a parent cares for him less when he is disobedient than when he behaves properly.

That is not how God loves us and it is not the way he intends we should love either. He disciplines his children just as much out of love as he blesses them. Even when discipline is meted out to a child, parents should take special care to reassure the child of their continued love.

- Eight, we go right over the top in our response.

When a child does something wrong, we can so easily over react. In moments like that, the punishment is not commensurate with the crime—it is the sledgehammer to crack a nut syndrome.

There is no point in using a cannon to kill a mosquito!

I heard someone say: 'I either get away with murder, or I get blamed for everything.'

It is a matter of striking a balance, being fair, and consistent. Sarcasm achieves absolutely nothing. Saying one thing and doing something different only confuses a child. Saying we are going to do it and not doing it only indicates to the child that we cannot be trusted. Sometimes we say things to our children that we would not dream of saying to anyone else for fear of ruining our reputation.

Remember, it is always dangerous for parents to discipline their children when they are annoyed, or when their pride has been injured, or when they have lost their temper.

Squaring the family circle

Paul does not rest content with a negative instruction to parents, he complements it with a positive instruction: *bring them up in the training and instruction of the Lord.* We are to lead our kids by setting a good example before them:

- we are to be totally loyal to them at all times and in all situations,
- we are to correct them when it is needful,
- we are to love them with no strings attached,
- we are to pray with them and for them, and
- we are to share biblical truth with them in a positive manner.

Training is not a one off event, it is an ongoing role. And it is one which can be enormously rewarding. It is interesting to note that the verb translated *bring them up* is the same word that is translated 'nourisheth' (KJV) in 5:29—it is almost as though we are going round in family circles, this is how the husband is to look after his wife and it is how he as a father is to relate to his children as well.

No passing the buck

The implications of this exhortation from Paul are many. One is that Christian parents must jealously guard their colossal responsibility— they may delegate some of it to both church and school, but they should never entirely surrender it. The ball is firmly in their court!

It is their God given task and nobody, nannies and baby sitters included, can adequately or completely replace them.

Another factor is that parents need to take quality time, unrushed time, to spend with their children. Failure to give them the attention they need and deserve when they are young will cause massive problems later.

'If parents but gave as much thought to the rearing of their children as they do to the rearing of animals and flowers, the situation would be very different.' (D. Martyn Lloyd-Jones)

Discipline matters

How then should parents rear their children? Answer: *in the training and instruction of the Lord.* The second word, whether translated *instruction* or 'warning' seems to refer primarily to verbal education, while the first word means training by discipline, even by punishment. This is the same word which is used in Hebrews 12:5-11 both of earthly fathers and also of our heavenly Father who 'disciplines us for our good, that we may share in his holiness'.

The need for such action is spelled out with remarkable clarity in the Old Testament. We have a couple of helpful insights in the book of Proverbs: 'He who spares the rod hates his son, but he who loves him is careful to discipline him,' and 'Folly is bound up in the heart of a child, but the rod of discipline will drive it far from him' (Proverbs 13:24; 22:15).

These verses in no way justify an excessively stern, draconian approach to discipline as evidenced in the harsh Victorian era. On the other hand, in our generation, we have witnessed an over-reaction leading to excessively *laissez faire* permissiveness. The pendulum has swung in the opposite direction!

'Spare the rod and spoil the child—that is true. But beside the rod keep an apple to give him when he has done well.' (Martin Luther)

It seems to me that, above all else, parents must be clear about their motives. Howard Hendricks says: 'Children are not looking for perfect parents, but they are looking for honest parents. An honest, progressing parent is a highly infectious person.'

A hug goes a long way!

The testimony of the distinguished painter Benjamin West is a superb illustration of this principle. He was young and one day his mother went out leaving him in charge of his younger sister, Sally. In his mother's absence, he discovered some bottles of coloured ink and, without giving it a second thought, decided to paint his sister's portrait. He made an awful mess.

When his mother came back she said nothing about the terrible ink stains. Instead she picked up the piece of paper on which he had been working and exclaimed: 'Why, it's Sally!' Then she stooped and kissed him.

Benjamin West used to say that 'my mother's kiss made me a painter!'

God is in the business of building homes! And when he builds it, he will bless it!

6:5-9

On the shop floor

Paul moves on to look at a slightly different topic when he addresses the hot potato of labour relations. What is the proper attitude for a Christian to adopt in relation to his work and how should he feel about those who occupy positions of management?

I believe those two pertinent questions bring this brief section into the third millennium. If we do not update it to the realities of life in today's world, we will still be thinking in terms of *slaves* (*doulos*) and *masters* (*kyrios*) which was par for the course in the first century. Slavery was part and parcel of the social and economic fabric of the ancient world.

In Paul's day, there was reckoned to be around 60,000,000 slaves in the Roman Empire—that is, one half of the total population was enslaved to the other half!

By and large, they constituted the work force, and included not only domestic servants and manual labourers but educated people like doctors, teachers, and administrators. Slaves could be inherited or purchased, they could be acquired in settlement of a bad debt. Prisoners of war were considered fair game and more often than not they ended up as slaves. Nobody queried the *status quo*, nobody dared challenge the arrangement, such was life in the first century, and that was that.

No human rights

Slaves were not treated as persons, they had no standing, they had no rights. To all intents and purposes, they were *persona non grata*. They were regarded more as 'things' as if they were some kind of inanimate object.

The dehumanisation of slaves in the public mind was mirrored in early Roman legislation. Legally they were only chattels without rights, whom their master could treat virtually as he pleased—he could do whatever he wanted with them.

The Roman state left the problem of the discipline of the slaves to their owners and some of the stories which emerged from this period are grim and gruesome, to say the least. Some of the awful atrocities committed against them were nothing short of barbaric, such as the slave of Augustus who was crucified because he killed a pet quail.

The reality is, some of these masters were no better than mindless and senseless thugs. Slaves were sometimes whipped, mutilated, and imprisoned in chains, their teeth knocked out, their eyes gouged out, they were even thrown to the wild beasts or crucified, and all this for the most trivial and petty offences. The fact that some slaves ran away, risking if caught, branding, flogging, and even summary execution, while others committed suicide, is sufficient evidence that cruelty towards them was widespread.

'*The terror of the slave was that he was absolutely at the caprice of his master.*' (William Barclay)

Slaves and saints

It is quite remarkable that Paul should even address himself to slaves. The fact that he did indicates that they were accepted members of the Christian community and that he regarded them as responsible people to whom, as much as to their masters, he sends a moral appeal.

If children are to *obey* their parents (*cf.* 6:1), slaves are to *obey* (*hypakouō*) their earthly masters (*cf.* 6:5). The same word is used in both instances. And they are to do it for the same reason, namely that behind them they must learn to discern the figure of their *Master* (*kyrios*) in heaven, Jesus Christ (*cf.* 6:9). In each of the four verses dedicated to this subject, Jesus Christ is mentioned in each one:

- They are to be *obey* just as they *would obey Christ* (6:5),
- they are to behave as *slaves of Christ* (6:6),
- they are to *serve* as if it was *the Lord*, not men (6:7), and
- they are to do it, knowing *the Lord will reward them* (6:8).

Jesus—super slave

My heart is moved when I see the Christ centred nature of this instruction. So striking, it hits us between the eyes. You see, the slave's perspective has dramatically changed. His horizons have broadened. He has been liberated from the slavery of men pleasing into the glorious freedom of serving Jesus Christ. His mundane tasks have been absorbed into a higher preoccupation, namely *the will* (*thēlema*) *of God* and the good pleasure of Christ (*cf.* 6:6).

It seems to me that exactly the same principle and mindset can be applied by contemporary Christians to their work and employment. Our great need is the clear sightedness to see Jesus Christ and to set him before us.

I was impressed when I read what John Stott had to say on this matter: 'It is possible for the housewife to cook a meal as if Jesus Christ were going to eat it, or to spring clean the house as if Jesus Christ were to be the honoured guest. It is possible for teachers to educate young people, for doctors to treat patients and nurses to care for them, for solicitors to help clients, shop assistants to serve customers, accountants to audit books, and secretaries to type letters as if, in each case, they were serving Jesus Christ.'

Sound of silence

When we are on this theme, now is probably the best time to answer the question which a few folk are fairly keen to ask. What do we say to those who condemn Paul because, when he had the chance, as here, he did not denounce slavery outright? I think there are three lines of argument.

One, although Paul did not condemn slavery in Ephesians 6, he certainly did not condone it. Two, Paul's discussion of the duties of Christian slaves and the responsibilities of Christian masters transforms the institution, even if it falls short of calling for its abolition. Three, it was this transformation which came from viewing all persons as made in God's image that ultimately destroyed slavery and continues to transform work relationships today.

A different agenda

I want us to fast forward Paul's teaching and bring it right up to the present time as we focus on the relationships which we experience in the workplace. The emphasis in these verses can be transferred across to all employees and how they get along with their employers, it is what happens on the shop floor that really counts, albeit what takes place in the boardroom with the CEO is also of some significance. When all is done and dusted, it is a relatively simple matter to earth Paul's comments to life in the fast lane of the third millennium.

Verse 5 indicates that, in all our work, we should exhibit an attitude which is not the 'do as little as you can for as much as you can get' mindset! Nor should it be an obsequious 'Yes, sir! No, sir! Three bags full, sir!' Charles Swindoll is right when he says that 'the way we conduct ourselves at work speaks volumes more than all the hours we spend at church.'

Being a Christian should always make a person a better, more productive, and more agreeable worker.

People will not be inclined to listen to the testimony of a Christian whose work is never up to scratch. They will immediately switch off when someone who is always complaining opens his mouth and tries to tell them about Jesus. No matter how good, bad, or indifferent our employer is, we should always give him our best and we must always do our best.

Wax free

The phrase *sincerity (haplotēs) of heart* speaks of integrity and that is what Paul is advocating we should all display. He urges us not to have any ulterior motives and he pleads with us to do our work without any shades of hypocrisy in our heart. The word actually comes from two Latin words: *sine* meaning 'without' and *cera* meaning 'wax'.

In the ancient world, where the making of pottery was an important industry, dishonest potters would sometimes cover up cracks or flaws in the pottery by filling them with wax. In normal usage this might not be detected. But it could be seen if the pottery was held up to the light before it was purchased and, when that happened, the wax would show up as a lighter hue.

Good pottery was often stamped with the words *sine cera* (without wax) as a proof of its excellent quality. In the Greek language there is a corresponding word that means 'sun tested'.

The word which Paul uses in this sentence is a slightly different word which has the idea of generosity or liberality as well as sincerity. It suggests that the employee should not hold back from his best but that he should actually pour himself out liberally in honest service.

The photofit is that of an exemplary worker being one who is enthusiastically keen to do his best at all times—he will do that and be that—even when his boss is not the easiest person to get along with.

Look! The boss is coming!

Verse 6 challenges us to be diligent for it reads: *obey them not only to win their favour (anthrōpareskos) when their eye (ophthalmodoulia) is on you, but like slaves of Christ, doing the will of God from your heart.* You see, it is not a matter of having one eye on the clock and the other eye on the boss, it should be both eyes on the job in hand, only then will we be doing the will of God. There is a need for us to be conscientious and punctilious in all that we do.

It is not a case of us working flat out when the boss is around in order to curry favour with him, we are servants of Christ no matter what the environment may be and the Lord is watching all the time and he is not impressed with shoddy work. We need to remind ourselves that there is no dichotomy between the secular and the spiritual—no matter what kind of work we are doing, it should always be carried out as a ministry unto the Lord. Solomon challenges us: 'Whatever your hand finds to do, do it with all your might' (Ecclesiastes 9:10).

Motivation

Paul elevates work to a higher plane with his upbeat remarks in verses 7 and 8: *Serve wholeheartedly (eunoia), as if you were serving the Lord, not men, because you know that the Lord will reward (komizō) everyone for whatever good (agathos) he does.* When it comes to work,

- we do it—not out of a sense of discipline—I have to,
- we do it—not out of a sense of duty—I ought to,
- we do it—out of a sense of devotion—I want to.

Our work should be done with a willing heart and when we do it we should be smilingly cheerful in our disposition. It does not matter if the job is boring or if it keeps us on our toes, we need to put our heart and soul into it. It is not the attitude that says: 'How can I soar with the eagles when I have to work with turkeys like you!' The exciting prospect at the end of the day is that God's pay day is coming.

Perhaps you have seen the Norman Rockwell-style painting of the man asleep with a grand smile across his face, and above him in the sky a deliciously beautiful apple pie—the focus of his dreams. Here, for all of us, is the great incentive, the ultimate in terms of motivation! And it is not pie in the sky!

The story is told of an elderly missionary couple who were returning home on a ship after many years of sacrificial service in Africa. On the same ship was Theodore Roosevelt. He had just ended a highly successful big game hunt. As the ship docked in New York harbour, there were thousands of well-wishers and dozens of reporters to welcome Roosevelt home. There was not a single solitary person there to welcome the missionaries home.

As they made their way to a cheap hotel for the night, the man turned to his wife in the back of the yellow taxi and said: *'It just doesn't seem right. We give forty years of our lives to Jesus Christ to win souls in Africa, and nobody knows or cares when we return. Yet the president goes over there for a few weeks to kill some animals and the whole world sits up and takes notice.'*

A few hours went by and before they went to bed that night, the two of them prayed together and the Lord seemed to say to them: *'Do you know why you haven't received your reward? It's because you're not home yet!'*

Highly effective managers

Paul addresses the attitude of good management in verse 9 with the comment: *Treat (poieō) your slaves in the same way. Do not threaten (apeilē) them, since you know that he who is both their Master and yours is in heaven, and there is no favouritism (prosōpolēmpsia) with him.*

All those engaged in any kind of management role have a mutual responsibility—hence the phrase: *treat your slaves in the same way.* If the employer expects his workers to do their best for him, he must do his best for them. If we hope to receive respect, show it— if we hope to receive service, give it. It is the golden rule in action!

'You draw more flies with honey than you do with vinegar.' (Anonymous)

There is no way that middle and senior management can dispense with the very courtesies and *politesse* that they expect to be shown. One may be a worker and the other a boss, but when it comes to common civility, both operate on a level playing field.

Boss, yes! Bossy, no!

Clear guidelines are established when the apostle intimates that management should never abuse their power or take advantage of their position.

'The chief is servant of all.' (African proverb)

In the final analysis, threats are a weapon which the powerful wield over the powerless. A relationship based on threats is not a human relationship at all. Standing over someone with a big stick does not achieve anything.

Back in the days of Paul, slave owners were used to being flattered and fawned upon—they should not expect such discriminatory favouritism from the Lord Jesus. If they go looking for it, they are in for a shock, they just will not get it, for the Lord does not treat people like that!

I think what matters to most ordinary decent people—blue collar, white collar, no collar—is this: they want to feel as if they are genuinely appreciated, they detest it when they are taken for a ride, they feel it when they are taken for granted. People want to be treated as real persons and they want to be treated with dignity. And that is what Christianity unequivocally declares:

- We do have real worth!
- We are made in God's image!
- What we do does matter!

6:10

Fight the good fight

In this final section of his epistle, Paul handles the reality of Christian warfare as he focuses on the Christian and his battles. It goes without saying and, we know from personal experience, that the Christian life is not a playground, it is more like a battle ground. It is not a place for fooling around, it is a place where the fight is on. It is warfare on a grand scale. Robert Louis Stevenson once said: 'You know the Caledonian Railway Station in Edinburgh? One cold, east windy morning, I met Satan there!'

- There is a conflict to be faced, and
- an enemy to be overcome.

When God begins to really bless us, Satan begins to attack us.

Whether we like it or not, we will meet stiff and onerous opposition and, the further down the road we go with the Lord, the more intense the battle becomes. Be warned, it does not get any easier, if anything, the struggle becomes ever greater. When we are out there in the trenches, on the front line, we know we are operating in enemy territory, we know we are in a war zone.

But, thank God, there is victory in Jesus. Paul says elsewhere that 'we are more than conquerors through him who loved us' (Romans 8:37). Martin Luther reminds us:

> *The Prince of Darkness grim,*
> *We tremble not for him;*
> *His rage we can endure,*
> *For lo, his doom is sure;*
> *One little word shall fell him.*

Even though we may be caught in the crossfire, it is quietly reassuring to know that the battle is the Lord's. Sure, there are times when it is extremely hard to tell who the real enemy is and where he is firing from but, even then, our hopes and our sights are pinned on Jesus.

Facing reality

Having marvelled at the sheer breadth of Paul's horizons in the previous chapters, the same man now brings us down to earth with a bump when he challenges us to face realities harsher than dreams. He reminds us of the opposition—the ugly blood and grime of war with the devil—for it is not all plain sailing when we give our lives to Jesus, it is not all sunshine when we walk in ways that please the Lord.

Paul introduces us to the devil and to certain aides at his command. He supplies us with no biography of the devil and no account of the origin of the forces of darkness. He assumes their existence as common ground between himself and his readers. In any case, his purpose was not to satisfy our curiosity, but to warn us of their malevolent hostility and teach us how to overcome them.

Is God's plan to create a new society? Then the minions of darkness will do their utmost to destroy it! Has God through Jesus Christ broken down the walls dividing human beings of different races and cultures from each other? Then the devil through his emissaries will strive to rebuild them! Does God intend his reconciled and redeemed people to live together in harmony and purity? Then the powers of hell will scatter among them the seeds of discord and sin! It is with these unfriendly powers that we are told to wage war.

No hiding place

Paul emphasises the reality of our engagement with the powers of evil and the grim necessity of hand to hand combat. The abrupt transition from the peaceful homes and healthful days of earlier chapters to the hideous malice of devilish plots in this section causes us a painful shock, albeit an essential one.

I suppose we have all wished at one time or another that we could spend the rest of our lives in undisturbed tranquillity among our loved ones at home and in the sweet fellowship of God's people. Such an aspiration, I am afraid, is living in cloud cuckoo land. Dream on!

You see, the way of the escapist has been effectively blocked. Christians have no alternative other than face the inexorable prospect of conflict with God's enemy and theirs. We have no option but to accept the implications of this concluding passage of Paul's letter.

'It is a stirring call to battle. We are being roused, we are being stimulated, we are being set upon our feet; we are told to be men.' Dr D. Martyn Lloyd-Jones goes on to say that 'the whole tone is martial, it is manly, it is strong.'

The struggle continues

The fact is—we need to keep this to the front of our minds—there will be no cessation of hostilities, not even a temporary truce or ceasefire, until the end of life or history is wound up and the peace of heaven is attained!

The chances are that is what Paul means when he uses the word *finally* (*loipos*) to kick start verse 10. Having said that, many of the better manuscripts opt for the word 'henceforward' meaning 'for the remaining time'. If this is the preferred translation, then Paul is indicating that the whole of the interim period between the Lord's two comings is to be characterised by conflict.

'The peace which God has made through Christ's cross is to be experienced only in the midst of a relentless struggle against evil. And for this the strength of the Lord and the armour of God are indispensable.' (John Stott)

Be encouraged!

With that in mind, I want us to explore these few verses together and take fresh heart from what Paul says to us. First, we have a tremendous word of encouragement: *be strong (endynamoō) in the Lord and in his mighty (ischys) power (kratos).*

That is all we need to know! We can depend upon the Lord and, with his touch upon our lives, we can face the enemy, eyeball to eyeball. If we did not have the assurance that we could draw on our divine resources, we would be doomed to failure. It would be one big flop for, in ourselves, we are no match for the enemy.

Normally, when we think of such a conflict, we shrivel on the inside, we get the shrinks syndrome, the legs get the wobbles and quickly turn to jelly, the heart beats faster—we just do not relish it. Period.

Most of us, at any rate, do not go spoiling for a fight so we feel seriously threatened, we feel inadequate, we sense that we are insufficient and it is all too much for us, we are out of our depth, we feel weak even at the thought of it. Sure we do!

But, we can do it, in his *strength*—we can do it, in his *mighty power.* On our own, we are impotent, our hands are tied behind our back. With the Lord, we have no qualms, we have nothing to quibble about for we are sure of victory.

Strength for today

The cardinal truth woven into the fabric of Ephesians is that we are 'in Christ' and we are 'one' with him. That means his life is our life, his power is our power, his truth is our truth, his way is our way and, as Paul goes on to say in verse 10, his strength is our strength.

It is the Philippians 4:13 principle which is not only good sound theology, it is better than that, it is excellent applied theology.

No matter what the enemy may throw at us, no matter how he may try to outwit us and outgun us, no matter what sinister tactics he may use to plot our downfall, we do not need to worry when we have the Lord on our side. We fight from the place of victory because Calvary and the empty tomb make all the difference.

6:11

Be enlightened!

Paul tells us to *put on the full armour (panoplia) of God so that [we] can take [our] stand.* In other words, if we want to take maximum advantage of the strength of God's mighty power, we need to put on the total armour that he has graciously provided for us.

The words *put on (endyō)* carry the idea of once and for all, of permanence. The battle kit is not something we put on and take off occasionally. No! It has to be put on and kept on permanently. It is not a uniform to wear only while playing a dangerous sport and then we remove it after a couple of hours when the ref has blown the final whistle and the game is over. The armour of God—our protective clothing—should be our lifelong companion.

Essential equipment

Then, and only then, will we be able to hold our ground. There will be no need to backtrack or even give the enemy an inch, we will not succumb to the sucker punch delivered from the hand of the enemy.

I imagine Paul was probably chained to a Roman soldier when he penned these words and, as he looked at the soldier's armour, he was inspired by the Holy Spirit to see in it the fitting analogy of God's spiritual provision for our battle with Satan and his angels.

To stand (*histēmi*) means to hold a critical position while under sustained attack. A similar sentiment is echoed in the words of the glorified Christ to the church in Thyatira when he said: 'Hold on to what you have until I come' (Revelation 2:25; *cf.* Revelation 3:11).

The devil's game plan

Why do we need the armour of God? That is the six million dollar question. It is to repel what Paul calls *the devil's schemes* (*methodeia*)—his *modus operandi*. Most of us realise that the enemy has many names in the Bible but the most common attributed to him are *devil* (*diabolos*) and Satan (*Satanas*).

- As the devil, he is the accuser—he constantly assails us before the Lord.
- As Satan, he is the adversary—he persistently opposes God.

The devil will do all in his power to prevent us from entering into our birthright as the children of God. In her autobiography, Agatha Christie described a trip she made in northern Iraq where she came across some conclusive evidence of the Yezidee people. She described them as a people who worshipped the 'peacock angel Lucifer'.

That is a marvellous name for him because it emphasises his strutting arrogance and theatrical attractiveness with which he has deceived so many. That is how he comes to us today—his breathtaking beauty is a major part of the charm offensive technique of deception.

The devil's ability to imitate and impersonate many of the gifts God gives to his children is something we need to also take into serious account when we find ourselves battling against him.

Victory!

The good news: the evil one is a defeated foe. We should never forget that 'having disarmed the powers and authorities, [Christ] made a public spectacle of them, triumphing over them by the cross' (Colossians 2:15). Ah, we stand in Christ on the victory side of the cross.

The enemy may rage and roar, he may act and look like a proverbial Goliath, he may appear a formidable foe. It is a bit like the walls of Jericho syndrome—at a glance he seems too big for us and too much for us. We could be forgiven for thinking that he is too hot to handle. That may be true, but the tamper proof facts remain:

- the devil is thoroughly powerless before a child of God who is clothed in the full armour of God,
- the devil is totally powerless before a child of God who is filled with the Holy Spirit of God, and
- the devil is utterly powerless before a child of God who is strong in the power of God.

Stalked by Satan

I am so glad and enormously relieved that God does not throw us unprotected into the theatre of battle against Satan's illusory empire. The word translated *schemes* or 'wiles' (KJV) carries with it the notion of craftiness, cunning, and ostensible deception (*cf.* 4:14).

It was frequently used of a wild animal who cunningly stalked and then unexpectedly pounced on its prey. That is how the enemy works—his schemes are built around stealth and plausible deception. 'Satan has us,' writes Charles Swindoll, 'in the crosshairs of his scope.'

The devil has a bag full of dirty tricks, we cannot possibly know them all, but God does.

Taking the devil seriously

The fall of the human race hinged on two pivots—deception and disobedience. Eve was deceived, Adam was disobedient. I believe Satan is unremitting in his efforts to take full advantage of those two beachheads he has established. He has done so with tragic success. Most of the world lies in his lap and most of the people around us are eating out of the palm of his hand.

Paul takes the devil seriously when he refers to him in the manner in which he does. It is because the devil seldom attacks openly, preferring darkness to light, that when he transforms himself into an angel of light we are caught with our guard down. He is a dangerous wolf, but enters Christ's flock in the disguise of a sheep. Sometimes he roars like a lion, but more often is as subtle as a serpent.

We must not imagine, therefore, that hostility, persecution, and open temptation to sin are his only or even his commonest weapons—far from it, he prefers to seduce us into compromise and delude us into error.

6:12

Know your enemy

Paul says two things about the enemy:

- this is not an ordinary run-of-the-mill battle for *our struggle (pale) is not against flesh (sarx) and blood (haima)*, and
- our principal enemies are not people.

We must see beyond people. Satan may use people to persecute us, to lie to us, to cheat us, to hurt us, or even kill us, but our real enemy lurks in the shadows of the unseen world.

He moves people as pawns on the chess board of time.

Oh yes, people are involved. But they are not the real problem. Our greatest enemy is not the world we see, it is the world we cannot see—'an invisible war' (John Bunyan). The ingenious opponent of God's people will get us in the ring and, when he does, he will try to trip us and throw us.

Sinister forces

There is more to it than meets the human eye. It is an occult battle. As I said, our primary struggle is not with human beings but with cosmic intelligences—our enemies are not human but demonic. Paul lists four distinct groups against whom we grapple:

- *the rulers (archē),*
- *the authorities (exousia),*
- *the powers of this dark world (kosmokratōr),*
- *the spiritual (pneumatikos) forces of evil (ponēria) in the heavenly realms.*

This quartet of ruthless evil forces who work against us are really descriptive of the different ranks in the army of demons. Each of them is prefaced in the chapter with the word *against (pros)*. They represent a particular category of demonic activity having different levels of authority.

Satan is alive and well on planet earth.

The enemy is real! The forces of hell arrayed against us are highly organised and superbly structured so that their impact can be devastating and deadly.

Five star generals

We wrestle against the *rulers*—the princes who share with Satan the power that he wields over fallen angels, evil spirits, and this world.

The word Paul uses to describe them can be translated 'chief ruler' which means they are high ranking officials in Satan's government— five star generals in his army.

We learn from Daniel that Satan actually deploys rulers or princes over various kingdoms of men on earth—for example, we read of the 'prince of Persia' and 'the prince of Greece' (Daniel 10:20). Remember Daniel prayed and for a solid three weeks the answer to his prayer was delayed because this prince was powerful enough to frustrate the efforts of God's angel as he left heaven to minister to Daniel upon earth (*cf.* Daniel 10:12-14).

These emissaries of hell wield enormous power but, thank God, through prayer and the help of the Lord, we can win the fight.

Damage limitation

We also wrestle against Satan's understudies as this is what is meant by the term *authorities*. Satan can do so much and no more. He can go so far and no further. He is limited. Significantly limited.

- He knows a lot—but he is not omniscient. God alone is!
- He has incredible power and can even work miracles—but he is not omnipotent. God alone is!
- He can be here one moment and somewhere else the next—but he cannot be everywhere at once for he is not omnipresent. God alone is!

So how does the devil compensate for his obvious limitations? His calculated strategy is to use those to whom he has delegated authority and a measure of power—they gather information, influence events, implement his schemes, inflict woe and bondage on men, laugh at man's blindness in refusing to even believe they exist, manipulate men, and encourage sin.

It would appear that most people in today's world do not believe in evil spirits *per se*. Some may be interested in the occult or fascinated with the paranormal, others are spellbound with ghosts and witches. However, the man sitting on the fringe laughs at the idea of the devil playing havoc with the lives of millions. Some hard questions need to be asked in today's climate:

- Why can we not put a halt to the drug trade?
- Why has it been so hard to pass tougher laws against drink driving?
- Why has homosexuality become an acceptable way of life in our society?
- Why is pornography such big business?
- Why can we not stamp out child abuse?
- Why the horrors of war?

Make no mistake about it, our world has been invaded from outer space by hordes of demons. They are there and they are hyperactive in our day and generation. If we hope to overcome them, we need to bear in mind that they have no moral principles, no code of honour, no higher feelings, no scruples, and no Geneva convention to restrict or partially civilise the weapons of their warfare.

In a word, they are savagely ruthless!

Global connections

The third clip Paul shows us—*the powers of this dark world*—is a clear indicator of their chicanery and duplicity. The word only occurs here in the New Testament and it means 'world rulers'. This would indicate something of the devil's masterplan for holding the world in subjection by shifty dealings.

The devil keeps people in a state of spiritual blindness, he has invented every false religion, he is behind every false philosophy which is peddled in our universities and colleges, he is the brain behind every false ideology and every false theory.

Think of the huge number of cults that are a caricature of the glorious gospel of sovereign grace. Think of the vast range of philosophies which control the mindset of millions of people around the world. Where do these all come from? Why are they so attractive? How can they recruit people and then hold them in fanatical devotion? How can they multiply their adherents? At the end of the day, that is Satan's task.

He specialises in blinding men and women, boys and girls. He pulls the wool over people's eyes. He has no qualms about leading people up and down the garden path or taking them into a blind alley. But he does more, he keeps them blind.

- Why do so many eminent scientists teach evolution as a fact, when it is only a theory?
- How can anyone be so callous and desensitised as to extinguish human life in the mother's womb?
- What leads ordinary people to suppress their innate knowledge of God and to declare themselves atheists?
- From where do men and women get the idea that there is no absolute right and wrong?

There is only one answer to each of these pertinent questions. It is the devil who has successfully conned them. Such people, whether they know it or not, are doing a ceilidh in the dark with the devil.

Hell's angels

We also wrestle against Satan's countless demons, referred to by Paul as *the spiritual forces of evil in heavenly realms.* They are 'spiritual agents from the very headquarters of evil' (J B Phillips). The unseen world is swarming with millions of demons. The devil has countless hordes of evil spirits at his disposal and each one is totally committed to the cause. The word translated *evil* implies that the decadence and depravity of our age is demon inspired.

The devil's agenda

Demons are obsessed with holding people enslaved to their senses. The devil drives them over the edge so that they fall headlong into all sorts of sexual and sensual sin—perversion, pornography, and permissiveness are encouraged, promoted, and aided by evil spirits whose goal it is to destroy the human race. We are engaged in a spiritual war of cosmic dimensions.

It is almost an understatement to say that men are slaves to sin and in bondage to Satan. The devil has them where he wants them—under his control. That is why it is as bad as it is and that is why it is not getting any better, if anything, it is getting progressively worse.

I do not want to minimise the capability of his strike power, but let us not fall into the trap of making him bigger than he really is—in other words, do not overestimate him. Having said that, let us not swing the pendulum to the other extreme and underestimate him either.

'*In the New Testament it is not believers who tremble at the power of Satan, but demons who tremble at the power of God.*' (Stephen Travis)

Well said!

6:13

Be enabled!

The apostle begins with the word *therefore* for what he says now is linked to what has gone before. Because of who the enemy is, because of where he is, because of what he is doing, we are to *put on the full armour of God*. What is the prime reason behind this two times repeated command? It is so that we might be able *to stand!* In other words, we are to give no ground to Satan, not even as much as a centimetre.

Stand up, stand up for Jesus

I think it is obvious from the words which Paul uses that the big concern on his mind is for Christian stability. He wants us *to stand*

and that posture is of such importance that he says it four times (*cf.* 6:11, 13, 14).

Wobbly Christians who have no firm foothold in Christ are an easy target for the devil.

And Christians who shake like reeds and rushes cannot resist the howling wind when the principalities and powers begin to blow. Paul's aspiration is to see Christians so strong and stable that they remain firm against the devil's wiles in *the day of evil*, that is, in a time of special pressure. For such stability, both of character and in crisis, the armour of God is essential.

The danger is that we can become far too comfortable in our Christianity—cosy, cushioned, and complacent—that we become oblivious to the seriousness of the battle raging all around us. We cannot opt out as a draft dodger or run away as a defector. There is no such a thing as being AWOL and there are no exemptions granted.

We are in a battle and we are meant to be crack troops in God's army, not spiritual softies in dad's army!

Not forgotten heroes

A lovely running commentary that illustrates this is found in 2 Samuel 23 where David's mighty men are listed. The grand review comes at the end of his illustrious reign and just before Solomon's glorious kingdom was established.

Adino was true to David in the place of great danger when he faced 800 men in one skirmish and ended up killing them all (*cf.* 2 Samuel 23:8). Much could be said of Eleazer who stood for God in the face of desertion. The Holy Spirit says after his great victory that the troops returned 'only to strip the dead' (*cf.* 2 Samuel 23:10).

Shammah stood for God in the place of discouragement. We might expect to see valour blaze in the defence of some strategic pass or bridge, not for him. He saw value 'in a piece of ground full of lentils' when he bravely stood against the Philistines and won the day (*cf.* 2 Samuel 23:11, 12).

Never say die!

That is what we need to do. We need to be loyal to great David's greater Son, the Lord Jesus Christ. And in spite of what the enemy can do and may do, we should remain standing. In such scary moments it is always helpful to recall the words of the Lord to Jehoshaphat as he faced the greatly superior forces of Moab and Ammon: 'Do not be afraid or discouraged because of this vast army. For the battle is not yours, but God's' (2 Chronicles 20:15).

Some of the greatest thrills come in the greatest victories and, invariably, the greatest victories come from the greatest clashes.

Enemy showdown

When we engage the enemy, there is no need for us to bend, go blankety blank, or buckle under pressure! We can look him straight in the eye when our confidence is rooted in the Lord. We need to remember that the Lord—the strategist *par excellence*—is on our side and he is committed to looking after us. But he expects us to keep our side of the bargain and follow his operational plan by putting *on the full armour of God*. Why? So that we can stand up to the enemy in the fierce heat of the scrum.

The adversary will do all in his power to knock us down and take us out. He will attack us from every conceivable angle. He will come at us day and night and, with a deft touch, he will try to catch us when we are off guard. He will oppose us, left, right, and centre. How does he go about it?

- He seriously undermines the character and credibility of God.

That is what he successfully did with Adam and Eve in the plush, idyllic surroundings of the Garden of Eden and, because he got away with it then, he has been doing it ever since. He will try to get us around to his way of thinking by coming up with all kinds of innovative ideas that cause us to doubt and distrust the Lord.

He will pull out all the stops in an attempt to get us to question the will of God and the motives of God.

Whenever things go disastrously wrong in our lives and our cherished hopes have not been realised, when our castles have tumbled and all that we held dear has been taken from us—in such difficult and trying circumstances, the devil wants us to point the finger in blame at the Lord.

- He pours cold water on the momentous victories we have enjoyed by generating trouble that makes life more unmanageable and unbearable.

It could be some form of persecution or peer pressure that he tosses into the lap of our lives, we may end up with a tarnished reputation among our close circle of friends and colleagues, we may lose our freedom and find our movements seriously hampered and restricted for one reason or another, we may face redundancy from our job and have to suffer all the ensuing pressure that goes along with that, we may suffer the misfortune of seeing the once solid support of our families begin to slip away from us, he may put us under so much pressure that we begin to feel as if we are losing our grip on things.

The trouble is, when life starts to crash in smithereens all around us, we often become introverted. In moments of devastation like that, we can, understandably, become fearful and wary of any kind of criticism because we want to be accepted by our nearest and dearest.

The old devil is no fool and he may even reverse his approach and give us an unbelievably easy time. When that happens we are prone to rely on ourselves and we fail to depend on the Lord Jesus. Either way, he will have accomplished his mission.

It does not have to end with us licking our wounds and feeling sorry for ourselves!

- He liberally sows the seeds of doctrinal confusion in our hearts and minds.

Christians who are untaught in the fundamental and foundational truths of Scripture are leaving themselves wide open to all sorts of wrong ideas about the eternal truths of God. The believer who is confused about God's word and the things of the Lord cannot be effective in the wider work of God.

- He hinders our service for the Lord Jesus.

The devil opposes every faithful life and he sets himself against every effective ministry. He stood against Paul's work in the city of Ephesus through 'many adversaries' (1 Corinthians 16;9). He even gave to Paul 'a thorn in the flesh' to buffet him and harass him, he tried to bring the worst out in Paul because he wanted to sideline the servant of God (2 Corinthians 12:7). He blocked the apostle Paul's plans for going to Thessalonica (*cf.* 1 Thessalonians 2:18).

God, however, has a lovely way of bringing blessing out of buffeting. The Lord used the thorn to strengthen Paul's ministry by keeping him dependent on his sufficient grace and he used that hindrance to accomplish his priority work elsewhere. You see, we make our plans and, sometimes, they are in apparent disarray, our dreams are often shattered, but God knows what he is doing!

The Lord may lead us around but he will always lead us aright.

Satan's ultimate goal and purpose is to always undercut and undermine the work of the Lord. Thank God, there are many instances where he bites off more than he can chew!

- He causes division among the Lord's people.

That is why Jesus prayed so earnestly and fervently for his followers that 'they all may be one' (John 17:22). We should be reconciled to one another as a testimony to the super-glue bonding that we have in the international family of God.

Paul's concern for the Ephesian Christians was that they should *make every effort to keep the unity of the Spirit through the bond of peace* (4:3). The enemy knows if we are fighting with one another we will not be any bother to him, so he lets us get on with it.

When we are at loggerheads with each other, the devil is watching from the sidelines with a gleeful smirk on his face!

• He persuades us to trust our own resources.

You see, for us to attempt to do the Lord's work in our own power is not to do his work at all. Remember David! After many years of successful rule over Israel when he roundly defeated all his enemies, he was hailed as a national hero, then we read: 'Satan rose up against Israel and incited David to take a census of Israel' (1 Chronicles 21:1).

Instead of totally relying on the Lord, David decided to do what a lot of evangelical preachers do, he counted his own resources in terms of manpower. God was not impressed with what David did, he was less than happy with David's action. But, true to form, David confessed his sin (*cf.* 1 Chronicles 21:8). We play into the open hands of the enemy when we depend upon ourselves and, in the process, we leave ourselves exposed and vulnerable.

• He leads us into sanctimonious spirituality.

It hurts me to say it but one of the devil's greatest success stories throughout the entire history of the church is that of filling the church with religious unbelievers and with real believers who are not totally committed. So many are more concerned about themselves— empire building—than they are about the Lord Jesus and extending his mission to the ends of the earth—kingdom building.

When we choose to go down that dodgy road we play Satan's game and, consequently, we play right into his hand. We should be aware of the end result—we are losers, short term and long term!

- He dangles the juicy carrot of worldliness in front of our eyes.

He does it by enticing us to permit the world to squeeze us into its own mould (*cf.* Romans 12:2). When the going is good and everything in the manicured garden is beautifully rosy, the devil finds it relatively easy to sidetrack us into materialism. He has no real problem getting us to look after Number One!

- He encourages us to disobey the word of God.

Because God wants us to adopt a lifestyle of faithfulness, the devil encourages us to be disloyal—because God wants us to live in glistening white purity, the devil solicits us to live immorally—because God wants us to consistently speak the truth, the devil tempts us to lie—because God wants us to show authentic love, the devil tempts us to hate—because God wants us to be content with what we have, the devil tempts us to covet—because God wants us to live and walk by faith, the devil tempts us to live and walk by sight.

Battle ready

That is how the adversary operates. And so, when he comes to attack us, we want to be able to stand. So, says Paul, in words full of wisdom: *put on the full armour of God*, and when we get it on, be sure to keep it on, for if we do, we will be victorious in the hour of conflict. We need to keep in mind the second verse of Martin Luther's gripping hymn:

Did we in our own strength confide,
Our striving would be losing;
Were not the right man on our side,
The man of God's own choosing.

Dost ask who that may be?
Christ Jesus, it is he—
Lord Sabaoth his name,
From age to age the same
And he must win the battle.

'This equipment,' according to William Hendricksen, is 'forged and furnished' by the Lord. In the Old Testament it is God himself, the Lord of hosts, who is depicted as a warrior fighting to vindicate his people. For example, we read that the Lord 'put on righteousness as a breastplate, and a helmet of salvation upon his head' (Isaiah 59:17). Still today, the armour and the weapons are his—the difference, however, is that now he shares them with us.

6:14

Dressed up

Aerobics is big business! The Christian life, however, is no 'go at your own pace' tone up exercise class, it is no genteel engagement. It is warfare. Battle. Conflict. It is not for the faint hearted. In that sense, it could be described as a contact sport for we find ourselves in the fray against the devil.

That is why it is essential for us to step into the ring wearing the right gear—it is imperative that we wear the appropriate battle dress if we are to resist the tigerish onslaughts of Satan. What is the armour? There are half a dozen items of equipment detailed in verses 14-17: a belt, a breastplate, shoes, a shield, a helmet, and a sword.

- The first five pieces ensure there is ample provision for our security in the battle—defensive weapons.
- The last piece gives us adequate provision for our success in the battle—an offensive weapon.

Dressing down

No one needs to remind a soldier going into battle: 'Don't forget your rifle!' And yet, so often in our lives, when it comes to spiritual combat, we have a built in tendency to forget. We forget our armour, we forget our weapons, we even forget the reason why we are fighting the good fight.

It must be a strange sight for the Lord looking down from his throne in heaven and seeing so many of us carelessly walking on to the battle field each day casually dressed in a pair of jeans and a tee shirt. Whether we realise it or not, therein lies the danger.

Now, in a valiant attempt to ditch that crazy attitude, Paul tells it like it really is, he spells it out. I want us to look at each item of equipment in precisely the same order that a Roman soldier would have put it on prior to going on duty. Before we do that, let me remind you of a story culled from a bygone era.

Achilles' heel

Homer's great hero, Achilles, was assumed to be invincible, that was, until one fateful day dawned. That was the day Paris discovered his heel was not protected! So what did he do? Like any good marksman, Paris aimed his arrow at that single defenceless spot. As they say, the rest is history!

Thankfully, God's armour does not leave us with an Achilles' heel.

Belt up!

The first item on the list is *the belt* (*osphys*), sometimes called the girdle. To all intents and purposes, this was a protective apron. It was a thick leather belt about six inches wide which had a number of thongs hanging down from it. They often had metal plates attached to them.

It protected the lower part of the body for it belonged to his underwear more so than his armour. It also gave the soldier freedom of movement for he was not restricted or impeded in any way. It was particularly effective against horizontal swipes of the sword.

As he buckled it on, it gave him a sense of hidden strength and confidence. To 'tighten one's belt' can mean not only to accept a time of austerity during a food shortage but also to prepare oneself for action, which the ancients would have called 'girding the loins'. By the same token, a slackened belt meant 'off duty'. Christians, however, must face each day with a fastened belt, ready to fight the battle when needed. We are never off duty!

Truth trafficking

In the same way, as soldiers in the Lord's army, that is what we are to do. We are to bind ourselves with truth. We are to put on the *belt of truth* (*alētheia*) and *buckle* it tightly round *our waist* (*perizōnnymi*). I think what is envisaged here is the objective truth of God's word, the plain truth of Scripture, the revelation of God in the Bible. We are to know what God has said in the Bible and we are called upon to believe it as well.

Perhaps we need to remind ourselves that the belt also holds the other parts of the armour together—it gathered his tunic together and it also held his sword. This means that truth is the integrating force in the life of the victorious Christian. A man of integrity, with a clear conscience, can face the enemy without fear. As Philip Brooks put it: 'Truth is always strong, no matter how weak it looks and falsehood is always weak, no matter how strong it looks.'

Truth is a transparent, practical honesty that gives a sharp cutting edge to our lives.

As I mentioned earlier, the girdle also held the sword—unless we practice the truth, we cannot use the word of truth. John S B Monsell's (1811-75) hymn focuses on the dedication required:

Fight the good fight with all thy might;
Christ is thy strength, and Christ thy right.
Lay hold on life, and it shall be
Thy joy and crown eternally.

Run the straight race through God's good grace,
Lift up thine eyes, and seek his face;
Life with its way before thee lies,
Christ is the path, and Christ the prize.

Cast care aside, lean on thy guide;
His boundless mercy will provide;
Trust, and thy trusting soul shall prove
Christ is its life, and Christ its love.

The breastplate

The second item of the Christian soldier's equipment is the *breast-plate* (*thōrax*). Once the belt was buckled, the Roman soldier fitted on his breastplate. This was a very tough leather smock that protected the body from the neck to the thighs, and sometimes his back as well. Usually the front part was reinforced with metal—bronze or chain mail (overlapping slices of animal hooves or horns or pieces of metal). It was a major piece of armour for it protected all his most vital organs. If it was not securely fastened, the soldier knew his chances of survival were slim.

Our breastplate is *righteousness* (*dikaiosynē*). In the New Testament the word has two meanings and it is highly likely that Paul has both in mind here.

- It can refer to right living.

To know that something is right and not to do it is to leave a gaping hole in our armour.

The Christian soldier is to be sure to put on righteousness. If he has not got it on, how can he stand true in an increasingly pagan and godless environment?

- It also refers to the perfect life of Christ which is credited to the account of every believer.

The devil is always telling us that we are no good. We know he is right! The downside is that we fall into discouragement, the fight goes out of us, and we lose heart. What are we meant to do when we succumb to such feelings? We are to remember that our acceptance with the Lord does not depend upon how well we are doing in our Christian lives. It is in no way linked to our performance.

We are welcomed by the Father because our sins were all dealt with when Christ died for us at Calvary. Perhaps the next time the devil reminds us of our past, we should take the opportunity to remind him of his future. The righteousness of Christ has been imputed to us and that makes us glorious in his sight. When we put on such a mindset, all of the devil's attempts to say otherwise, come to nothing.

Luther said that when the devil came knocking on the door of his heart, he would send the Lord Jesus to the door. Christ would say: *'Martin Luther used to live here but has moved out ... I now live here.'* *'Then,'* said Luther, *'when the devil would see the nail prints on the hands of Christ and his pierced side, he would take flight immediately.'*

When all is said and done, to put on the breastplate of righteousness is to live in a daily, moment by moment obedience to our heavenly Father. If we do not put it on, apart from losing the battle, it will also cost us our joy. And it will lead to a life of barren fruitlessness for we are unproductive when we are living in disobedience to the Lord. And it will bring a loss of reward for we will have nothing to give to him when we meet at the Bema, the judgment seat of Christ (*cf.* 2 Corinthians 5:10). Sadly, it will also bring reproach on the glory of God.

We can tie up some of the loose ends by looking at it like this: if cultivating *truth* is the best way to overthrow the devil's deceits, then cultivating *righteousness* is the wisest way to resist his temptations. This is what Count Zinzendorf (1700-60) had in mind when he wrote his great hymn:

Jesus, thy blood and righteousness,
My beauty are, my glorious dress;
Midst flaming worlds, in these arrayed,
With joy shall I lift up my head.

Bold shall I stand in that great day;
For who aught to my charge shall lay?
Fully absolved through thee I am,
From sin and fear, from guilt and shame.

6:15

Mobility matters

Ever wondered, what did the Roman soldier wear on his feet? Paul provides the cryptic answer when he says: *with your feet fitted (hypodeō) with the readiness (hetoimasia) that comes from the gospel (euangelion) of peace (eirēnē).*

Generally speaking, he would have worn hobnailed sandals—the *caliga* or half-boot—that were attached to his feet and ankles by intertwining strips of leather. The secure fastening and the heavily studded soles combined to give him a firm footing which was so vitally essential in combat. A man fighting for his life does not want to be slipping and sliding all over the place.

'It is one thing to stand fast, it is quite a different matter to be stuck fast!' (Anonymous)

We too must have a firm footing if we are going to fight well in our spiritual warfare. We find it in the prepared foundation of the *gospel of peace.* We need to reflect on the timeless truth that we are at peace with God. We should treasure it up in our minds for it is worth more than acres of diamonds.

We passionately believe God's truth. We are declared righteous in Christ. And so we are at peace with God. There is nothing between us and him. All obstacles to our enjoying him have been removed. Peace prevails. The conflict may be fierce and raging, it may be long and wearisome, but when we stand foursquare on the peace of God we will not be moved.

6:16

A protective screen

The next item on the equipment list is the *shield* (*thyreos*) *of faith* (*pistis*) and Paul speaks of it as an indispensable addition to our battle dress! I found it most interesting to note that different regiments of the Roman army used different sorts of shields. Paul has in mind here one particular type—the *scutum*.

From the front it appeared rectangular, but it was curved in such a way so as to protect the soldier's sides. It was approximately four feet high and two feet wide and was made of solid wood which was then covered with metal or heavy oiled leather. It completely obscured a crouching man from view, no matter how hard you tried, you just could not see him. It was as if he was not there!

Incendiary missiles

The enemy would frequently shoot arrows with flaming tips at the soldiers in the opposing army. But hiding behind the shield, the soldier had nothing to fear from these burning missiles. Apart from anything else, they burned out fairly quickly.

In fact, groups of soldiers could put their shields together in such a way that they carried a protective roof which resembled a giant tortoise. Whatever the enemy fired at them, it had little or no effect, it came to absolutely nothing. The opposing troops were wasting their time and their energy and, more often than not, they finished up a spent force or a damp squib.

Paul's language emphasises the potentially destructive nature of the *evil one's* constant onslaught—his prolific use of *flaming* (*pyroō*) *arrows* (*belos*). It comes upon us with all the burning hatred and fury that he can muster. Having said that, faith is the Christian soldier's shield. The devil can do nothing against it. His worst attacks are frustrated. Faith offers total protection and makes advance possible. Where there is faith there is nothing to fear.

Faith is ...

- Faith is believing what God has said,
- faith is taking God at his word,
- faith is accepting his teaching,
- faith is obeying his commands,
- faith is heeding his thoughts,
- faith is laying hold of his many promises.

The story is told of the Scottish pioneer missionary John G Paton (1824-1907) who was translating the Bible for a South Seas island tribe. In the course of his exhaustive work, he discovered that they had no word for trust or faith.

One day a native who had been running hard came into the missionary's house, flopped himself in a large chair and said in his own dialect: *'Phew! It's good to rest my whole weight on this chair!'* *'That's it,'* said the alert John Paton, *'I'll translate faith as "someone resting their whole weight on God".'*

Such is faith! Where there is faith, defeat is unknown and unthinkable. The soldier who has faith is never floored by anything for faith is invincible. Apollyon taunted Christian with the threat: 'Here will I spill thy soul.' 'And with that,' Bunyan continues, 'he threw a flaming dart at his breast; but Christian had a shield in his hand, with which he caught it, and so prevented the danger of that.'

6:17

Don your helmets!

The Roman soldier's helmet is the last piece of equipment he would normally put on. It was usually made of a tough and resilient metal like bronze or iron. Military historians tell us that an inside lining of felt or sponge made the weight bearable. Nothing short of an axe or hammer could pierce a heavy helmet and, in some cases, a hinged visor added frontal protection. Helmets were decorative as well as protective and some had magnificent plumes or crests.

In the same way, every soldier in the Lord's army is to *take the helmet (perikephalaia) of salvation (sōtērios)*. What does it actually mean? Isn't the Christian believer someone who is already saved? Well, yes he is! But, in the Bible, salvation is used in three different tenses:

- past—we have been saved,
- present—we are being saved, and
- future—we shall be saved.

It is used of what God has done for us in the past, that was our experience of Calvary. It refers to what God is doing for us right now for he is changing us to be more and more like Jesus. It speaks of what he will yet do for us in the future for one day he will take us home to heaven to enjoy himself for ever and ever.

A cool head

The helmet has to do with the head and he is telling us to keep the coming salvation very much in mind (*cf.* 1 Thessalonians 5:8). The reality is that we will not be on the battle field for ever, the conflict will soon be over, before very much longer we will be in the glory.

It seems to me that it is not hard to fight well when we keep thinking about such an exciting and exhilarating prospect—an irrepressible hope.

Forward be our watchword

The Lord will always protect us when we are in the thick of things. At the same time, he also expects us to go forward into enemy territory. It is not enough to remain on the defensive. It is not sufficient to hold our ground. We must invade and capture, go forward and advance.

'*The best form of defence is attack.*' (Napoleon)

Cut and thrust

We need to take the sword in our hands for it is our hand that holds it. I am glad to say, however, that a stronger pair of invisible hands is placed over them. We wield the razor sharp *sword* (*machaira*) as best we can but it is the unseen hands which give it force, direction, and cutting power. God's work is not done without us. It is nonetheless God's Spirit who does God's great work. The Spirit's sword is the word (*rhēma*) of God.

The Scottish pastor and writer Thomas Guthrie said: 'The Bible is an armoury of heavenly weapons, a laboratory of infallible medicines, a mine of exhaustless wealth. It is a guidebook for every road, a chart for every sea, a medicine for every malady, and a balm for every wound. Rob us of our Bible and our sky has lost its sun.'

How are victories won in the spiritual dimension? How is the enemy put to flight? How are we to advance behind enemy lines? By the word of God. There is no other way! Oliver Cromwell's soldiers, his Ironsides, fought with a sword in one hand and a Bible in the other—we can never win God's battles without God's book!

Spiritual work is done best by using spiritual weapons.

In the rousing words of Charles Wesley (1707-88) we say:

Soldiers of Christ, arise
And put your armour on!
Strong in the strength which God supplies
Through his eternal Son.

Strong in the Lord of hosts,
And in his mighty power;
Who in the strength of Jesus trusts
Is more than conqueror.

6:18

Winning the battle on our knees

In this section, Paul deals with the conflict the Christian must face. Most of us realise that living for God in a secular society is an uphill struggle. Believe it or not, there is a war going on and we are soldiers on the front line. We have been enlisted as spiritual squaddies in the Lord's army. We have been instructed to *put on the full armour of God* and here we are challenged by yet another command—to be men and women who pray at all times.

What is the link, where is the obvious connection? Well, the battle may be fought out there, but often times, it is here where the victory is won. Maybe this was what inspired the poet George Duffield (1818-88) to write:

Put on the gospel armour,
Each piece put on with prayer.

Charlotte Elliot (1789-1871) wrote the words for another hymn:

Christian, seek not yet repose;
Cast thy dreams of ease away;
Thou art in the midst of foes:
Watch and pray.

Principalities and powers,
Mustering their unseen array,
Wait for thy unguarded hours:
Watch and pray.

Watch, as if on that alone
Hung the issue of the day;
Pray, that help may be sent down:
Watch and pray.

In the timeless classic, *Pilgrim's Progress*, John Bunyan tells of Christian's weapon called prayer.

'*When everything else failed, this would enable him to defeat the fiends in the valley of the shadow.*' (John Bunyan)

Artful dodgers

It is abundantly clear, therefore, that prayer is a potent force, a powerful factor. However, for some people, prayer is about as exciting as changing a flat tyre on the motorway. This is probably because the regular practice of prayer is just plain hard work. It takes time, effort, and discipline.

Indeed, some people find prayer so boring and difficult that they have become extremely creative and innovative in dodging the responsibility. For many Christians, prayer has become about as commonly utilised as a fire escape—it is there for emergency use only, a fallback position—nice to have it when we need it.

This is definitely not God's perspective on prayer. If the truth be told, he views it as the most profound and significant discipline of the Christian life. It is interesting to note that prayer is not mentioned as being part of our armour. That may seem rather strange at a first reading. It is not merely another weapon we can bring out of the kit bag. It is much more than that.

Inhaling the air of prayer

The thought is that all the while we are fighting with the armour on, we are to be in prayer. It is the very spiritual air that the soldier of Christ breathes. It is the all pervasive strategy in which warfare is fought.

Recall the words of Jesus when he urged his disciples to 'always pray and not give up' (Luke 18:1). He knows when the battle gets hard, soldiers easily become tired, weak, and discouraged. In the epic struggle with Satan, it is either pray or faint.

Believing prayer is the climax of his epistle because prayer fills all of the Christian life. Prayer is the electrifying crescendo at the end of Paul's anthem of Ephesians. Amazing!

'Ephesians begins by lifting us up to the heavenlies, and ends by pulling us down to our knees!' (John MacArthur)

Prayer all sorts

What can we learn then about prayer that will encourage us to talk less about it and get down and do it? The first thing that really impresses me with these verses is the many-sidedness of prayer. Paul speaks about *all kinds of prayers* (*proseuchē*) *and requests* (*deēsis*).

- *Prayers* refers to that which is general.
- *Requests* are geared to that which is more specific.

Put the two of them together and we have a clarion call to come to God with our burdens and our needs. The scope is all embracing and he is all powerful. He is omnipotent, he is a God who can do anything, but fail. It does not matter how we do it, just do it!

R. Kent Hughes tells the story of Floyd Pierson, a retired Africa Inland Mission worker, a man who literally prayed *on all occasions with all kinds of prayers and requests*. So habitual was this that in his seventies, when he went to take a driver's test, he said to the examiner: 'I always pray before I drive. Let's bow our heads together.' The official likely wondered what kind of ride he was in for! I can see him checking his seat belt and settling his sweaty hand on the door handle. Pierson passed! But apart from the humour, there is something quite beautiful here—the unaffected witness of a vibrant inner spiritual reality which bubbles up with *all kinds of prayers and requests*.

A prayer's portfolio

They can be long prayers or short prayers, they can be prayed out loud or said in the quietness of our hearts, they can be born out of a time of refreshing fellowship or they may be a desperate SOS, they can be written out on a page of paper or they may be spontaneous, they can be spoken or they may just be a sigh or a whisper from deep within.

- It can be anywhere, anytime, about anything!

Prayer is simply telling it to Jesus, it is clearing our chests before him, it is getting a load off our minds as we storm the gates of glory.

The best definition I can think of for prayer is probably the simplest as well: prayer is talking to God.

Prayer in 3D

When we pray we enter three different realms. One, we enter the hidden place. This is the special moment when we are alone with the Lord. It is what Jesus aptly called 'the closet religion' (*cf.* Matthew 6:6). It is the quiet place where we commune with him as friend with friend.

In such a place, all else is shut out and we are shut in with the Lord.

Two, we enter the heavenly place. This is the sphere mentioned in Ephesians where our blessings and battles are. It is there that the devil's emissaries gather to hinder and harass us, to distract and discourage us. This is where we need the whole armour of God. This is where we need the Spirit's mighty sword. This is where prayer is a real engagement with the enemy.

Intrusive thoughts

We struggle against wandering thoughts. Concentration is a problem for many of us. So often when we pray, our minds begin to daydream and we so easily go off on another tangent. In moments like that, the devil is busy trying to deflect us from the matters in hand.

We battle against bad thoughts and these can come with startling suddenness. It happens when our mind becomes aware of something from our past, or maybe something we have seen, or even words which we have heard during the course of the day. How we need the Lord to come and sharpen our focus.

In such awesome moments with majesty, we need to have clear minds and clean minds.

We encounter selfish thoughts. All too often we are immersed in our own little world, totally wrapped up in ourselves—the me, myself, and I syndrome; when things material become number one on our personal prayer agenda, when we are preoccupied with those things which are only of temporal value.

Three, we enter the holy place when we find ourselves on the other side of the rent veil. Thank God for that *place of quiet rest near to the heart of God.* This is where by faith we reach out and touch the Lord. This is where we see one who is invisible. This is where we realise that God is bigger than all our problems. This is where we are overwhelmed with the greatness of our God and the majestic wonder of his throne.

Praying round the clock

There is a rich variety in prayer, but there is also a frequency to prayer which Paul alludes to. This is suggested by the all encompassing phrase: *pray ... on all occasions* (*kairos*).

There is no time when we do not need to pray. There is no time when God will not hear our prayers. To 'pray at all times' does not mean we take it literally, even Jesus himself did not do that. It is impossible to carry on a running verbal dialogue while we do our business and get on with living. No one can walk around all day with their eyes closed! It does mean, however, that we keep the channels clear and ensure that the lines of communication are always open.

We know the Lord is only a prayer away and, because of that, we will live in such a way so that in an instant we can touch the throne. It is living with a conscious sense of the intimate presence of the Lord. It is not some form of *crème de la crème*, super spiritual experience. This is a life in tune with the Lord.

It is where everything we see and experience becomes a prayer.

Praying outside the box

Another facet of prayer is hinted at when we think of the extra-ordinary power of prayer. The apostle indicates that when we pray it should be *in the Spirit*. This has nothing to do with speaking in tongues or in some other ecstatic or dramatic manner. If that is what it isn't, let me tell you what it is!

It is to pray in the name of the Lord Jesus. It is when we pray according to his sovereign will. It is when we intercede in a way that is consistent with his nature and character. It also implies that we will pray in concert with the Holy Spirit as intimated in Romans 8:26, 27.

What an enriching experience. It means that for us to pray the way we should, we will pray as he prays. We will join hands with him and together our petitions will be in beautiful harmony. Every request of ours can be linked to his and our will can be united to his.

We say 'amen' to Jesus!

It is what happens when we are both on the same wavelength and marching to the beat of the same drum.

Praying with our eyes open

There is the manner of prayer: *be alert and always keep on praying* is how Paul puts it. Jesus told his disciples to 'watch and pray' (Matthew 26:41). Paul advised the saints in Colosse that they should 'devote themselves to prayer' (Colossians 4:2). It is the Nehemiah principle (*cf.* Nehemiah 4:9).

We need to be steadfast in prayer. Perseverance is the name of the game (*cf.* Luke 18:2-5). It is keeping at it, not giving up or giving in, not doing it in fits and starts; it is holding on, watching and waiting for the answer to come. Dogged persistence. When it comes to prayer, it is always too soon to quit.

We need to be sensible in prayer (*cf.* 1 Peter 4:7). We need to pray with our minds and our understanding as well as with our hearts and spirits. We need to be precise in prayer. Be particular. Be focused. Name names. Single matters out for special emphasis. It is not praying around the world for a short cut, it is homing in on specifics.

The word translated *be alert* (*agrypneō*) actually means 'lying sleepless'. What a vivid description. Many of us know what that means when we lie awake at night. Been there, done that! So, says Paul, use such moments wisely.

Watching sights the enemy! Praying fights the enemy!

We would do well to have some sleepless nights over the state of our country, over the woes of the world, over the condition of many of our churches, over the needs of our family and friends, over our own spiritual lives and our walk with the Lord. When God sends sleepless nights, pray! Let us seize insomnia as a gift from the Lord so that we can be alert and pray.

We can turn those quiet night hours into golden moments of communion with the Lord.

Prayer partners

There are also the objects of prayer. This is reflected in the final few words where Paul says we are to *pray for all the saints*. The bottom line is that God's people need one another and we should pray for each other. Alone it can be a real struggle to get through and at times it may seem as if it is all too much for us to handle and cope with.

To know that someone, somewhere is upholding us in prayer helps to keep us going. It recharges our batteries. I often think of the words of 1 Samuel 12:23 where we read: 'Far be it from me that I should sin against the Lord by failing to pray for you.'

6:19, 20

It's me, it's me, it's me, O Lord

Pray also for me, that whenever I open my mouth, words may be given me so that I will fearlessly make known the mystery of the gospel, for which I am an ambassador in chains. Pray that I may declare it fearlessly, as I should. Typical of Paul, isn't it. He tells us what to do, then he shows us how to do it.

Paul did not plead with them to pray for him so that his ankles might be healed. After all, they would be raw and extremely sore because of the shackles he was in. He did not even ask them to pray that he might be set free from prison and released from his suffering. No!

His deep concern was that he might be able to tell the message of Jesus Christ at every opportunity. All he wanted was that every time he opened his mouth, he wanted to speak well of Jesus, and he wanted to do it *fearlessly (parrēsia)*. He wants the church family to pray long and hard for him—he was cooped up in Rome, they were across in Asia Minor.

Prayer spans the miles.

Think of Paul's humility. He is a man—an ordinary bloke—and he is standing in the need of prayer. He is big enough to know his many shortcomings and small enough to beg for their prayerful support.

And his honesty. It is exactly the way he feels. If he did not, he would not have asked. It is genuine, real, and sincere. How unashamed he is of such a request. I hope he is not sad or disillusioned at the possible lack of response.

Bad things happen to good people!

Their prayers on his behalf would give him enormous assurance and he would be able to speak with unfettered boldness. Paul may have been in chains, but he was not tongue tied. He still sees himself as an *ambassador* (*presbeuō*), still very much aware of the high calling of God upon his life. It is almost a contradiction in terms: *an ambassador in chains* (*halysis*).

Ambassadors normally have diplomatic immunity to represent their country without restraint. Here is Paul, and that is what he is, an ambassador—and this is not where we would expect to find him, in chains! In a funny kind of way, he is bound, but he is also free; he is down in a dungeon, but he is also up in glory; he is handcuffed to a guard, but he is also seated with Christ in heaven.

The same can happen in our lives: we could be standing at the kitchen sink washing the dinner dishes and, at the same time, be in the throne room of heaven.

Their prayers would make a world of difference! That is the whole point of prayer, and that is the power of prayer. In a single sentence of two words: prayer works! Here is the power of effective kneeling. Satan trembles when he sees the weakest saint upon his knees.

6:21-24

A benediction of blessing

Paul brings his stirring epistle to a fitting close with his final greetings—a wonderful finale with his last few specially selected words.
They are beautiful in their clarity. There is a simple dignity to what
he says because it reflects the theme of his mighty epistle. In his
wish list, he talks about *peace* (*eirēnē*) and *grace* (*charis*), *love*
(*agapē*) and *faith* (*pistis*):

- *Peace* is the Hebrew greeting.
- *Grace* is the Gentile greeting.
- *Love with faith* is the Christian greeting.

Peace to the brothers, we may be in a battle, but we are not at
war with the brethren. If we are, we are fighting the wrong battle.
Satan's dogs of war will bark at our heels and hound us right down
to the river. But in the midst of the storm, we can still have peace
ruling within.
Love with faith is a delightful combination.

- Love is the source and faith is the force.
- Love reaches down, faith reaches up.
- Love is the beginning and the end, faith lies in between.
- Love reaches out the hand of God, faith takes hold of it.
- Love provides all that we need, and faith appropriates it.
- Love says: 'here you are' – faith takes it and says: 'thank you'.

The March 1978 *Readers Digest* carried this little vignette from
a Sunday School teacher: 'For St. Patrick's Day, I asked the five
year olds in my Sunday School class to bring "something green that
you love". The next Sunday they brought the usual green hats, green
sweaters, and green books. But one boy entered with an especially
big grin. Behind him, wearing a green dress, came his four year old
sister.'

Marvellous grace

Grace is how Paul started his letter (*cf.* 1:2). He ends it the same way. He has gone full circle. At the beginning of the letter he said to them: 'Hello, grace to you.' And now, at the end of the letter, he says to them: 'Cheerio, grace be with you.'

Grace is God's unmerited, unlimited favour that shines upon us all the time, and is with us along all the way. It is grace that sets our feet on the highway to heaven, it is grace that keeps us company all the journey through, it is grace that will see us safely home at last.

The story is told of a man who appeared at Heaven's gate and was met there by an angel who told him: 'It will take 1,000 points to get in. Tell me about yourself so that I will know how many points to give you.' The man smiled and said: 'Well, I've been going to church almost every Sunday all my life.' 'Excellent,' the angel said. 'That will give you three points. What else?' The man was shocked. 'Only three points?' he gasped. 'Well, I was a Sunday School superintendent for a while, and I tithed, and I tried to be a good neighbour.' 'Very good,' the angel said. 'That will give you ten points.' The man gasped again. 'At this rate,' he said, 'I'll never get in except by the grace of God!'

Grace saves us, sustains us, and strengthens us. It is ever sufficient for us in that it is immeasurable. Grace is undeserved and unearned. And it is unrepayable for God does not expect any favours in return!

Why grace?

'What is it that frees us to be all he means us to be? Grace! What is it that permits others to be who they are, even very different from us? Grace! What allows us to disagree, yet stimulates us to press on? Grace! What adds oil to the friction points of a marriage, freeing both partners from pettiness and negativism? Grace! And what gives magnetic charm to a ministry, inviting others to become a part? Grace!' (Charles Swindoll)

You see, Paul knows all about their surroundings, he is familiar with their worsening situation, he is conscious of their many problems and challenging difficulties, he is aware of their changing circumstances. And so, he warmly and prayerfully commends them to the torrents of the grace of God and to the God of all grace.

Undying love

The final challenge of the epistle is in relation to our love for the Lord Jesus. We should love him with a love that is without corruption, we should love him with a love which is *undying*, we should love him with a love that never fades.

What a massive difference that would make to all of our lives. To be able to say today: 'I love you, Lord.' And when tomorrow comes to be able to gladly affirm: 'Yes, Lord, I still love you.'

Never ending grace

Well, believe it or not, we have come to the end of the book but, thank God, his grace is lasting and limitless. He says to each of us: 'My grace, it's there for you! Make the most of it!'

A big God, big on grace!

The icing on the cake is that he just keeps on loving us and blessing us. To me, that is what makes being a Christian the greatest experience this side of heaven, it has to be the ultimate adventure on planet earth. Pure and simple, that is the genius of grace!

Study Guide

~ compiled by John White ~

Chapter One

1. List at least five major things from verses 3-10 that God has done for us that should make us 'praise' him (verse 3).

2. What do you understand by being blessed 'in the heavenly realms' (verse 3)? Does this mean we will only be blessed when we die?

3. Discuss how it makes you feel to know God chose you 'before the foundation of the world' (verse 4).

4. What are some of the implications of being adopted as God's 'sons' (verse 5)?

5. 'Redemption' (verse 7) means to be set free and it is through 'the forgiveness of sins'. What does being forgiven set us free from?

6. 'Riches' or wealth is a word Paul likes to use, and here Paul links it with 'grace' (verse 7). What does that tell us about what God is like?

7. Along with his 'grace', God has 'lavished' on us 'wisdom and understanding' (verse 8). Why then do we so often lack these qualities, and what can we do about it?

8. What do verses 9 and 10 tell us about the where, when, and how of God's masterplan for the universe?

9. Is Paul's practice of giving thanks and praying for other Christians in verses 15-19 the same as yours? What practical steps can we take to support each other better through our prayers, and what do these verses tell us about what we should pray for?

10. What do verses 20-23 tell us about the dignity and authority of Jesus Christ? And how should verses 22 and 23 affect the way we act as churches?

Chapter Two

1. In what ways do verses 1-3 help us understand people's reluctance to accept or even hear the gospel?

2. What does the fact that we are both 'objects of wrath' (verse 3) and the recipients of God's 'great love' and 'mercy' (verse 4) tell us about him?

3. Verse 6 speaks as if we are already in heaven which clearly we are not. So what point is Paul making by speaking like this?

4. Summing up verses 1-6, how do they demonstrate 'the incomparable riches of [God's] grace' (verse 7)?

5. Being given something 'by grace' (verse 8) means we have not earned it and do not deserve it. Why can this be so hard to accept, not just at the start of our Christian lives, but every day?

6. If we do not do 'works' to earn a good relationship with God, why do we do them (verse 10)?

7. In light of verses 11 and 12, who are the 'uncircumcised' in today's world and what do these verses tell us about their spiritual condition? What does that mean for our involvement in the church's task of sharing the good news about Jesus with the world, and what is the ultimate goal of this task (verse 13)?

8. What do you think Christ would say to Christians who do not get along together (verses 14, 15)? In what ways should these verses determine how you think, feel, and act towards *all* Christians, of whatever church or denomination?

9. What practical difference can it make day by day in our personal lives and Christian relationships that 'we both have access to the Father by one Spirit' (verse 18)?

10. Based on verses 19-22, how would you define a local church, its purpose, and your place in it?

Chapter Three

1. What understanding do we get from verses 2-6 of the way that God communicates his truth to us, and what a privilege it is to have it?

2. In verse 6 Paul again refers to the great theme of Ephesians—the unity of all believers in Christ. Someone has written: 'Ephesians calls us to build bridges not minefields.' What specific things could you do this week, this month, and this year to build bridges? Now go and do them!

3. What is God's big picture as outlined in verse 6?

4. How can we be sure that God's inclusion of Gentiles among his people is not just an afterthought?

5. What would it mean for you to be a 'servant of this gospel' (verse 7)?

6. How did Paul—and how can we—'make plain' (verse 9) or illuminate God's truth?

7. What is God doing 'now through the church' that shows his 'manifold wisdom' (verse 10)? Why does it matter that 'the rulers and authorities in the heavenly realms' know about it?

8. What do you think about kneeling to pray (verse 14)? Why?

9. What are the implications of the fact that we can only fully know Christ's love 'together with all the saints' (verse 18)?

10. God can do 'immeasurably more' than 'all' we can even 'imagine' (verse 20). Are we living individually and as a church in the reality of that fact? Discuss ways in which God's 'glory in the church' (verse 21) can become more real in your situation based on the 'immeasurably more' that he can do.

Chapter Four

1. Why does Paul remind the Ephesian believers that he is a 'prisoner for the Lord' (verse 1)?

2. What aspects of our 'calling' (verse 1) motivate us to live worthily?

3. Living out verses 2 and 3 is not easy (although God expects us to do it). Can you suggest ways in which we can help each other to be more successful than sometimes we are?

4. If verses 4-6 are true, why do we have so many denominations? Should we do anything about it, and if so, what?

5. The giving of 'grace' and 'gifts' (verses 7, 8) refers to the abilities that Christ gives to all of us to work for him in the church and the world. In what ways are you using the 'gift' he has given you? How can your church be organised differently so more people can discover and use their gift?

6. What do verses 9 and 10 tell us about Jesus? What help does that give us about receiving and using his gifts?

7. The purpose of the four groups mentioned in verse 11 is to 'prepare God's people' (verse 12). What have some of them done and what do the others do that makes God's people prepared?

8. What is it that God's people are being prepared for, and what should be the result (verses 12-16)? What does this actually mean in practical terms in your church?

9. Verse 17 starts an intensely practical section that goes right through to the end of the epistle. It is about living the different kind of life implied by being a Christian. Why does Paul start this section by talking about the mind and heart? How can we be 'make new in the attitude of [our] minds' and hearts?

10. Verse 25 repeats the 'put off/put on' idea of verses 22 and 24. Reading from verse 25 down to 5:2, what are some of the characteristics of Christian behaviour? What are the basic reasons why we should behave like this, and how important do you think it is that we adopt

<u>Chapter Five</u>

1. How does the behaviour Paul lays down in verses 3-7 contrast with today's society? What reasons does he give for Christians to behave in the way he tells them to? What practical steps can churches take to help their members obey what Paul is teaching?

2. There is a link in verses 3-7 between what we do and what happens to us (see especially verse 6). Do you think this applies to Christians or do we somehow escape the consequences of what we do? Should Christians be motivated by fear when trying to avoid sin?

3. What advice does Paul give here which will help to give us a balanced view of sexuality?

4. How do we 'find out what pleases the Lord' (verse 10)?

5. How do we expose 'deeds of darkness' (verse 11), and does this apply just to the church or to the world as well? What good does it do to expose these things?

6. What is 'being filled with the Spirit' (verse 18) and how do we experience it? What difference does it make that the Holy Spirit is in us (and in every part) and not just with us?

7. What are a) the similarities and b) the differences between being under the influence of alcohol and being filled with the Holy Spirit?

8. What is Paul saying in verses 22-24 is the relationship of a wife to her husband? What would you say to someone who dismissed these verses because either they were out of date or because they demeaned women?

9. In marriage, does God intend one partner to be the other's doormat? If so, which? Why?

10. What do we learn from verses 25-33 about a) a husband's relationship with his wife and b) Christ's relationship with the church?

Chapter Six

1. What does the fact that Paul addresses children directly (verses 1-3) tell us about how he regarded them? And what are the reasons he gives here and in Colossians 3:20 for doing what he says?

2. How do we 'honour' our parents, and can you explain how this results in things going 'well' with us and enjoying a 'long life' (verses 2, 3)?

3. Why does Paul address verse 4 to 'fathers' and not parents?

4. Verses 5-9 are addressed to slaves and masters. Do you think they also apply to our employee/employer relationships today? If they do, give some specific examples of how they might applies in today's workplace?

5. What does it mean to be 'strong in the Lord' (verse 10)? And how can we be strong?

6. Who are the 'rulers, authorities, powers, spiritual forces' (verse 12) we struggle against and how do they influence things? What difference should that make to the way we think and act in the world?

7. There are many good things in our world, so in what sense is it 'dark' (verse 12)? And how come it is nevertheless so good?

8. What is the 'full armour of God' (verses 13-17) and how do we put it on (verse 11)?

9. The one offensive (as against defensive) weapon is the 'sword of the Spirit, which is the word of God' (verse 17). In what situations would it be appropriate to use this weapon, and just as important, *how* are we to use it in an appropriate way?

10. Verses 18-20 are, strictly speaking, not part of the 'armour' of the preceding verses. How, therefore, do they complement what Paul said there?

twr

TRANS WORLD RADIO
where hearing is believing

- 1.5 million listener letters per year
- responses from 160 different countries
- aired in 185 different languages and dialects
- more than 1,800 hours of programming each week

> 'THEIR VOICE GOES OUT INTO ALL THE EARTH,
> THEIR WORDS TO THE ENDS OF THE WORLD.'
> (Psalm 19:4)

- a biblical ministry
- a multimedia ministry
- a faith ministry
- a global ministry

THAT'S RADIO . . . TRANS WORLD RADIO!

For further information write to:

Trans World Radio	Trans World Radio	Trans World Radio
Southstoke Lane	P.O. Box 8700	P.O. Box 310
BATH	Cary	London
BA2 5SH	NC 27512	Ontario N6A 4W1
United Kingdom	USA	Canada